Good for Women

Stories of notable women of faith

Also by Michele Guinness

Child of the Covenant (Hodder & Stoughton)
Tapestry of Voices (SPCK)
Reflections on Women's Lives (Zondervan)
Woman – The Full Story (Zondervan)

MICHELE GUINNESS

God is Good for Women

Stories of notable women of faith

Contents

Acknowledgments   vii

Introduction   1

1   **The Entrepreneur:** Helen Taylor-Thompson, MBE   7

2   **The Superintendent of Police:** Ruth Clark   35

3   **The Writer:** Susan Howatch   53

4   **The Fashion Consultant:** Nellie Thornton   77

5   **The Army Officer:** Lieutenant-Colonel   99
    Jan Ransom, MBE

6   **The Rabbi:** Julia Neuberger   123

7   **The Health Trust Chairman:** Carolyn Johnson   151

8   **The Politician:** Hilary Armstrong, MP   177

9   **The Priest:** Joy Carroll   199

10 **The Chief Executive:** Angela Sarkis   221

11 **The Survivor:** Mandy Moore   243

12 **The Consultant Gynaecologist:** Anne Garden   259

Conclusion   279

Acknowledgments

A special thank you to the dedicated women of Crusade for World Revival, who in their deep commitment to encouraging the faith of their sisters everywhere, have taken the risk of republishing this book. It seems very much in keeping with the ethos of the lives of the twelve women whose stories are told here.

It is difficult to express my gratitude fully to those remarkable women. They not only took time out of their frenetic schedules, but also enriched my life with their experiences and challenged me with their courage and determination. It has been so exciting to find out how each have fared since I first wrote about them, and to discover that all have been given even greater opportunities to confront the status quo and make the world a better place. Because of them, my life has not been the same. Thanks to their example, I have grabbed hold of, and enjoyed, opportunities I never dreamed I could, and in the process, become a committed, if rather diffident, pioneer.

Introduction

Does God have a down on women? Anyone who judges His personal preferences by the history of religion could be forgiven for thinking that He does.

Traditionally, religion does not seem to be good for women. It has tended to side with a status quo that keeps women in their place, dutiful, domestic and dependent, self-effacing creatures, more valued for their mildness and insipidity than their passion or their clout. And while traditionally male-dominated institutions such as the police, politics and the army are slowly, albeit reluctantly, offering women access to authority and opportunity, the Church is still the last to allow them to rise through the hierarchy. Yet, paradoxically, many of the pioneers who have risen to the challenge, who have dared to excel in a very male world, have done so because of, not despite, their faith.

This isn't new. There have always been women whose faith in a just and good God inspired them to break through the system and herald a new justice: Florence Nightingale, Elizabeth Fry, Catherine Booth, Mary Slessor, Amy Carmichael, Octavia Hill and Josephine Butler, to name but a few. Judaism also had its heroines: Rosa Luxemberg, Bertha Pappenheim and Ernestine Rose, no more accepted or valued in their own culture than any Christian equivalent. The very fact that the women of their day were denied leadership forced them, often unwillingly, into the role of pioneer, battering on the closed doors of institutions, if not a glass ceiling, sometimes until their fists bled.

Attributed to a woman, the very word 'pioneer' can conjure up images of aggressive, pushy behaviour, of a harpy mowing over every unsuspecting man and woman in her path. But the women whose stories are told here are neither strident nor loud. One or two were inspired by Margaret Thatcher's achievement in becoming the first British female prime minister. Most struggle with her rather less than feminine approach to leadership. They are all feisty, determined, passionate, wilful and obstinate when the cause makes it necessary. Their behaviour in a man would never be called aggressive.

They realise that this is how they might be seen. But they are prepared to take the flak that seems to fly when women are up-front, which means an almost inevitable rejection of cultural conditioning and of society's expectations of dainty feminine behaviour. And in that they are unusual. Women tend not to be the risk-takers. When they do, it is often for the sake of others, rather than themselves.

The majority would not call themselves feminists. It would not occur to them to do so and they would be horrified if others suggested they were. The only two who do are a priest and a rabbi, Joy Carroll and Julia Neuberger, and they have reservations about what they see as its more unhelpful extremes. None thinks men are expendable. On the contrary, they speak of influential fathers, supportive husbands, encouraging male colleagues and friends. Metaphorically speaking, men still open doors for women.

They are trailblazers because they have no choice. They tread where no woman, and sometimes no man, has trodden before. All women priests are pioneers, says Joy Carroll. They are among the first. But so are the rabbi, the police superintendent, the army lieutenant-colonel, the chief executive and even the gynaecologist. Nellie Thornton began designing clothes for people with special needs because it was the obvious thing to do, and no one else was doing it. Had she known the consequences in advance, the political manoeuvring and heartache she would have to face, she might have thought twice.

All the women here in their own way break new ground. And,

like their predecessors, their chosen field is predominantly education, health and social welfare. They stand at the interface between human beings and the establishment. I make no apologies for including a consultant gynaecologist and, though Julia Neuberger sees herself as a rabbi first, two Health Trust chairpersons. (Julia firmly calls herself a chair, Carolyn Johnson a chairman, which highlights major differences in their approach, and provides me with a headache when I want to find a word to include them both.) Women have always been in the forefront of caring, though Superintendent Ruth Clark wouldn't thank me for saying so, feeling that their other, less traditionally female gifts such as capability and efficiency, are often overlooked. Like it or not, the nurturing, maternal role appears instinctive and is the foundation for a variety of themes that overlap and recur, like tiles on a roof: the fight against poverty, inequality, and injustice; the meaning of beauty and human dignity; the nature of health and wholeness. Even for the lieutenant-colonel and MP, caring seems an inescapable aspect of the uniquely female way in which they understand their job.

The women reflect on similar issues: career and celibacy, marriage and motherhood, ambition and power, loneliness and teamwork, juggling a frightening number of commitments, the ageing process, the peculiar joys of being a woman. It is probably no coincidence that four are single, two married late in life, and five do not have children, though Carolyn Johnson with her six boys almost makes up for them. She, Julia Neuberger and Angela Sarkis successfully combine career and motherhood. Some of the others speak of the sacrifice involved in being unable to do so. They see it as an inescapable part of their calling.

Here are women who often struggle with the religious establishment, but whose basic belief is the foundation of everything they do. Unlike feminist theologian Daphne Hampson, who left the Church because she could no longer stand its patriarchal view of God and its paternalism, their God is a liberating, sustaining life-force. That is, for all of them, their understanding of the biblical view of woman. Woman's story is there written large, according to Rabbi Julia Neuberger, though it may be hidden in the text, and finding it may be like digging for gold. Whether woman is in a supporting role, such as Sarah, Rebecca or Miriam, or takes centre stage like Hannah, Ruth and Esther, all have found a God who met their deepest desire and inspired them to play a major part in the history of their people.

At a conference I attended on women and religion, Morna Hooker, Lady Margaret Professor of Divinity at the University of Cambridge (this is the oldest chair at the university), spoke up passionately for poor apostle Paul, often dubbed a chauvinist for verses taken out of context, pilloried for promoting an image of woman as demure and quiet, while critics ignored his unspoken, basic assumption, running like a thread through his letters, that women would be ministers and leaders in the new churches. Jesus himself had a robust, easy, equal relationship with women, often affirming them for their faith, while criticising men for their lack of it.

Personally, I find Daphne Hampson's desertion a bit of a cop-out. If you disapprove of a system, stay in it and change it, I say. But then, like the women I have interviewed, I can't resist a challenge. Raised in a fairly orthodox Jewish family, given every advantage of education as Jewish girls are, I soon discovered that to be a wife and mother was nonetheless the only real expectation. That raised several major questions in my mind about my value in society. I wanted a husband and children, but what if I didn't get them? And if I did, what would I be worth once they left home, or if, God forbid, I lost them?

Years later, a graduate and member of a Free Church, I realised that, though the setting and decade had changed, the expectations had not. Visiting, counselling, baking pizzas and quiches for faith suppers, cleaning the pews and arranging the flowers were eminently womanly tasks. Preaching and leadership were not – unless you were a missionary. And that was apparently by default, because the men preferred to stay at home.

Timidly, I started to write, had my first article published, and waited, if not for awfully un-English applause, at least for a pat on the back. In vain. Motherhood, I was told, usually by older women, was the ultimate calling. Only, I was a mother and it wasn't enough, not for me, at any rate. That's why I became a journalist. Indeed, it seemed to me there were great dangers in living for one's children. Like others in this book, I began to wonder whether women, as much as men, collude in limiting our horizons.

I looked around for role models, but there appeared to be few. Not many women of my mother's generation had gone out to work. Some had found satisfaction in working in the home, some in voluntary work. But a frightening number seemed prone to long-term, low-grade depression, born of a restless sense of waste and unfulfilment. I had dreams of using the pen to challenge the foibles of society, but writing is as heavy a commitment as any other, and there were still the problems of prioritising career, children, home, and inevitably, as the wife of a clergyman, the demands of the church. It was a profound comfort to me, years later, to watch a highly professional Julia Neuberger come out of chairing a meeting, pick up a phone in a public lounge and say, 'What have you done to your knee? Don't you think you ought to go to casualty?'

The writing of this book became a personal pilgrimage. If God was good for women, our lives must have meaning and purpose in their own right. They would make a difference. Sure enough, I discovered that the role models were there all the time. The heroines of yesterday have their counterpart today. Helen Taylor-Thompson took up Josephine Butler's banner and pushed out the boundaries on caring for the sexual outcast. Angela Sarkis demands justice for the poor as loudly as Octavia Hill. In her own inimitable way, bearing superficially little and yet essentially so much resemblance to Mother Julian of Norwich, Susan Howatch made the fundamental spiritual themes of forgiveness and redemption accessible to a very unchurchy society.

Women's stories may be hard to find, but they are there and must be told for future generations. Not all represent my personal views. But together they have widened my perspectives, challenged my egotism, enriched my spiritual life. Believing you can achieve the impossible, knowing others have done it before you, will be an important spur for my daughter and her generation – and for those of us who still have enough time left to transform our small corner of the world. These stories prove it is never too late to change track, or discover a life's calling. Susan Howatch was in her forties when the course of her life changed dramatically, Nellie Thornton in her fifties when she started her fashion workshops for disabled people, and Helen Taylor-Thompson had said goodbye to sixty when her great crusade to save the Mildmay Hospital began.

There are times when I have been ashamed of my gender: when we allow ourselves to be excluded or exploited, when we are weak, fearful or terrified of being without a man, conversely, when our insecurities make us behave more like a man than men. But my pride in women has grown immeasurably as I have met those whose lives feature here. They cover the entire political spectrum. Some are well known. Some are not. Some have had the advantages of material security, education and parental encouragement. Some, like Mandy Moore of Croxteth, have not. That is why she is included. She represents all the women through the centuries who have had to wrestle against overwhelming social odds. All appear to be living proof of an old saying recounted to me by the preacher Eric Delve: 'When God has a difficult job to be done He looks for the best possible person to do it. When He has an impossible job on His hands, He looks for a woman.'

CHAPTER 1

The Entrepreneur: Helen Taylor-Thompson, MBE

'Dear Mrs Guinness, I have been reading your book *The Guinness Legend* with great interest. Our vicar's wife lent it to me because of the references you have made to Mildmay. I would very much like to have the opportunity to meet you and to show you round the hospital, in particular, the new Family Care Centre.'

I went. I'm not sure why. After *The Guinness Legend* was published I received dozens of letters from people telling me they were related distantly by marriage or misfortune to the Guinness family, that I had referred to old friends, contacts of their parents and grandparents, their second cousin three times removed, from whom they had had neither word nor news for many years. They recognised buildings where they went to school, colleges where they studied, houses where they had stayed or visited once on a rainy day. It was all very interesting, and I replied, 'how nice', and put their letters in a file for possible future research purposes.

But this letter, from the President of what was once the Mildmay Mission Hospital, refused the filing system and fired my curiosity. 'It is so exciting to know how Mildmay has not only risen from the ashes since being closed in 1982, but how the work has continued and grown,' she wrote. Little did I guess what an understatement that was.

I had of course heard of Mildmay in the last few years, but with little more than the hazy half-interest with which most suburbanites register happenings in the capital. Princess Diana had visited the hospital and sent the press photographers into a paroxysm of pure delight by holding the hand of an AIDS patient. That sounds like a journalist's cynicism. The Princess was, of course, responsible for debunking some of the fear and prejudice surrounding a terrible disease. And so was Mildmay. AIDS, I said to myself at the time with some surprise, recollecting the Mildmay's evangelical, Christian foundation: the hospital must now belong to the National Health Service.

Not so, according to the letter. I was intrigued. Most philanthropic or missionary ventures, sprouting up profusely in the miserable human rabbit warrens of Dickens's London, had long since disintegrated into dust, superfluous with urban redevelopment and the advent of the welfare state. Then how and why had Mildmay survived?

Its long-term history was very familiar to me. At the end of the nineteenth century the poverty-stricken East End was a Mecca for radical Christian social entrepreneurs. William and Catherine Booth of the Salvation Army, George Holland, founder of the Ragged Schools, and Amy McPherson, who ran the first home for destitute children, were all committed to alleviating the appalling misery and deprivation on their own doorstep. So too were my husband's grandparents, Henry Grattan Guinness and his wife, Fanny, who set up the first 'faith' Bible college in Bow, where students paid no fees, prayed for food, and trained on the London streets for missionary work abroad, running night classes, surgeries and dispensaries. One of their first students was a young man called Tom Barnardo, who never pursued his original dream of sailing to China, once he became aware of the hundreds of hungry children who lived on roofs, under bridges and in shop doorways.

The Earl of Shaftesbury, politician and social campaigner, used to gather this exceptional band of visionaries for what he called 'regular tea-fights', so that they could help furnish him with ammunition to use in government debates, and he could help resource their projects by introducing them to his wealthy, upper-class friends. Clearly, this was an early example of effective networking. Among the group were the remarkable Pennefathers of Mildmay.

The Pennefathers personified the pioneering flair of the time. A Men's Night School, Sewing Class for Widows, Flower Mission, Lad's Institute, Servants' Training Home were just a few of the initiatives spawned by the highly fertile imagination of William Pennefather, Vicar of St Jude's, Mildmay Park. Collectively his expanding little empire was known as the Mildmay Institutions, and for a motley band of costermongers, match- and factory-girls were as integral a part of their social life as the music halls and taverns. Their chief originality, however, was that they were run with immense dedication by an exceptional team of female ministers, the first in Britain.

The Mildmay Deaconesses were the brainchild and personal responsibility of Catherine Pennefather. Young women of 'consistent Christian character, with a reasonable education' were taught cookery, sewing, housekeeping, book-keeping, biblical knowledge and singing. Some specialised in nursing, though their medical training was rudimentary in this pre-Florence Nightingale era. Nightingale herself held the Mildmay Deaconesses in great respect as precursors of the professional nurse. Unremarkable as their work may seem by today's standards, it was daring at the time. Do-gooding in a dangerous environment, nursing undesirables and preaching were not considered suitable occupations for a lady, and earned them a great deal of scorn, criticism and downright hostility.

Yet in 1866, when a massive cholera epidemic swept through the dirty, overcrowded alleys of an area in Bethnal Green known as The Jago, renowned for its squalor, prostitution and drug addiction, no one else was willing to care for the dying or their dependants. In three months, 4,000 were dead. In desperation the local vicar, James Trevitt, had begged the Pennefathers to send him two of their deaconesses. From a base in what was appropriately called Cabbage Court, they organised a soup kitchen, provided 80 children's meals a day, and ran a makeshift medical centre. And there, for ten years, they went on caring for the sick and the destitute until an old warehouse was finally converted into the first Mildmay Mission Hospital.

Several years later it was demolished by the London County Council as part of their first slum clearance scheme, and in November 1892 a purpose-built hospital with 50 beds was opened on the present site, in a less noisy part of the East End, by Shoreditch Church. Catherine Pennefather, who had been invited to plant the plane tree that still stands in the courtyard, was too unwell to attend the official opening. She died two months later.

Several decades after her death, Henry Grattan Guinness's daughter, my husband's Aunt Geraldine, who had been a pupil at Mrs Pennefather's Day School, was asked whether Catherine Pennefather wasn't something to do with Mildmay. 'Something to do with Mildmay!' she retorted. 'She was Mildmay.'

And that was the limit of my knowledge of the hospital. The remainder of its history, spanning a century, was little more than a blur, until I realised from the national news that it had been reborn. Perhaps that was why I went – to fill in the gaps, because I found it difficult to make a quantum leap from a hospital reflecting the Victorian piety of the Pennefathers to the first specialist AIDS hospice in the country. Or because it was a story that appealed to my fascination for social history and health issues. Or because the name Helen Taylor-Thompson had such a commanding ring to it that it begged obedience. Or perhaps it was a mixture of all three, heavily laced with a deep-seated intuition that an institution that had played its part in the life of my husband's ancestors was now about to take its place in mine.

'It is quite extraordinary how so many contacts of the past tie up with those of today,' she wrote. Yes, I thought, perhaps more than either of us realise at this particular point in time.

It was not at all what I imagined. Hidden in an arterial mass of tiny back streets, it certainly doesn't look like a hospital. In fact, no one would know Mildmay was there. I couldn't see how to get in and rang the wrong doorbell – to the administrative, not the medical block. Someone threw up a window and pleasantly pointed out the front door. My sense of direction is rudimentary at best. There are buildings old and new all slotted together like StickleBricks into a relatively small space, and surrounded by smart new town houses.

I finally find my way into a spacious reception area more reminiscent of a small, comfortable hotel than of a hospital. It's pinkish, pleasant and beholden to a gifted flower arranger, who has done her best to compensate for the lack of greenery outside. But before I have the time to appreciate all the finer points of the decor, the President herself appears and whisks me off. 'I'll show you round later; first let's have tea.'

In classic woollen suit, and with rich, refined voice, her fair hair streaked with grey, Helen Taylor-Thompson is genial and dignified, a disarming combination of a worldly-wise grand-mother and a benevolent lady of the manor. Everything about her speaks sound common sense. She is the epitome of growing older not only with grace, but with all her faculties so finely honed by experience that they are quite capable of slicing through the nonsense of fools and, presumably, a great deal of red tape. For this, I soon discover, is the woman who fought Goliath, who took on the National Health Service and transformed the dilapidated charity hospital it had shut down into one of the foremost centres in the world for the treatment of HIV.

'You will have tea?' she asks with a smile, once we are ensconced in a cosy little sitting-room.

I nod, knowing already that it must materialise simply because she has spoken the word. Moments later a tray appears. There are real china cups, home-made shortbread, pink serviettes and an elegant pot.

'Where did that magnificent teapot come from, TT?' asks John, one of the young managers she has invited to join us.

'Ssshh,' she says, handing me my cup. 'We're trying to create an impression.'

I am impressed, not with the quality of the crockery, but because this attractive woman, whose face lights up when she speaks with an almost girlish enthusiasm, tells me she is 72. It's a fact she obviously recollects with some surprise herself. That's why, she explains cheerfully, she is no longer chairman of Mildmay, but president, a more honorary, less high-profile role befitting her ancient state, but still providing an outlet. Most spring chickens, I reflect ruefully, would be satisfied with half her energy.

Why, I ask her, when she could have been enjoying a tranquil retirement in her armchair, has she spent such a large part of it fighting to reopen an antiquated medical institution? I anticipate lofty concepts such as calling, mission or even divine guidance.

'Probably sheer bloody-mindedness,' she says, laughing.

She can't stand pretentiousness, and will debunk any attempt to turn her into a contemporary Joan of Arc inspired by visions and voices.

'Well, I had no idea then of what it would become,' she admits, 'I simply remember thinking, "You want to close my hospital down? We'll see about that!" Had I appreciated the extent of the battle ahead I might have thought again.'

The story is as remarkable as any Catherine Pennefather might have told a century ago. It starts in 1952 when Helen Taylor-Thompson's involvement with Mildmay began. A successful businesswoman, young and single, unusual by any standards in the 1950s, she was invited by Commissioner Motee-Sladen, granddaughter of William Booth, to join the management committee. In those post-war years, while maintaining its particularly Christian ethos, the hospital had been happily absorbed into the new NHS. By the 1970s, when Helen became chairman, local health authorities had begun to be seriously worried about the ever-expanding shortfall in their budgets. Beeching (the Minister of Transport in the 1960s) had closed the small country railway stations. District and cottage hospitals risked being the next victims. 'I saw the writing on the wall,' Helen says ominously, 'and with a view to being in the right place at the right time, so that I could have the maximum influence for Mildmay's sake, became a member of both the community health council and the District Health Authority.' When the axe finally began to fall in 1982, just as she was about to retire from business, she was strategically placed to mount the campaign of her life.

'I had no experience of saving a hospital,' she reflects, as if we're discussing the rescue of a favourite family pet, 'but it was a good hospital, much loved by the local community. I believed there was still great work for it to do, and that driving passion was all I needed. The rest was instinctive – just plain common sense.'

Common sense told her she couldn't fight alone. She needed a vanguard of people with gifts and talents supplementing those she lacked. The Hospital Advisory Council (HAC) had originally been created as a forum for the staff. It was now reborn as a driving force. 'They fell from heaven,' she says of the small group of individuals who became her right-hand women and men. 'I was becoming increasingly swamped beneath a mound of letter-writing and photocopying, and simply didn't have the technical resources, let alone the time. I remember sitting at the top of the stairs at home, praying in desperation that someone would come along to help. At that moment the phone rang. It was a man called Lawrence Twinam, whose daughter nursed at Mildmay. He asked me what he could do. He worked for the Greater London Council – and had access to all the machinery we needed.'

Behind the HAC was the Hospital League of Friends and an ever-swelling mass of public support. There were weekly prayer meetings and days of prayer. On 29 January 1983, a protest rally attended by Ian Mikardo, MP, culminated with a petition of 11,000 signatures being sent to the government urging it to save Mildmay.

To no apparent avail. In July, after a temporary reprieve, the District Health Authority voted by a majority of nine to five to inform the Secretary of State, 'with great reluctance, that the least unattractive alternative, given the reduced allocation of money, was to close Mildmay and to concentrate on the DHA's shrinking resources within its remaining facilities'.

For many of Mildmay's supporters that sounded like the death-knell. For Helen Taylor-Thompson it was a rallying call. She immediately requested an interview with the Secretary of State, Norman Fowler. It was his second-in-command, the Minister for Health, Kenneth Clarke, who finally received the delegation, headed by Peter Shore, the Labour MP for Tower Hamlets. Clarke was not a man known to give way to pressure. But for well over an hour he listened to proposals for running a community hospital with a combination of public and voluntary funding. He seemed impressed – but not enough. Four months later, in March 1984, he approved the plans to close Mildmay – permanently.

Helen still refused to admit defeat. A new and extremely daring idea was slowly taking shape in her head. 'I wrote to all the authorities concerned and said, okay, if that's the way you want to play it, give us Mildmay and we'll run it and pay for it ourselves. They must have thought I had taken leave of my senses.'

Whatever he thought, the minister gave his approval to the reopening of the hospital on a 99-year lease, at a peppercorn rent, on condition that the Regional Health Authority were satisfied that her proposals were financially viable, and the District Health Authority, which had closed the hospital on the grounds that it was superfluous to requirements, agreed there was a need for it. 'No one,' commented one health official later, 'had ever been known to get any concession out of Kenneth Clarke.' Several years would pass before Helen had the chance to thank the minister personally, and make one final request.

After almost 40 years Mildmay had reverted to its status as an independent charity hospital, with the freedom to develop its own particular character in a way it might never have been able to do had it remained within the NHS. Euphoria, however was tempered by the sobering realisation that members of the District Health Authority, who had the final word, were not going to find it easy to take a decision that countered all their reasons for closing Mildmay in the first place.

After months of wrangling, mainly over funding, they finally met to discuss Mildmay's future one last time. The occasion is as vivid in Helen's memory as if it had been painted in oils. 'There were five of us and we sat together on one side of the long, polished table, facing a very hostile row on the other. The battle lines were drawn, the antagonism almost tangible. Before the meeting the five of us had met to pray together in a freezing room in Mildmay. The place was ramshackle, vandalised, a ghost hospital, and it suddenly seemed as if the whole thing was sheer madness. Yet as I drove through London to the meeting a childhood picture suddenly formed quite clearly in my mind. It was Daniel facing the lions, and underneath it were the words, "God closed the lions' mouths." By some great miracle that is exactly what happened. I was the first to arrive for the meeting. It was pitch black in the basement room where we were about to meet. I went in, reached for the switch, and as the room was flooded with light, asked the Holy Spirit to do the same in the spiritual sense. And from the row of lions facing us, not one voice was raised in opposition to our opening.'

The authority had, however, stipulated that the HAC must raise a further £250,000 on top of the £500,000 guaranteed by the Hospital League of Friends. Their surprising volte face, it appears, was partly induced by the conviction that Mildmay would be closed within a year. 'One of the members asked me how I thought I was going to raise that kind of money. I told him I would do what I always did. First, I get down on my knees and I pray. Then I get up again and I work.'

As far ahead as she could see, the next years of her life would be committed to fundraising – not the usual job of a chairman, but Helen was not a run-of-the-mill chairman. The hands-on approach never bothered her. 'I think that's one of the differences between men and women. Men tend to form committees of people who do things for them. We women are used to doing several things at once and just get on with it.'

'Getting on with it' included personally scrubbing the building clean from top to bottom. Ironically, in May 1985 the health authority's plans for accommodating chronically sick young people fell through and they put pressure on Helen to come to their rescue and reopen Mildmay by October. 'It was in a dreadful state, filthy, freezing, with broken windows. There was three-year-old cake crumbs in the tins and three-year-old meat glued to the mincer. We put on old clothes and rubber gloves, and for five months scraped away at the dirt. A mother-and-child clinic had been using part of the building for two days a week, which meant there was still a phone and a porter. He was jolly useful. He said to me, "Who's going to clean the men's toilets?" I said, "I am." He said, "No, you're not" – and cleaned them himself. When we opened exactly on time to fulfil our contracts – it was pristine. You could have operated on the floor.'

On 20 November 1985 St Paul's Cathedral was packed for a great service of thanksgiving. Mildmay's real destiny, unknown to everyone there, was yet to be revealed.

⌒

Mildmay has an annual Thanksgiving Service at a church around the corner, and this is the night. Many of the staff have disappeared to sing in the choir and, while the hospice is quiet, it's time for Helen Taylor-Thompson to take me on a guided tour.

'Oh, the first year was difficult,' she says dismissively, as we walk slowly back to the front lobby. 'I used to panic in bed at night. We never knew where the next penny was coming from. Yet somehow we survived. We had to – or I would have felt we were letting God down. We went ahead appointing key staff. I felt Mildmay needed a professional hand at the helm. It was while I was sitting in the bath one day in Mexico that I knew Veronica Moss should be the Medical Director. I'd met her, you see, when she came to do staff medicals, and was very impressed. I never thought of the problems. There was no money to pay her. What a fearful cheek – to ask her to leave the secure, well-paid job she loved in a busy, successful GP practice to take on a white elephant. She was flabbergasted when I asked, but rang two days later to say yes. And I was right; her vision and direction have been crucial.'

It was in February 1987 that the seed of a thought was finally planted in fertile soil. 'Someone asked me whether Mildmay might not be the ideal place to care for people with AIDS. At the time I knew very little about it, but there was something about the suggestion that made me sit up and think. People were referring to AIDS as a modern epidemic. Mildmay was born a century ago because Christians wanted to do something about the consequences of their particular epidemic – cholera. Was it possible that history was about to repeat itself?'

She put it to the board, she says, with her usual under-statement. I had been with her long enough to realise that when Helen 'puts' anything to anyone their emotional detachment is seriously under threat. 'There were real fears that this might make our precarious financial state worse, that we'd lose patients, nurses and money. So I suggested we went away to pray that God would show us what to do.' Four weeks later the board unanimously agreed to go ahead. 'We decided to convert our one empty ward on the top floor,' she says, as we wait for the lift. 'It was called Coventry Ward after Miss Coventry, who had founded the order of Deaconesses with Catherine Pennefather. "Well, that's a rather unfortunate name," I said, we'll have to change that, for a start.'

A mere 13 months later, a major achievement by any business standards, another miracle in the Health Service, the first hospice in Europe for people with AIDS was opened. 'I had to go to San Francisco to see first-hand what kind of accommodation would be needed. Well, there was nothing nearer, you see.' The lift doors part. The corridor is bright, homey, cheerful. 'Not easy,' she says, looking round with satisfaction, 'to convert a monster of a Victorian building into something attractive, cosy and warm.' Yet not impossible either, I realise, for someone of Helen's determination. The transformation into nine single-bedded units, achieved in so little time, was also paid for with a staggering £280,000. A further £1 million a year was needed to sustain and develop the new nine-bedded unit, and provide it with the calibre of professional nursing care Helen felt it required.

In many ways her real battles had only just begun. She toured the country, sharing her vision with regional health authorities, business organisations, churches, anyone who would listen and might help to find the necessary funding. Only now she was not only at odds with health bureaucrats, who rarely released promised funding on time, but with the League of Friends, who felt she might be compromising Mildmay's Christian foundation by getting involved with homosexuals, and were reluctant to hand over even part of the £750,000 of charity money they had amassed. Even the gay community was unsure at first, fearing they might be targeted for Bible-bashing. 'They asked us how we could look after AIDS patients when we thought all homosexuals were wicked. I said we didn't, that Jesus went among lepers and healed them. We would do the same.' There was also a certain amount of local ill-feeling – one or two residents who resented having the disease on their doorstep. A few bottles were thrown through the windows, but Mildmay, quietly encapsulating Christian care in the quality of the service provided, respecting the rights of every individual, slowly and effectively silenced all its opponents, as Helen knew it would.

'The more overtly crusading style of the old Mildmay had to go,' she says with feeling. 'I had a hysterectomy here. The nursing care was wonderful, but they would broadcast services over loudspeakers to the wards. I was so relieved when they put me in a side ward where I couldn't hear them. It was always during visiting hours, presumably to reach the maximum number of people. I did tell them a thing or two about that.' Now, prayer and specific Christian counselling are always available, but only when requested. They often are. The chapel, once the old accident and emergency unit's operating theatre, is used for regular communion services, baptisms, confirmations, funerals and even the occasional wedding, as well as large memorial services three or four times a year.

We have come to a male ward, and I'm aware that within many of the individual units there are patients being quietly cared for, without being exposed to the scrutiny of yet another visitor. 'Many of them have become my friends,' Helen says wistfully.

'You grieve when they die. We all do – we wouldn't be human otherwise.'

She takes me into an empty bedroom. The decor is pleasant, soothing. A curtain rail is hanging off the wall. 'John,' she says, pointing it out to him.

John has been faithfully following us round. 'I'll see to it, TT,' he says.

'He hates going round with me,' she whispers, just loud enough for him to hear, 'but these things do matter.' John winks at me behind her back, his admiration undisguised.

'It's nice being old,' she says merrily, 'You can get away with telling people what to do.' 'Now,' she says, 'You must see the glass conservatory on the roof.'

John groans. He knows what's coming. She won't wait for the lift this time. They're far too slow for someone who has so much to cram into so little time. 'Your back, TT,' he reminds her.

'Yes, yes,' she says, as she escorts me to the staircase. 'A bit dicky, since the war, but the hike will probably do it good.'

As we climb the stairs she tells me how the Mildmay team travelled to San Francisco and New York to observe and learn, and gain more expertise in the relatively new field of the rehabilitation, respite and palliative care of people with AIDS. Such was the demand that nine beds were soon too few. The remaining wards were gradually refurbished and converted into comfortable single rooms. A day centre and home care service were set up. The conservatory was built.

We emerge high above the roofs of London, where a large glass construction, filled with palms, comfortable armchairs and colourful cushions is perched, overlooking the city. I can see why this is one of her pièces de résistance. It compensates for the lack of garden. And the view is magnificent, stretching as far as the eye can see. Way below, Legoland houses are interwoven with ribbons of roads and motorways, dotted with Dinky Toy vehicles. The River Thames, a thick band of shimmering water, divides the city, meandering in and out, until it finally disappears into the distant horizon. All life-threatening disease robs the sufferer of any sense of control. Here, on top of the world, human existence takes on more manageable proportions. Everything has a different perspective.

Barely was the conservatory built when Helen took on her greatest challenge of all. 'Ruth Sims, the Director of Nursing, and I used to share all our thoughts, hopes and worries. It was she who first mentioned the need for a special place for women and children. I watched one little boy visiting his mother on one of the main wards,' she remembers. 'He was so disturbed when he realised someone had died in a bed nearby. No child should be confronted with the sadness of what they have to face in that way. That's when I knew Ruth was right. We had to build a brand new centre – to prepare and support the whole family together in a time of immense pain and bewilderment.'

We move on now to the family centre, the first of its kind in the world, built in eight and a half months, at a cost of £3.3 million, and officially opened early in 1994 by Diana, Princess of Wales. Apparently 38 per cent of the women in this country who are HIV positive are aged between 15 and 24. When the illness flares up, admission to an acute hospital usually means separation from their child or children. If both parent and child have AIDS, they may die on different wards or, worse still, in different hospitals. But not at Mildmay. The centre has 12 family rooms, all en suite and grouped in pairs with an interconnecting door. There are two fully self-contained flats where children, parents and even grandparents can stay together for what may be the last time in their lives.

There is also a day nursery. Here, children facing the loss of their mother or even both parents, some already infected by HIV themselves, are encouraged by specially trained staff to express their feelings in play. It's quiet this late afternoon. Toys are stacked in cupboards and corners. The paint easels have been wiped ready for tomorrow. Two mothers are quietly feeding their babies. This room, bright and cheery as it is, is perhaps more poignant than any other. All the tragedy of the disease is encapsulated in the small desks and crayons, a postbox toy, a child's drawing pinned to the wall. Yet, as we return to the sitting-room and I listen to Helen's excitement at the way the international side of Mildmay's work is developing, it is impossible to remain defeated by sorrow for any length of time.

Mildmay is now at the forefront of AIDS education. Health-care professionals come from all over the world to see Europe's largest AIDS palliative care centre, and to attend specialist training courses and conferences. A Mildmay team in turn went to Poland to advise on the setting up of a specialist hospice. They travelled to Greece and to Italy, where Helen had what she calls a 'semi-private' audience with the Pope, and addressed a Roman Catholic conference in the Vatican. There were invitations to North America and Japan. Then they received an urgent request from the Ugandan government to help them set up the first AIDS centre in Kampala. For Helen this turned out to be another, very personal, rerun of history, and the extraordinary fulfilment of a family ambition.

'My mother died giving birth to me. My father, who was descended from David Livingstone, had a life-long passion for Africa. He planned to build a hospital and was poisoned on his way there to lay the foundation stone when I was only nine. He's buried in Mombasa.'

Such an inauspicious start to life is fairly well guaranteed to turn a child into a loser or a survivor. Helen ascribes her independent-mindedness to a forward-thinking stepmother who shocked the establishment by teaching sex education in schools, and her determination and stamina to an extraordinary combination of parental genes. Her maternal grandfather, Sir Alexander Glegg, invented depth charges, which may explain a lot about her. He also chaired countless companies, including the Bible Society. Her father was descended from a long line of Scottish lairds who lived in a large baronial mansion in Blairmore. As the eldest son he was given a decent secondary education and £200, and told to 'do what you like because there's no more money'. He signed on with Cunard as a stoker in the ship's boiler-room, got himself to Cornell University and trained as an engineer, sharing a room with a Japanese student who worked nights.

The death of his wife during the birth of their second child, though an enormous blow, never diminished his spirit or his faith. Within two years, skating on the ice at a Varsity and Public Schools house party in Switzerland, he saw and fell instantly in love with the leader of the ladies' group. They married and, though they had no children of their own, she was a very loving mother to the two he already had, especially after he died, when she was left to care for them, along with three laundries and a dry-cleaning business.

'I couldn't cry when my father died. Africa seemed so remote. I bottled it all up and became anorexic at 14. The doctor bullied me, but Mother didn't. I think she knew what this was about. She simply waited. One day one of my aunts arrived with a box of Fuller's chocolates. It would have been terribly rude to refuse such a treat, so I took one, intending just to have a nibble. But once I'd had one, I couldn't stop, and ate the entire box. I think in that moment the grieving process was over.'

The following year, when her stepmother became ill, the doctor insisted she be sent away to school. She was taken out of Wimbledon High, a school she loved and found intellectually stimulating, and sent to Clarendon, a strict Christian girls' boarding-school in Malvern. For a spirited, free-thinking teenager raised in a warm and loving home, it was like being frozen alive. She hated it.

The rarefied atmosphere of Clarendon was created by a fairly Spartan evangelical piety. Inevitably, most of the staff were unmarried and somewhat out of touch with the budding sexuality of their 'gels'. The opposite sex was an alien species, to be viewed with suspicion and a certain amount of alarm. Among the girls there were one or two rebels, but many loved the school and most submitted to the system. Helen was amazed to see how some even tried to outdo one another in pious behaviour.

One particular memory sticks in Helen's mind – and her throat – typifying all that she found difficult about her time there. Twice a term a woman came in to wash the girls' hair.

'Twice a term, can you imagine? Mine was ram-rod straight, and before we sat in front of the fire to dry it, I put my curlers in. Well, what a rumpus that provoked. I was made to take them out, wet my hair again, and leave it to dry as straight as nature intended it.' Even at 15 Helen couldn't understand the virtue of looking unattractive. 'I think they thought we might incite male attention – the wrong sort – and,' she adds with a twinkle, 'that we'd never have the strength to resist.'

'You wouldn't think God was good for women if Clarendon was anything to go by. Girls with ideas of their own were put in their place. We were stripped of any sense of hope of achievement, the only expectation that we would become missionaries or sweet little missionary wives. If we complained about the lack of heating and frozen plumbing in the lavatories we were told it was far worse for missionaries. Perhaps that's why my worst fear was becoming a missionary in China – though, thanks to Mildmay International, I've been one by default virtually everywhere else.'

When Helen finally had her chance to create an institution with a Christian ethos it wouldn't resemble Clarendon.

Her stepmother saw how unhappy she was, and finally allowed her to stay at home with a private tutor. 'I thought I might like to be a nurse, but Mother said, "You'll never be a good nurse, Helen, you'll always be telling the doctors what to do." So I decided to become a doctor, and then war broke out, which rather scuppered everyone's ambitions. There were always the family laundries, of course. Mother had done her best to keep them going, and it occurred to me I might make a good businesswoman. "Do it properly, then, Helen," she said, so I trained in management and science at Hendon College, and learned all about boilers on the shop floor of Catkins in Putney.'

A young woman of Helen's spunk wasn't going to let the war pass her by. When it came to serving her country, gender was irrelevant. But the WRACs and WRNS offered women boring clerical jobs with little adventure, so she opted for the FANY instead and, because she spoke French, found herself a backroom girl with SOE.[1] For the first time she came face to face with sexual harassment and was deeply shocked. 'I was a rather naive young woman, raised in a sheltered Christian home, in a predominantly male environment for the first time. I couldn't believe how many of the men only wanted to get us girls into their beds. They would ring their wives and say they were too busy doing their bit for the war to come home that night, so that they could sleep with their secretaries or personal assistants. It taught me that a woman needs to stand up for herself and hold her own.'

But it was a lesson she learned the hard way. One night she and a friend were lured into a basement room by two sergeant majors. While one of the men took her friend into an adjoining room, Helen was subjected to what amounted to attempted rape. She managed to wrestle free and was about to escape when she heard her friend screaming in the next room and went back to rescue her. The officer set upon her again. She fought him off successfully, but during the struggle was rammed against a concrete wall, and suffered irreparable damage to her back. 'My war wound,' she says, smiling, 'and I got it from one of us, not from the enemy! Oh, it was a great life, there was such camaraderie, but I learned that men could be incredibly evil if they had set their minds on one thing.'

The discrimination she experienced in the Forces prepared her for entrance into the exclusively male business world of the 1950s, where she was viewed with a certain amount of suspicion and disapproval. An uncle told her she was letting the family down by not becoming a wife and mother. She ought to be out enjoying herself on the tennis courts, not worrying her silly female head with lofty matters of enterprise and finance. Looking back, she sees how she was learning the management and entrepreneurial skills that would one day serve a very different purpose.

When Derek Taylor-Thompson finally came into her life he was one of a rare breed of men – an instinctive egalitarian. 'Derek,' she says of the tax man who would become a high-flying civil servant, 'never expected a traditional stay-at-home wife, as long as he was fed and his shirts were ironed.' This was after all 1954, not 1994!

Thanks to a legacy, they settled into a mews cottage in Earl's Court and in 1957 a daughter, Catherine, was born. Helen paid for child care, and went on with her work, which caused one or two raised eyebrows at their church, St Paul's in Onslow Square. Her own faith, which had become lukewarm after the war, had been rekindled at a rally in the Central Hall by the preacher, Tom Rees. 'He appealed to me,' she says, 'He was down-to-earth, funny and liked jazzy music.'

Not so the Young Wives' Group, which she found irritatingly petty and irrelevant.

'They wanted to talk about silly things like the submission of women to their husbands. Well, really, it isn't God who puts restrictions on women. They do it to themselves with their blinkered view of their religion. They limit their horizons and possibilities.

'Derek always said you didn't need to discuss submission if you really loved one another. You know instinctively not to do what the other doesn't like. If he didn't like sausages I wouldn't give him sausages. I always consulted him about everything – but he would never try to stop me doing something I really enjoyed. In fact he took a retirement job when he saw how busy I was with Mildmay. After 42 years I don't go along with all this nonsense about working at marriage. If you have to work at it, it strikes me it's on the wrong footing. I think it's just the same with God. If there's something you know He doesn't like, don't do it. Do what He wants you to do. I have never divided my life into categories – one for religion, one for business, or even one for sex. They're all interwoven.'

In the 1960s, with the advent of the domestic washing machine, Helen saw that her laundries were running out of time, sold them and set up her own successful property development business. The only real gap in her life was a second child. 'Catherine's birth had been difficult. I was 38, and after what happened to my mother, Derek and I were a little anxious about having another child of our own.' It was a time of the war in Vietnam. The newspapers were filled with harrowing pictures of dispossessed children. 'Adoption seemed the obvious thing to do.

Bopha was a 13-year-old Cambodian orphan. It was quite a fight to get her. It may even have taught me a few tricks about how to handle bureaucracy. But she was well worth the struggle – a source of great joy to us.'

Helen's most fruitful and fulfilling years were yet to unfold. In many ways, as she looks back, she sees quite clearly how a variety of different experiences fused to prepare her for her greatest challenge. Unlike society's normal expectation, it came later rather than sooner in life. At that stage of their existence when her contemporaries were settling down to the more sedentary lifestyle of the archetypal British pensioner, Helen put away her slippers, packed her bags and followed in her father's footsteps – to Africa.

The outcome of her trip to Kampala was much more satisfactory than his had been to Mombasa, all those years before. Shortly before she went to Uganda she saw in the papers that the World Bank was supporting an AIDS Centre in Harare. Never outdone, she made up her mind to try and speak to someone from the World Bank at the soonest possible opportunity. 'On the plane out I was sitting next to a young American doctor. I looked across and on her lap were sheets of papers with facts and figures about AIDS in Africa. I couldn't believe my eyes. We started chatting and I soon discovered she just happened to be researching HIV in Africa – for the World Bank. She knew exactly whom I needed to see, and introduced us once we were in Kampala. He agreed to give me a quarter of a million dollars there and then.'

In Africa she felt an abiding sense of shame at the white man's responsibility for the AIDS epidemic, which is decimating the people. 'A hundred years ago, each man farmed his own land and there was little or no prostitution. Then whites altered the balance of the economy, created jobs in the town for the men, who had to leave their wives and families behind in the country for years on end, sending them money so that one day they could buy a retirement home.' It makes her query the traditional Western missionary approach to polygamy. 'My father always used to tell me that an African man might have up to ten wives, but he was always faithful to them.'

However, while some countries want only Mildmay's professional expertise and not their Christian ethos, Uganda has said it wants both. 'They need our faith, not our culture,' Helen says. 'They have such a problem with AIDS, they know the only hope is a radical change of lifestyle. And that can't happen without the help of a force far greater than government or medicine.'

With her usual foresight, Helen believes the Kampala project is just a first step into the desperate situation in the Third World. In response to increasing demand from all over the world, Mildmay International was formed on World AIDS Day, 1 December 1992, with a view to establishing consultancy, training and care centres in whatever country they are requested. The British Council now pays staff to travel to Africa on a regular basis, to run two- and three-week training courses for the people of Tanzania, Kenya, and Uganda. 'But we have our eye on India too,' Helen says, 'where there are 87 new cases of HIV every day. Can you imagine their plight?'

Despite the energy and time it consumes, Mildmay only accounts for one handful of the fingers Helen has in many different pies. Seeing what can be done if there is the will to do it has fired her imagination in countless directions, as various cracks, gaps and crevices appear in our social system. In 1992, as part of a working group of managers responsible for implementing the new Mental Health Act, she helped to draw up an exciting flagship policy document for the local health authority, challenging what she felt was a rigid and rather limited approach to people with mental illness who lived in the community. It began, 'The future of mental health services in Tower Hamlets has been the subject of substantial debate in recent months. The Mental Health Act managers have observed this process with growing alarm. We feel that the very substantial shortcomings of the present service and the inadequacy of the likely future resources to deal with the mental health problems of the Borough are not driving the process to look sufficiently radically at what is possible, realistic and desirable, and what is not.'

The tone was hardly guaranteed to win her friends in the cautious high places of health purchasing. Nor was the radical nature of the project she went on to describe. What she had in mind was the building of a special network centre offering both residential and day care, with a gym, swimming pool, art and craft workshops and nature reserve. It was ambitious and far-sighted, combining asylum, in the original sense of the word, with maximum therapeutic support. The financial implications alone killed the concept at source. The document was summarily buried under the mass of missed opportunities. For Helen the rejection rubbed a raw nerve. At best it was blind, at worst a tragic failure to pioneer and model a new approach to the care of those with mental health problems. Conservative committees, visionless bureaucrats, and narrow-minded cost-cutting are all anathema to her. Lack of money is never a good enough reason for saying no.

The Great London Banquet however was one of her more satisfying ventures. For some time she had listened carefully to debates on all kinds of possible public demonstrations of ecumenical strength during the Decade of Evangelism, but none caught her fancy, none seemed original or productive enough, until someone suggested the enactment of one of the best-known parables. The idea was to encourage people in positions of power and influence, both inside and outside the Church, to sit down and eat with the powerless, so that together they could share their stories, make new friendships and leave with an authentic new vision for the future of London. Helen became a director of this mammoth feat of organisation.

On Saturday 3 June 1995, the day before Pentecost, 30,000 people took part in 207 meals across the capital. It poured with rain, but the spirit of Dunkirk lives on in the hearts of the British people, and the event achieved all Helen hoped it would. Churches went out into the highways and byways to bring together members of their local community. MPs met unemployed youngsters. Sudanese and Korean churches shared their food and customs with traditional Anglicans. Bishops, mayors and dignitaries waited on the homeless and sat chatting to street-sweepers. Barriers between haves and have-nots, black and white were broken down.

For Helen this was a beginning, not an end in itself. It inspired her with the vision for a centre for social entrepreneurs, her very own millennium project, now firmly on her turn-of-the-century agenda. This will be a meeting point, a resource base, she says, where visionaries, generally misunderstood or underrepresented at national level, will be encouraged to regenerate their local community, especially in depressed urban areas, by developing a host of initiatives, from nurseries to nursing homes, drug rehabilitation centres to hospices. Initially she needed £45,000 to allow the idea to be researched and developed, so that a bid can be put together – peanuts for Helen, a fortune for anyone of lesser faith.

⌒

She is a director of her local hospice in Sussex, and sorting out their funding problems has been taking up a fair amount of her surplus time and energy recently.

That little piece of information just slips out as we drive through London to her club for dinner. I put my pad and pen into my handbag, and sink down in the car seat with sheer exhaustion, wondering how much else I've missed.

'So I said to Gerald Malone,' the Health Minister's name jolts me back into consciousness, 'I don't agree with your policy on nursing homes. Old people shouldn't have to spend all their capital on nursing care. They like to hold on to a lifetime's hard-earned savings. It gives them a sense of achievement. Fair enough if Mrs Jones can afford it out of her income – but why take her capital?'

'What would you do in his shoes?' I ask with curiosity.

'Cap the lottery at £5 million. Who needs more? Put the excess into a social fund to pay for nursing care for the elderly.'

There is an answer for every social problem. The sad fact is that most of us don't think of it – or if we do, don't say so – at least, not to those who matter.

'What did the Minister say?'

'He asked me to write him a report, so I did. Four sides of A4. I mentioned the Dutch example, where every new estate built has a nursing home at its centre, so that the elderly can stay in the heart of their own community. Goodness knows if he'll take it on board, but at least I've tried.'

We draw up outside the Oxford and Cambridge University Club in Pall Mall. Derek has been a full member for years, she explains. But until very recently, she, not as a wife but as a woman, was allowed only associate membership. It strikes me as a strange irony that any organisation should reduce a pioneer of her calibre to mere associate status simply for being female. But she likes it, she says, because it is so much cheaper and women are banned only from the bar, which is smoky anyway, so that is no great loss.

Could a man have saved Mildmay?, I find myself wondering, as we climb the elegant staircase of this magnificent Georgian building and, beneath the heavy chandeliers, take our rather obvious place among the predominantly male, gruff clientele in the muted whisper-filled dining-room. I can't imagine it somehow. 'We're going to open a hospice for gay men with AIDS, chaps.' Embarrassed shuffling. Polite coughing. They would probably form a committee to debate the possibility in the hope that it would go away, and reject it as unfeasible if it didn't – six years later.

Helen is merely one of a series of remarkable women who have made Mildmay what it is, from Mrs Pennefather and her Deaconesses, spurned by society for doing work unfit for a woman, to its predominantly female management and medical staff today.

'Why do you think so many women have been involved with Mildmay?' I ask her.

'Women have to excel to prove themselves in a world of men,' she says. 'I wanted the best, and they were the best. I'd camp on someone's doorstep to get them if I had to. A man wouldn't do that.'

She still believes it is a disadvantage to be a woman in today's world. God may well be good for individual women, but our social structures, dominated by plodding male bureaucrats, are not. 'Men always think, "Oh, she'll get married, have babies or change her mind," always some reason why you shouldn't be taken seriously. Never cry in front of them, no matter how much they bully you, no matter how awful you feel. They can't handle it. It confirms all their worst preconceptions. You have to stick to your guns or they'll walk all over you. But that isn't regarded as a feminine thing to do. It doesn't make you very popular.'

She remembers with huge amusement how, thumbing through the files one day, she found the copy of a letter from the League of Friends addressed to the Department of Health, dating back to the days when she was trying every means to retrieve the £750,000 of charity money they had collected for Mildmay and refused to release. It said, 'Methinks the lady doth protest too much. She goes on … and on … and on!' She drones slightly and pulls the kind of knowing face one man might make to another when discussing a difficult member of the opposite sex.

I suggest that might have been quite hurtful, but she chuckles with undisguised glee.

'I thought it an enormous compliment.'

We pause while the main course is served. Lamb noisettes cooked to perfection. We tuck in heartily, while around us men in city suits delicately move their food around the plate, sip their claret, and engage in restrained, important, meaningful conversation.

'Men always try to lump me with the aggressive type of woman,' she says, with more than a hint of exasperation in her voice. 'I try to be much more subtle. But you see, we are instinctively more intuitive, and they don't like it awfully. It shows them up. But it is a gift from God, and we can use it to great effect. It can protect us from succumbing to the committee mentality.'

Over coffee in the lounge Helen expands her vision for the future of society, for a more intuitive, 'female' way of making major decisions, while I hastily and surreptitiously make a few scribbled notes on a small pad. The Club does not approve of 'work' being done on its premises, and whenever someone appears she waves at me to hide my pad behind a convenient cushion. 'We'd have so many more exciting ventures if bureaucrats discovered more entrepreneurial ways of working. The world needs people, not committees, people who know instinctively what is needed at grass roots without working it out with a slide rule for ten years, then telling us it can't be done. Nothing is impossible if you have faith, imagination and determination.'

'But Helen,' I remind her, 'many of us have those, but we still don't achieve what you have achieved. What's missing today?'

'Gump!' she says quite simply, with a wave. The pad disappears and I look the very picture of polite innocence.

'Gump?'

'Oh, you know,' she says with a chortle, 'that drive which means that nothing and no one will stop you once you have the bit between the teeth.'

On the face of it her strength and stamina have never waned, though, when pushed, she admits that there were times in those early days when she held her breath and wondered if Mildmay would ever survive.

'You have to appear to have a hide like a rhinoceros. After all, your team is relying on you. They believe in you. What good are you to them if they see a quivering heap? Basically I'm a very optimistic person, and that keeps me going. I see the potholes, but they don't deter me. I lie awake at night wondering how I can get round them. If you do make a mistake and fall into one, climb straight back out and avoid it the next time round.'

Meanwhile, many potential pitfalls still lie in Mildmay's path. It has to take its place like any other hospital in the NHS market economy, fighting for contracts, while capital funding for any new buildings will continue to depend upon charity. 'We have changed a great deal over the years, or else we would still be fighting cholera, but the vision is basically the same: to alleviate suffering wherever possible'. According to the latest figures, every day five more people in the UK discover they are HIV positive.

Around 15 to 20 per cent of them will die in Mildmay.

Sometimes their stories come full circle. Helen was recently invited to speak about Mildmay to the 'lifers' at Wormwood Scrubs. 'It was rather a frightening prospect,' she says, 'until they came in and I saw a group of very sad, very needy young men, much like any other.' They listened intently and, after she finished speaking, one young man, a Ugandan with a lovely face, told her his brother-in-law had died in Mildmay. 'He had an impossible name, so I told him, that even if I could never remember his name, I would never forget his face.' Another young man, who looked absolutely desperate, white and wan, told her he had AIDS and a razor blade. He intended killing himself. 'I told him I realised AIDS was another life sentence, but that I knew many people who were living with it bravely, with hope and peace, because they had found the faith to do so.'

Convicted murderers or government ministers, they're all the same to Helen. She makes no distinction. By some strange coincidence she bumped into Kenneth Clarke again, then Chancellor of the Exchequer, at a party, and was able to thank him personally for his gift of Mildmay ten years previously.

'If it hadn't been for you,' she told him, 'Mildmay would not exist. No one thought we'd ever make anything of it, but now, when you look back over your life's achievements, it will always be one of the brightest jewels in your crown. And it was God who gave it to you.' Never one to miss an opportunity, she went on, 'Now I want to ask something else of you – the freehold.'

'Why on earth do you want that?' he asked her.

'Because it's a mucky lease. Ninety-nine years. It will pass soon enough, and what then? I've put £6.5 million into the project, so I think you owe it to me.'

He promises to deal with the matter forthwith. If he doesn't, one thing is sure, he'll never have Helen Taylor-Thompson off his back.

As she recounts this final anecdote, and I take my leave of her, I'm convinced I hear the sound from heaven of Catherine Pennefather laughing.

Note
1. WRAC stands for the Women's Royal Army Corps; WRNS for the Women's Royal Naval Service; FANY for First Aid Nursing Yeomanry; and SOE for Special Operations Executive, an Allied resistance movement active in France.

As the President of Mildmay, Helen spends less time working for the hospital but she still goes to Africa every year as the Centre in Kampala continues to grow, and from time to time opens a new children's project. As the result of her many experiences in Africa she is devoting herself to an exciting new charity which she founded in 2000. This new venture called Thare Machi *(the* Starfish Initiative*) is seeking through technological education to reduce HIV/AIDS and remove the causes of prostitution and slavery among the desperately poor and illiterate girls and young women in the Developing World, and to help them find a career.*

CHAPTER 2

The Superintendent of Police: Ruth Clark

In 1994, in a blaze of publicity, the Lancashire Police Force appointed the first woman Chief Constable in the country. And although Pauline Clare earned that post through her own merits, the fear and prejudice that tend to keep men in their great bastions of power and to keep women out are not vanquished overnight. Convincing men that a woman is capable of doing what has traditionally been seen as a man's job, of holding her own in a difficult, aggressive environment, and of proving she is an asset, not a threat, is a long, laborious process requiring a special kind of woman. Over many years one woman in particular so impressed the members of the Lancashire force that she paved the way for Pauline Clare's appointment.

When Ruth Clark became Superintendent at Fulwood in Preston, she was one of the highest-ranking female police officers in the country. And no one could have been more surprised by the appointment than Ruth herself, the woman raised in a strict Brethren home where submission to men was part of the natural order, and who left school at 16 to work as a machine operator in the treasury department of the Ormskirk Urban District Council.

The first time I saw her was at an official function at the Royal Preston Hospital where I was working as the press officer.

Representing the authority of the local police, she was tall and striking and looked every inch the part, from her sensible shoes to the shiny navy bowler with its crisp white band of braid. She had taken time with her appearance, her hair, her make-up. Commanding she may have been, but here was no male look-alike.

I remember, as she appeared, being overcome by a wave of intense pride that the Super should be a woman, and not just a little bemused by the way the young policemen around her bowed and scraped and called her 'Ma'am'. A number of senior male managers and a consultant or two all turned their heads to stare in surprise. Was it the impressive uniform that rattled them, or the bearing of the woman who wore it? Even when they finally forced their faces into models of bland indifference, their body language went on betraying a certain unease with this unexpected reversal of the usual hierarchical pattern.

It would have been impossible to ignore her when she walked into any room. She had what can only be described as presence. It wasn't simply her height, the severity of the uniform, which suited her nonetheless, the iron grey hair or the strong set of the jaw. The authority seemed innate. It came from within, from someone calmly at peace with her role and her own femininity.

I caught her eye and she smiled, a broad smile, which lit up her entire face. Any sense of intimidation I may have felt gave way to intense curiosity. I still had painful memories of a visit to the police station in Manchester some 20 years ago to report a missing cassette-player. The catcalls as I walked along the corridors, the thinly veiled sexual innuendos from the constable on duty were threatening and offensive. I realised then with shock and a sense of loss that the friendly family bobby, the *Dixon of Dock Green* image I had been sold in very early childhood, was a thing of the past, and I vowed never to be put in that situation again. Media accounts, years later, of policewomen claiming discrimination did not surprise me. This woman, however, had not only survived such a hostile environment and all the obstructions to promotion, but also had managed to penetrate that most fortified of all the glass ceilings.

I went to meet her at Fulwood police station in Preston shortly before she was due to retire. The station is police-standard-issue, functional, Spartan, unwelcoming with its gloss-painted brickwork, mottled glass doors and the constant rumbling echo of distant boots. It is entirely devoid of any aesthetic touch, and reminds me, I realise, of the penitentiaries I have seen on TV documentaries. No world of women, this. She smiles warmly at the gangs of policemen who scatter and make way for her in the corridor and nod respectfully in return as she passes. She is neither brusque or abrasive yet still very much in command, in a quiet, gracious sort of way. Here is someone, I think with envy, as I follow the long, strong, culotted legs up the scrubbed linoleum staircase, who has learned the art of never having to raise her voice to establish her control, an art I wish I had mastered as the mother of teenage children.

I follow her into her room, surprisingly airy and pleasant, comfortable in a basic, modest way, with two armchairs well away from the large paper-strewn desk that dominates one corner. A young constable brings in coffee in a pot.

'At least policewomen don't have to make the tea any more,' she says wryly, beckoning me to one of the chairs.

'How does a woman get to the top in an organisation like this?' I ask, as she fills two china mugs. Our walk through hard, alien territory has left me feeling a little unsettled.

'I don't really know,' she says, reflectively. 'If you'd told me years ago it would happen, I would never have believed you. My male colleagues planned their career moves. They worked hard at their performance to get to where they wanted to be. But I never expected promotion. I thought I was no better than anyone else.'

Is the self-deprecation that goes hand in hand with unsought achievement personal to her or to all women?, I wonder. Was there really no ambition?

She pauses to think, and I can almost see the mental rerun of her career. She is apparently at home with ruthless self-analysis, and will not give me glib, unconsidered or knowingly dishonest answers.

'No, there was a time, after a series of rapid promotions, when I seemed to stagnate and it worried me. But I remember thinking, "If this is as far as I'm going to get, so be it. I'd rather be content with my lot than try and force a back door."'

Is that resignation?

'No, positive acceptance,' she says, smiling, and for that she has her faith to thank. 'I wasn't prepared to sacrifice my integrity by pretending to be anything but who I was. I know I was downgraded because I was seen in tears after dealing with certain cases. But it didn't matter. There was a point to be made, that policemen and women are human beings too, that we are affected by what we see and hear. If promotion was meant to come my way, it would – without my resorting to a performance.'

Women, she concedes, do tend to pursue different goals from men. Personal fulfilment is much higher on their agenda than professional fulfilment. 'I never wanted to be a man. I would have hated that pressure to succeed. On the other hand, women have to overcome a number of often unwitting, negative childhood messages that undermine their confidence and keep them out of leadership roles.'

In the rather restrictive, dour world of the Lancashire Brethren in which Ruth was raised, children were meant to be seen, not heard. As the youngest of three girls, she felt that her opinion was never worth very much. It was, however, a loving, if materially struggling, family. Her father was a draper who travelled around Lancashire farms selling his wares. Her mother was a furrier who made her children's clothes and sent them to chapel in their Sunday best. That didn't alter Ruth's sense of indignation that they were pitied for living in a Nissen hut and being poor, while the well-to-do received deference and respect. 'Take no notice, Ruth,' her mother said. 'Beauty and goodness come from within.'

If beauty came from within, the external adornments of jewellery and make-up and a decent hair-do were out. Plainness was to be applauded. The three girls were encouraged to blend in, not stand out. Ruth was left feeling highly sensitive about her appearance for the rest of her life.

Although the Bible was instilled into her from babyhood, she had no faith of her own until a visiting evangelist terrified the teenager half to death with a sermon on 'the Rapture'. When Christ came again, he thundered, those who followed Him would be taken up to heaven, while those who did not would be left behind. 'I didn't want to be the woman who was left behind.' She was baptised and, shortly after, started work with the Ormskirk District Council. 'I didn't know what I wanted to do with my life. Mother said that while I was thinking about it I might as well be bringing some money into the family purse.'

It was one of the 'temps' there, married to a retired police sergeant, who began to pester her into applying for the police force. 'I was big, bossy and had large feet, ideal material in one way – but not in another.' Her sheltered upbringing was hardly the best preparation for what lay ahead. Though she was accepted for training, even her trainer thought she wouldn't last the course. 'It was a total culture shock. I was as green as I could possibly be. On a very basic level, I'd never worked with men before and found them rather coarse.'

Her first posting as a constable was to Fulwood in Preston, where she ended her career much nearer the top of the ladder 30 years later. In 1965 a policewoman was not regarded as an equal to a man. They worked a seven-and-a-half-, not an eight-hour day, for nine-tenths of the pay. They had their own separate division, dealing mainly with offences committed against and by women and children. But there were not enough so-called 'women's incidents' coming into the Fulwood station, so Ruth found herself involved in general policing from the very start.

Her first 'on-duty' was the first Sunday in her life she couldn't attend chapel, and it felt very strange. 'Any kind of work was absolutely out in our home on the Lord's Day. I'd never even been allowed to do my homework or read a secular book. It was reserved for holy activities.' She was called out instead to a house where a 15-year-old girl lay dead in the bath. The teenager had killed herself trying to abort a pregnancy. 'I was deeply shocked – on every level. For someone brought up to respect the sanctity of life, I suppose I felt this was the terrible consequence of tampering with nature. I was still very rigid in my thinking, wasn't ready to face the wider questions.'

Ruth had the terrible task of waiting for the girl's parents to come home, so that she could inform them of what had happened.

Later, back at the station, she felt very shaken, but there was no one to help her come to terms with what had been a harrowing event. In those days that kind of incident was regarded as routine policing. It was the first of many situations, completely alien to her own experience, which Ruth was forced to face alone. She was made to understand very quickly that to reveal emotion of any kind was unacceptable. Any copper who couldn't cope shouldn't be in the force. She learned to cope – fast. Being out of her depth became a way of life.

One night she and a male police officer were called out to a secluded country area to resolve a domestic dispute. 'We arrived at a cottage in the middle of nowhere to find a couple in their seventies having a violent quarrel over the amount of time he was spending in the greenhouse. The police officer was 23. I was 20. And neither of us were married. Yet we were expected to become marriage guidance counsellors on the spot and sort the old pair out. I have never felt so inadequate in my life.'

Working on instinct she sent the men out to the greenhouse, made a cup of tea and sat the old woman down for a chat. 'By the time we left peace and harmony was restored. They sent us off with a bag of home-grown tomatoes each.' And from that relatively minor incident, Ruth grasped a crucial fact, which would stand her in good stead in the future, both within and outside the police force. 'I realised then that all anyone needed was someone to listen.'

It would be years, however, before promotion would give Ruth the opportunity to put her listening skills to their greatest effect. Meanwhile, there was the daily grind of basic policing, the threats and curses, being spat upon by drunks, who then vomited down her uniform. It was all part of a normal working day.

Her family were not very positive about her chosen career. It was hardly what they expected from the child whose opinion didn't count for much. Nor did it seem entirely right for the daughter of serious, God-fearing, chapel folk. 'My elder sister was teaching in Africa. My middle sister was in the civil service. Until they married, most of the young women at church were teachers and nurses, well-meaning, caring vocations for nice Christian women. I broke the mould. I don't think anyone really understood what I was doing or why I was doing it. But to their credit, they never tried to stop me.'

For Ruth, despite the struggle of being confronted with human degradation on a level she barely thought possible, there was a deep sense of fulfilment, a growing certainty that she was doing what she had been born to do. With the calling would come the strength to do the things she found most difficult. She had to keep reminding herself of that fact, sometimes through gritted teeth. 'I thought I knew what poverty was. My home was poor, but I'd never known the filth or the deprivation I was seeing now. I'd never been given a cup of tea in a jam jar before. Or been forced to deal with someone who was like a caged animal and could only pour out a torrent of foul, offensive abuse every time he saw a woman.'

'I've known policemen,' I say to her, 'who in order to survive, have become jaded, cynical. Everyone they meet is a potential criminal. Was that never a temptation?'

'People outside the force sometimes think I'm hard,' she says, bemused.

I can't quite believe it, then remember that, the first time I saw her, I noticed a certain tendency to pierce those around her with an eye which seems to fillet flesh from the bone. Teachers have it too, that look which says, 'I don't think you're telling me the full story, Jones, and it will be the worst for you if you don't.'

A professional hazard, she agrees.

'But that's why my faith has been so important. It prevented disillusionment with humanity from setting in. What was I seeing that the Bible hadn't led me to expect?'

Some church members, she imagines, thought she ought to be standing outside the cells, Bible in hand, preaching hellfire and damnation. There's always the temptation for every policeman or woman to become judge and jury as well as arresting officer. 'But I forced myself to try and see people with

God's eyes. And it can be very illuminating. It shattered the preconceptions forced upon me by my childhood teaching. Jesus didn't feel demeaned in any way by mixing with outcasts. He treated everyone with dignity and respect. Once you take off the blinkers and put your prejudices aside, it changes your perspectives.'

That change can be dramatic. For Ruth it was the realisation that Christians were not always the most honest, generous-hearted people in the world. And sometimes prostitutes were.

There is a certain warm glow in Ruth's eyes when she speaks of prostitutes, of sympathy, if not affection. She certainly isn't naive. 'They'd have scratched my eyes out if I'd let down my defences for a minute.' On the other hand, she feels they have more integrity than the punters. 'Prostitutes are women who see through the hypocrisies of a patriarchal system. They see what lurks beyond the male status symbols, the designer suit, the flashy car. They see the fundamental selfishness and ill-discipline that hide behind a thin veneer of respectability.'

It was at this time that the Director of Public Prosecutions resigned over allegations that he sought the services of prostitutes, sending shock waves rippling through the judiciary system.

'Why do they do what they do?' I want to know. 'Is it only for the money?'

'They despise men, but they despise and devalue their own bodies even more.' Long before the horrors of child abuse were uncovered in the public arena, Ruth had made the connection between the damage done to a girl and the woman who is a victim for the rest of her life. 'Rosemary West's descent into evil, for example, was almost a classic case.'

She admits she wasn't the most sympathetic of police officers with the female criminal fraternity. She was taken aback not only by the violence of women, but by their habit, more common than among men, of finding heart-rending justification for their criminal behaviour: married young, couldn't feed the children, premenstrual, menopausal. 'It must be said that for the majority of my working life I was single and didn't understand the pressures of family life. Some of my male colleagues, as husbands and fathers, were much more tender-hearted than I was in dealing with child or female criminals.'

Promotion was comparatively easy within the women's police division. Ruth rose quickly through the ranks, from Sergeant in 1969, to Inspector at Leigh, near Wigan, in 1971, and then in Blackpool in 1973. The Blackpool job was probably the most stressful of all. The large seaside town hosts 17 million visitors a year, and was packed, she says, with everything except common sense. Maintaining law and order could be a nightmare. To add to her pressure, her working life was about to undergo a major revolution. When the Sexual Discrimination Act was passed in 1975, few institutions were as radically affected as the police force. The separate women's division was abolished almost overnight, and Ruth's empire was reduced from a spacious, comfortable suite of offices, to the right-hand bottom drawer of an inspector's desk, shared with four male colleagues and a chief inspector.

Ruth now found herself responsible for ten male constables and a sergeant, all of whom had more service and a better knowledge of the area than she did. 'I'll never forget my first parade. All I could see ahead of me was a row of heavy male jaws, and I was terrified. A verse from the book of Jeremiah found its way to my befuddled brain, and armed me with the courage I needed. "Don't be afraid of their faces, for I am with you and will rescue you." I felt I was going into battle.'

⌒

Her fears were well-founded. Managing the men wasn't easy. It called upon all the powers of assertiveness she had managed to acquire over the years, and one or two new ones. Lynda La Plante's portrait of Detective Inspector Jane Tennison's struggles in *Prime Suspect*, as a lone woman leader in the boys' club, has an uncanny way of taking Ruth back to those early days of mixed policing. 'La Plante has it right. Because I was a woman, the men constantly played tricks on me or tried to catch me out. I had to be one step ahead of them all the time. They watched to see whether I had the stamina to deal with incidents like pub fights. I once had to supervise the observation of a male strip show. They really enjoyed that.'

There could not be the tiniest chink in her professional armour.

'One night I was contacted on my way back to the station and asked my location. When I got back I stopped at the communications room and asked who wanted me. No one, apparently. I went up to the inspector's office, and found the door closed and the lights off, which was very unusual.

'Suddenly I became aware of two large black mounds of fur moving on the desk. Fortunately I love animals, and went over and picked one of them up. That was when I realised there were people behind me in the darkness, laughing. A constable had put two Peruvian guinea-pigs in my in-tray. I ask you, would they have done that to a male officer? It was very amusing, but it made me realise that it would take more than government legislation to eradicate sexual discrimination.'

Prejudice, Ruth says, was as alive and well in the police force as it ever was, but she would dispute with any colleague who said it was a bar to her rising to the highest ranks. 'The glass ceiling is much more in evidence in the Church, where women are frequently relegated to flower arranging and hospitality, than it is in the police.'

Although she wasn't in a position to let it show, the most distasteful part of her entire working life was the raids carried out in Blackpool under the Obscene Publications Act. 'I couldn't take vile stuff like that home. My parents had become very frail and were living with me by then. That would have finished them off. I didn't want to take it into the house anyway, so I watched it at the station behind closed doors.' It was more disgusting than she ever imagined possible. 'How evil could people become?' What worried her most was that months of being subjected to such filth might make her immune to it, and she rang round several of her Christian friends, asking them to protect her with their prayers.

She found it lonely being the only woman at the top. The male managers were chummy and clubby. They went out together for a drink or to play golf, leaving her behind. There were very few people with whom she could share in the strains of the job. Eventually, in the early 1980s, she decided to take a break from policing, so that she could make up for missed opportunities in her education. At Bradford University she took a BSc in Psychology, specialising in interview techniques, non-verbal communication and the effects of drugs on the brain. She returned in 1983 as Chief Inspector for Lancaster.

It was a crucial time for a woman to head up a force. The 1980s would see the introduction of many new, humane guidelines in the treatment of female and child victims of crime. For Ruth they were fascinating years, providing the opportunity to pioneer in the way she had always wanted. 'Inevitably I read the Bible as a policewoman. I saw quite clearly that from the beginning of time that God was aware of the plight of women in a patriarchal society and cared passionately about their domination and exploitation. Traditionally, a woman who was raped became an outcast, a social reject through no fault of her own. The Old Testament made it clear that the perpetrator should either marry her or make provision for her, radical views at the time, missed by subsequent generations. God was good for women. But successive cultures with man in warrior mode have been nothing less than cruel.'

It was apparent to many policewomen that for years, because the police force and judicial system were male-dominated, rape and child abuse victims were not handled sensitively. Ruth thought of acting locally, but felt it would have been interpreted as a personal crusade and provoked counter-productive hostility. What was needed was a radical change of policy at national level. Inevitably, that meant women lobbying for attention. 'I did my share at grass roots, not from a professional vantage point but as a member of the Soroptimists, and it was immensely satisfying to see how influential we and other women's groups could be in challenging the status quo.'

In 1986 the Home Office issued a new set of directives on the treatment of victims of rape and domestic violence. With help and advice from social services and police surgeons, Ruth helped to set up the Rape Crisis Centre in Lancaster. 'We provided bright, sympathetic surroundings, a bath where women could sit for a long, warm soak, a comfortable change of clothing. It was all so obvious you wonder how it could have been missed for so many years.' There was also a play area for children, with a two-way mirror so that they could be interviewed while they were playing. The first little girl asked Ruth where the doll's house was. 'It was an oversight, but fortunately, a local garage generously came to our rescue.'

But Ruth believes that the most significant change of all was in the traditional male attitude to crimes against women. 'There had always been the suspicion, in the days before the morning-after pill, that a woman was claiming rape to cover herself in case she was pregnant. What was she doing walking home alone at one in the morning? What did she expect if she wore her skirt that short? If a wife didn't like domestic violence why did she put up with it? There was an underwritten assumption that a woman must deserve what she got – even if it was abundantly obvious, for example, that a woman with four children and no money could hardly walk away from tyranny.'

Today it saddens her that despite such a radical shift, convictions in rape cases are still so hard to get, and the outcome relies so heavily on the woman's reputation. But injustice always has been one of her greatest frustrations. 'It infuriates me that before a trial the prosecution has to put its entire case before the defence, while the defence need reveal nothing. I lost count of the times I watched someone I knew was guilty walk from the court scot-free because of inadmissible evidence. Those are the times I thanked God I believed in an ultimate judgment and an afterlife.'

That was the certainty that enabled her to keep her calm when she was confronted with parents who had maltreated a child. 'All I could think of was the pain of friends of mine who were infertile. But it's a dangerous way to proceed. You dare not let your personal feelings take over. Self-discipline is essential.'

The most volatile situation is when a member of the police is involved with the victim and then has to deal with the offender. 'It takes an almost superhuman effort to control your own anger.

You know you could pass the flashpoint at any moment. Impartiality, honesty, fairness, all the qualities around which I built my career, and even my life, could vanish in a second. There is this overwhelming urge to hurt as they have hurt – especially if their victim has been a child. "Judge not that you be not judged." I would say it to myself over and over again. "This is a man or woman for whom Christ died. Who are you to judge, Ruth? Since when are you so perfect?" If I hadn't had that resource, I don't know how I would have coped.'

The innocent suffering of children – in road-traffic accidents, when they have been beaten or held against the fire – has always been the greatest challenge to her faith. 'Every part of me seems to cry out, "How could a God who loves children allow it?"' There's no definitive answer, she admits, simply a sense that if human beings are free to behave as they wish, then we are each responsible for our own actions. She herself knocked down a child shortly after she learned to drive. The child survived, but the trauma of the accident has never left her. She feels responsible, though it was probably unavoidable. All human selfishness, she says, whether it is the criminal kind or the petty variety that manifests itself in countless different ways – both at work and in the Church – is never acceptable.

From Lancaster she went, for a brief interlude, to St Anne's on the Fylde coast. Now in her forties, and feeling desperately alone after the death of both her parents for whom she had been caring for some years, she felt she needed someone to care for her for a change. It was here that romance blossomed for the first time in her life, and died almost as quickly. 'I was swept off my feet. Everyone thought it was an ideal match.' But it was a disastrous marriage, lasting a mere two years, leaving her with a profound sense of sadness and failure. 'Despite what he said, he never could come to terms with the demands of my job.'

There was the added pain of discovering that in certain church circles there was still a stigma attached to divorce. Speaking invitations were cancelled without reason. One or two old acquaintances were suddenly rather scarce just when she most needed them.

Meanwhile, she was faced with the greatest challenge of her career. After 25 years, she was sent back to where she started, Fulwood in Preston, initially as deputy to the Superintendent, and then, when he retired, as Superintendent in her own right, the only senior policewoman in the entire Lancashire Constabulary. 'Times really had changed,' she laughs. 'That's when I knew for certain I was no longer expected to make the tea.'

If that was now true of the police force, it certainly wasn't of her church. 'A friend asked me one day how I reconciled having such power at work with being denied any in church. She wanted to know whether it was my humility. I told her I didn't think of what I had as power, more as responsibility. A superintendent should look after the staff, listen to their problems and their pain.'

I ask whether her male colleagues see it that way.

She doesn't think so. But nor have they had her struggle to overcome the childhood voices that threatened to sap her confidence and hold her back at every stage of the way. She always found it difficult to accept criticism positively, to distinguish professional assessment from a personal attack. The self-consciousness she inherited as a teenager made her feel very vulnerable in such a strident male environment.

The challenge, when promotion came, was how to take the opportunity without sacrificing the femininity she had taken so long to discover. 'I remember being told that if I wanted to get to the top in the police I would have to learn to drink, curse and swear like a man. They were so wrong. My femaleness was meant to soften and mellow a male-dominated world, to make it an easier place for the men.'

Everyone is more aware of work stress among the police at last, she says with a certain measure of relief. Marriage breakdown is endemic. It almost goes with the job. And she can't see it getting any better. 'We're under constant scrutiny. The government has made the police responsible for crime, but doctors are not responsible for the health of the people. The crime rate continues to rise no matter what we do. And then the public expect more of us than ever. Once upon a time neighbours would sort out the children misbehaving in the street. Now they're intimidated. They call in the police. Once we walked to the scene of the crime, and had time to compose ourselves between cases. Now we're at incidents within seconds.'

It was as a superintendent she found she could do what no man could do, simply by dint of being a woman. 'I gave the men permission to cry. They would never have cried in front of another man. It would have been station news. It would have affected their promotion prospects. And policemen need to cry. Oh, they develop mechanisms for self-preservation, but you can only harden yourself to a certain degree. I've seen very powerful men break down. And I've cried with them over their domestic problems, or over a job that was just too hard to bear. I didn't want any young policeman or woman in my care to feel the lack of support I felt for all those years. I hope that as a woman I've been able to give the men permission to be real about how they feel.'

After 30 years in active service Ruth has decided the time has come to hang up her hat. She looks around the room, like so many other rooms she has known in so many other stations, in virtual disbelief. The world as she knows it is coming to an end, and there's a mixture of excitement and apprehension. 'I want to wake up in the morning and look forward to what the day will bring. I want to go to my wardrobe and not take out a white shirt. I want to hear the phone without a sinking feeling in the pit of my stomach that it may be a major incident. I want to live without constantly listening for a bleep.'

She is only in her early fifties. Won't she miss the status?

'Status never mattered to me. It makes me sad to see how a label affects people, how they invest their selves in their role, and then become pompous – especially men. They like a little servility, and mistake it for respect. I was always glad to leave it behind at the station. At parties I breathed a sigh of relief when no one could guess what I did for a living. Once, a man was convinced he knew. I was horrified. I thought the fact that I could hold my own in a corner had given the game away. Then he said triumphantly, "You're an actress." I suppose I was in some ways, but I hope I've been real too.'

What she will miss is bringing reassurance to the fearful,

restoring harmony to families, hearing 'thank you' from children, having their furry sweets pressed into her hand – 'oh, and crying with relief when a lost child turns up, like the day a little girl we were looking for in Blackpool and had almost given up hope of finding, was discovered fast asleep among the donkeys.'

There will be one unexpected, wonderful bonus: marriage to Max Winterbottom, Deputy Clerk of the Lancashire County Council. Their paths crossed when Ruth was supervising the handling of a sit-in at County Hall. Max, a widower with two grown-up children, was at home with the flu, but he rang to say that he would struggle in to work if he was needed. 'I've had quite enough of their bureaucracy, let him stay at home,' Ruth replied. They actually met the following week to review the situation, and romance took them both by surprise.

After her previous experience, Ruth found it hard to commit herself. But Max was gentle and persistent. His first wife had died of cancer after a long and happy marriage. He had had his own share of pain and sorrow, and had confidence enough in the future for both of them.

Not all her nearest and dearest entered into the joy she had found at last. The Brethren do not condone remarriage. The strain shows on her face. It's a face, I note, that gives away every emotion, never rigidly trained to keep feelings at bay, not a stereotypical 'police face'.

As I leave her and walk back down the stairs, my footfall joining the dozens more in countless different parts of the building, I have the feeling that had I been a criminal I would have been fortunate to find myself in Ruth's office, for I would have found integrity and compassion, qualities developed not overnight, but on the long, hard road of discipline and self-discovery. But woe betide me if I had tried to manipulate her simply because she was a woman. In justice tempered with mercy, I might also have found a glimmer of God in the least likely setting.

～

I saw Ruth in her new home several months later. The retirement parties were over, and marriage had turned her into the very model of domesticity. An enticing smell of home-made soup wafted out of a pristine kitchen. A Christmas cake, lovingly prepared months in advance, was already tucked in its tin.

'The whole experience of making that cake, the smell of it, the feel of moulding and making it, the sense of being mistress in my own kitchen, was a sheer delight.'

She's in jeans and jumper these days, still imposing, but relaxed now, manifestly, radiantly happy, as she shows me proudly round, loving the chance of looking after Max. 'He's been on his own for four years. I want him to have a meal to come home to, to sit and chat together every evening. I want to enjoy the simple things, observe the cameos of human experience in village life. Do you know, I can buy chicken carcasses for 20 pence in the village, and make all my own soups. A £300 designer dress couldn't have given me as much pleasure.'

'Do you ever pine to be back,' I asked her, 'particularly when you see Pauline Clare in charge of your old force?'

The connection between the two women did not go unnoticed at her retirement do, though she still rather balks at the way the word 'caring' kept cropping up in the speeches, 'as if caring was a female prerogative. They kept saying, "Everyone you work with is touched by the experience in some way." Apparently I had a soothing effect on the most abrasive of colleagues, which is nice to know.'

Afterwards, in private a sergeant said to her, 'You were the only one who wrote to congratulate me when I was promoted. I wish someone had said what a good boss you were,' and that gave her the greatest pleasure of all.

The boss. She never sought it or expected it, but she made it. 'And somehow I managed to fulfil all the functions of the office without resorting to playing a man. Doesn't that prove God is on woman's side?

'The potential of women is limitless,' she says, as we stand gazing out of her floor-to-ceiling picture window at the Lancashire hills rolling gently away to the horizon. 'Look at what some of the women in the Old Testament achieved. Rahab, the prostitute, who protected spies and saved her family; Naomi, left childless and a widow, who became a mother of her people; Deborah, the judge and leader. I think there's a progressive awareness in the New Testament of the influence women can have.'

'Who are you?' I prompt her. 'With whom do you most identify?'

She thinks for a while.

'I'm like the woman with the haemorrhage, hardly daring to touch the hem of Jesus' robes. Typical of a woman, isn't it? We don't want to trouble Him, or intrude. We feel worthless. Our needs are not enough to claim His attention. Then He turns and touches us. Perhaps it's only now, released from cultural expectations, that we're beginning to feel brave enough to fulfil our full potential.'

Feminists might claim a compromise, that Ruth's refusal to play the men at their own game, her lack of ambition to get to the top prove that only the stereotypical weak woman leaves the men unthreatened. But Ruth is not weak. It was no small achievement for the little girl who felt her opinion didn't count to become an influential leader. She learned to hold her corner in the most aggressive circumstances, to be assertive without being unfeminine. She proved a woman could earn respect in a very male world, by being herself and therefore making it more human. She showed that the police do not have to become hardened, but can draw on hidden reserves of compassion for the toughest criminal without excusing crime. Ultimately she has become the satisfied housewife without lamenting power, position or status.

Inspired, I went home and baked a cake.

Ruth has a busy retirement. She is currently chair of the Lancashire Ambulance NHS Trust, a more than part-time position.

CHAPTER 3

The Writer: Susan Howatch

The lot of the clergy, however the media may portray them, is not all tea and sympathy, or even a glass or two of sherry. I say this from grim personal experience. When I took on my particular clergyman in his pre-ordained state, for richer or poorer, for better or worse, I had no idea how those vows would be tested, or that I would live them out in competition with a force mightier than a mistress: the Church of England. So often, caught in the crossfire of clerical life, mystified by the political machinations of clergy and congregations, mangled by their strange, manipulative games, I have blessed the wisdom and insight of one woman, who appears to understand the twists and turns of this complex psychological maze, and to have found the way out. Sitting up in bed with Susan Howatch, in the shape of one of her Starbridge novels, can be a revelation. My husband, book in hand, without dog-collar (stripped of their accoutrements, they are, as Howatch describes so well, men like any others), has gasped on more than one occasion, 'She's been here. She's seen it. It's uncanny.'

Is she novelist or prophet? Living a stone's throw from Church House, Westminster, Susan Howatch would be ideally placed to play the seer – if she chose. There would be no shortage of clergy queuing for the pearls of wisdom she might throw in their direction, if she were to cast herself as a modern Julian of

Norwich. She shares Mother Julian's love of silence and solitude, her mystical, yet earthy approach to spirituality. Both translated their visions into words, but the Starbridge novels, whatever truth they may encapsulate, are essentially fiction, and Susan Howatch would be horrified to be thought of as anything but a writer. Perhaps, however, the most stimulating, satisfying fiction writing is prophetic, challenging our accepted preconceptions, warning us of the consequences of our behaviour, exploring and interpreting divine intervention in the lives of ordinary people. And the message Susan Howatch proclaims from book displays in shops and supermarkets is that the will of God is redemption from the folly of our all-too-human ways.

She certainly doesn't look the quintessential wild and hoary prophetess, in her baggy, black polo sweater and easy-fit trousers, the comfortable working uniform of the writer. The first time I met her, in 1989, when I was a raw researcher in religious programmes for Central Television, I'm not sure what I expected but remember being relieved by the bobbed hair, hearty laugh and jolly, down-to-earth normality. Journalists have since made much of her predilection for Marks & Spencer, as if they can't quite believe that someone who can afford to endow Cambridge University with £1 million, for the first lectureship in theology and natural science, could eschew designer clothes. Though why a taste for Marks & Spencer should be a certain sign of asceticism is beyond me. She has, she admits grudgingly, a couple of 'good' outfits for special occasions, but she says it dismissively with a wave of the hand. She is simply not interested in that kind of superficiality.

Every visitor is stunned by the contemporary decor of her flat, probably because they expect something more befitting a writer who inhabits an imaginary world full of gracious, old buildings reeking of age and incense, and who obviously loves them. This bold, ultramodern contrast comes as a complete shock. Black wrought-iron furniture stands in stark relief against dazzling white walls displaying an array of dramatic Celtic bronzes. Neither plant nor ornament soften the straightness of the symmetrical lines. This is a single woman's working flat, too bright to be austere, too bold to be completely comfortable. The melting wall-to-wall carpet is a vivid cat's-eye green. Her bathroom suite would look better through sunglasses on a morning after a night before. 'Is this the lambent amber of Bishop Jardine's eyes?' I ask her as I emerge. 'Peach,' she exclaims, laughing, 'that's peach!'

She throws on a jacket, pulls a brush quickly through her hair and we set off for one of her favourite haunts – a posh hotel rooftop restaurant. There, while we share some diverting diocesan tales, we sit giggling under the palms like two naughty schoolgirls. She is vivacious and entertaining. The straight brown bob swings from side to side as she tosses her head. Her eyes twinkle with merriment and mischief. The foibles of humanity, and especially the clergy, are an endless source of wonder and amusement. 'I looked down on them from my window when I lived opposite Salisbury Cathedral,' she confides, 'and imagined, as they scurried backwards and forwards, what guilty secrets lay hidden behind the austere clerical garb. We put them on a pedestal. We invest them with all our desire for holiness and piety, and the glamour of the role blinds us to the fact that playing the part is a man with the weaknesses, fears and insecurity of any other man.' It doesn't take a great deal of insight to see that for her the clergy are a prime example, a symbol perhaps, of how all humans hide their real selves behind a 'glittering image', which we fabricate for ourselves or allow others to fabricate for us.

For a researcher who had not long since completed a network documentary on clergy stress called *Great Expectations*, begging the viewer to see and accept the clergy for who they were, her words were music to my ears. But in the end, the television programme I had planned to make about Susan Howatch came to naught. At that time she had written only *Glittering Images*, the first book in the Starbridge series, and a novel about the salacious goings-on in an episcopal palace wasn't deemed seriously 'religious' enough by my head of department to merit its writer a religious documentary. He, like many men, couldn't shake off the image of the airport novelist.

I first heard of *Glittering Images* at a deanery do, a jolly event inflicted annually on the clergy, allowing for an exceedingly good nosh-up, some hale and hearty back-slapping among the men and some contrived, rather embarrassing attempts at social intercourse among their wives.

'Have you read *Glittering Images*?' asked one clergyman loudly over a plateful of quiche and coleslaw, sending a spray of puff pastry in every direction.

'A load of twaddle,' interjected the then suffragan bishop, now retired. 'Pure fantasy,' he said with a disarming smile, and magnanimous wave of the hand, while the other fiddled frantically with his large pectoral cross.

'Do you think so?' the clergyman persisted, with the innocence of a hedgehog trying to cross the M25. 'I thought there were some very profound home truths in it, some familiar characters perhaps.'

'Scandal and corruption in the bishop's palace? Wishful thinking. Don't you believe a word of it.'

And as the bishop marched off to find himself a stiff drink, I decided there and then that this book was likely to be the best read I had found in a long while. I must have it – and wasn't satisfied until it was in my hands.

From the opening pages I was almost hypnotised, irresistibly drawn into the illusory world of Starbridge, revolving like a diamond in the light to reveal a myriad different facets of reality. It made me wonder, of all the people I thought I knew, how many were merely letting me see what they wanted me to see, their 'glittering image'? What of my own front? Was I little more than the sum of my chosen, glamorised parts?

The clergyman at the party was right. Written large on every page, like it or not, there was my ex-bishop, with his cigars, his brandy, his manicured hands and well-tempered voice, reproduced in the charm and sophistication – if not in the tortuous and tortured relationships – of Alex Jardine, her 1930s Bishop of Starbridge. Susan had never met my bishop. I checked. He, in the late 1980s, was a member of a dying breed, still at its height in the 1960s and 1970s, when savoir faire was as important as piety, and worldliness a distinct advantage to any cleric bent on climbing the ecclesiastical ladder.

The narrator, a brilliant, handsome and ambitious priest and academic Charles Ashworth, is sent undercover by the ecclesiastical hierarchy to investigate rumours of an unconventional relationship in the Bishop of Starbridge's household. Ménage à trois or triangle of total innocence, the truth is almost impossible to grasp, and what he finds forces him to confront the ghosts in his own murky past. Ashworth's fragmented psyche is dismantled and put back together more cohesively during a course of intense spiritual direction with the enigmatic Anglo-Catholic monk, Jon Darrow, who, in a single sentence, hands him the key to spiritual and emotional wholeness, 'You'll never be master of your future, until you're master of your past.'

To weave and then unravel the complex web of a psychological thriller with the aid of contemporary counselling techniques, was innovative, even ambitious. If psychotherapy, spiritual direction, counselling, call it what you will, could enable an anguished young theologian to come to terms with the deprivations and failures of his past, rework his present and face the future in stronger, saner mind, there must be hope for the most desperate cases. I could think of at least a dozen people in my local church who would benefit from a session with the extraordinary Jon Darrow. Come to think of it, I wouldn't have minded an hour or two with the mystical monk myself. We all need someone to haul us out of our human mess from time to time.

Small wonder Susan Howatch was repeatedly asked where he was, usually by desperate clergymen. 'He's a figment of my imagination,' she would explain.

'How can he be? I need him. He's my only lifeline.'

And she would refer them to a monastic order whose reputation for restorative therapy and inner healing she knew she could trust.

The part of the book I found most intriguing and yet couldn't quite grasp was her own religious experience, weaving its way enigmatically through the pages, there, yet not quite tangible, like the Cheshire cat in *Alice in Wonderland*. Instinctively I knew there had been some major mental upheaval in the woman who used to write those historical family sagas such as *Penmarric* and *Cashelmara*, thicker than and almost as heavy as the telephone directory. But what? Not that I had been an avid reader of her earlier books, but then I wasn't an avid reader at all in the early 1970s. It took a particularly debilitating, nauseous pregnancy in 1977 to lay me low enough to introduce me to some of the women writers I had missed: Jane Austen, the Brontës and Elizabeth Gaskell. My reading continued and the twentieth century was just about in sight when, in 1979, the BBC televised her epic saga, *Penmarric*, a serial lasting as long as it must have taken her to write the book. Like millions of others, I was hooked, glued week by week to the TV. Nationally, Susan Howatch became a household name.

By the time I had read *Glittering Images* I knew enough about the medium to realise it must have served her well financially. Successful writers were a tough little breed – or so I thought – given to a certain amount of angst, of course, enough to give an edge to their work, but all the time fairly sure of themselves, well worked-out and full of happy endings. They were not, on the whole, overcome by sudden, dramatic, Damascus-road-style revelations. Yet here was dynamic religious experience so raw it had to be recent. Was this new literary departure simply evidence of a hitherto unknown ability to communicate in convincing theological language, or was the spiritual psyche of the real Susan Howatch, hidden from view by her personal need for privacy and the glittering image of fame and fortune, communicating through her characters? That was the mystery I set out to solve that day in 1989 when we had lunch together on a London rooftop, the capital winking alluringly below us, Starbridge-like, through the large picture windows.

'I merely woke up one morning, and realised everything I had thought important was in fact unimportant and everything I had thought unimportant was vital.' That was what she said in the *Church Times* in 1991, and that was the gist of what she said to me. Her own personal religious drama was no romanticised, television-style conversion in mystical soft focus, with a choir of heavenly beings cooing at the dawning of inner peace and tranquillity. It was in fact the most uncomfortable experience of her life. 'When one has lived for many years with the conviction that God is of no particular relevance to one's life and that one can do very-nicely-thank-you without Him, it comes as a great shock to realise that there's something out there closing in – or, as the mystics might have put it, something in there welling up.' She felt bruised and battered, as if God had got hold of her by the scruff of the neck, slammed her against the nearest wall and shaken her until her teeth rattled. It was, she admits, probably the only way to get through to someone who had built around themselves such an inviolate glittering image.

Fame, fortune, to write a blockbuster by the time she was 30: these were the major goals of the young Susan Howatch. She ascribes her ambition and her ongoing penchant for the solitary life, to being an only child. Born in 1940, raised by a mother who taught bridge in Leatherhead after her father was killed in the war, she was writing stories virtually from the moment she learned how to form a sentence. By the time she completed her education at Sutton High School and began a law degree at King's College in London, she had already submitted the manuscript of her first novel.

The rejection slips kept on coming. One particular refusal from her present publishers, Collins, proved a turning point in her life. She was invited to their premises in St James's Place, fussed, cosseted and encouraged to make certain alterations to her manuscript, only to receive a polite, but casual brush-off after months of slaving on the text. Numb with rage she decided she was finished with Britain, with rejection, humiliation and a dreary administrative job.

New York welcomed her with open arms and published her at

once. 'Britain in the 1960s was very male-oriented. There was little room for a woman with brains. America was different. They weren't suspicious of clever women. They didn't frown on ambition, or despise success the way the British do with our inverted snobbery – which is merely a thin veneer for a culture of envy. In America you were judged on what you produced.' And she produced a best-seller.

When she was 29, *Penmarric* was accepted for publication. Destiny was on course. Her agent told her only Norman Mailer had ever been offered a larger advance, and she thought, 'Oh-ho, terrific, the fairy story comes true.' Much later she wrote, 'In all the euphoria attending my success I quite forgot that according to the Greeks, when the gods want to destroy a man they give him what he most wants.' She would probably now agree with the great mystic Teresa of Avila, that it was not the unanswered, but the answered prayers we should worry about.

Published in 1971, *Penmarric* was the first grand-scale family saga of obsession, love and tragedy since Galsworthy, and the only black spot on Susan Howatch's otherwise clear horizon was that the land of the *Forsyte Saga* lumped her with Barbara Cartland on the shelves marked 'Romance'. Would that have been the case had she been a man? She doubts it. The old prejudices die hard. Racy tales of glamorous folk who get their come-uppance might sell in their millions, but are hardly considered the stuff of great literature – not if written by a woman, at any rate. 'I never have become part of the literary establishment in Britain,' she said to me years later, with just a hint of regret. 'I make too much money to be taken seriously.' Sadly, popularity still equals mediocrity and the Starbridge novels, devoured by bishops, theologians and academics, are only just beginning to dent the stereotype.

Meanwhile, with American sculptor husband, Joseph Howatch, and baby daughter, Antonia, in tow, 'I jet-setted away in the fast lane of life, indulging in a time-consuming and futile preoccupation with champagne, Porsches, large houses', and a whole variety of other, equally meaningless pleasures, which she finds too boring to spend time discussing today. 'When you have all you ever wanted by the time you're 30, there isn't a great deal left to enjoy at 40.' Nonetheless the 1970s were highly productive years. *Cashelmara* appeared in 1974, *The Rich are Different* in 1977 and *Sins of the Fathers* in 1980.

There were by now, however, darker shades in her writing, a hint that all was not well in the world of make-believe, a certain gloom amid the glamour, the suggestion that there might be a price to pay for the self-indulgence of the past, that there must be more to life than material success. But if there was, what was it, and how could it be found? Manifestly, at this stage she hadn't a clue. In 1975 her marriage had fallen apart. It was a profound shock, leaving her with an immense sense of failure and a huge void somewhere at the centre of her being, which she tried unsuccessfully to fill with a series of transient relationships with men. Unable to face returning straight to England, she took advantage of the special tax concessions for writers in Ireland, and lived in Dublin with her daughter, wanting only peace and quiet and to immerse herself in the therapy of writing. A shocked *Daily Mirror* reported, 'Millionairess Sue lives in one room and sleeps on a sofa.' More shocking – she didn't wear make-up or jewellery or eat caviar for lunch. In fact, 'How she spends her money is hard to fathom.'

In 1980 she moved into a flat opposite the west front of Salisbury Cathedral and completed the book that would force her to face the fact that salvation was not to be found in writing either. It was called *The Wheel of Fortune*, and it was an ambitious attempt, she says reflectively, to say something of more significance to mankind. 'I was exploring the nature of time and certain elements in the philosophy of Boethius. I became hopeful that both my publishers and the critics would realise that my work was maturing.'

Far from it. One day in 1983 she rang her editor at Hamish Hamilton and told him she would be late in delivering the manuscript. 'Susan,' he replied, in desperation, blissfully unaware that his innocent few words would ultimately cost him thousands of pounds in future book revenue, 'what am I going to tell the accountants at the board meeting?'

That was the moment she realised that in the rat race she was the bait, not a front-runner, a means to an end for her publisher. To compound her sense of aggravation and frustration, the book, when published, though a huge commercial success, was snubbed by the critics, relegated to the usual 'airport novel' status, and stocked, as ever, with the bodice-rippers. Her serious novel had been trashed.

A worse blow was to come. Thirteen-year-old Antonia decided to return to her father in the USA. Susan now felt a failure as a writer and a mother. The glittering image was in tatters. She made no effort to hold the final remnants together, but retired from the public eye, determined, if she could, to discover the real person hiding behind the public persona. And what she found filled her with a sense of complete and utter desolation. 'As my entire world turned itself inside out to become alien and meaningless, I slipped into deep depression. Why bother to publish if all that was required of my books was to keep my publishers in the black and give employment to my lawyers and accountants? I had my fame, I had my fortune; I had served myself to the very best of my ability, but I had wound up profoundly unhappy and unfulfilled.'

For three years she became a virtual recluse, rarely answering the phone, aware only of the cathedral, 'vibrating and coruscating' away beyond the window of her study, drawing her with an irresistible magnetism the way Starbridge would lure its lovers to their downfall in her books one day. In her case, however, it was the first tiny glimmer of possible salvation. She slipped in surreptitiously to sit at the back while the offices were said, to listen for a message from God or simply imbibe the atmosphere. The casual observer, she admits, would have thought she was becoming unhinged, but in fact her experience wasn't unusual for someone of around 40 having a mid-life crisis. Could she have come through it without God, one journalist asked her. That never occurred to her, she said, since, in Jungian terms, it felt as if God Himself were exerting pressure on her psyche. 'Theologians call it "the Second Journey", a restructuring of one's life. I was coming to my spiritual senses. I'd lived for me. Now I wanted to do what God wanted.' What did He want? She didn't know. And He didn't seem to be in a hurry to tell her. That was the problem.

Since her theological education was schoolgirl-rudimentary, she decided to research God, much as she would any subject material of her books, and took an A level course in religious studies. She devoured the works of such great spiritual writers as Charles Raven, Austin Farrer and Dean Inge, whose wisdom she later passed on to a wider public through the mouths of her characters, and who, at that time, cast light on her own sense of disorientation. Some words of Dean Inge gave her great comfort: 'The silence of God has always been a great trial to mankind.' Nevertheless, her trial continued unabated. The vicar of the Close mopped up her tears of despair, administered the laying-on of hands and prayed for her. 'He rode round on a bicycle. I would run after him and catch him and ask him questions. He used to say, "Keep listening for the word of God, Susan, it will come", and pedal off.'

Revelation came at last, as promised and, when it did, it was so obvious that it was the easiest message in the world to miss. 'Do for me what you've always done best. Write!' So from the back of a drawer where she had stuffed it, she pulled out the manuscript of a novel she had written about the Church of England and went ahead with publication. It was called *Glittering Images*.

Little did I guess at that first meeting that my own professional crisis was waiting in the wings. 'I see from the *Sunday Times*,' she wrote to me, a few weeks later, 'that your Guinness book is shortly to be published, and I wish you lots of luck with it.' In fact it was a disaster. My own real-life family saga, based on my illustrious in-laws, had a libel writ slapped upon it by those not-after-all-so-illustrious relatives within weeks of publication. All hard-backed copies were promptly burned. Any hopes I might have had of overnight fame and fortune went up in smoke, but I suspect Susan would have suspected that I had been saved from a great deal of folly and heartache.

Her old motives had gone. So had the old drive. She had been left, for a time, faltering with uncertainty. How could she explain what had happened to her? In this hell-bent materialistic world, would anyone take her seriously? Should she go on writing novels at all? She had written *Glittering Images* because writing gave her pleasure, because she felt compelled to write it, but put it away because she wondered whether it might be nothing more than an exercise in self-indulgence. When her American agent asked for a peep, she had tried to put her off, saying, 'Oh, it's just a little church thing.' But 'the little church thing' was the beginning of a major series. It turned Susan Howatch into a woman with a mission: to communicate to the widest possible audience the eternal realities of failure and redemption.

After several ostensibly uncreative years the Starbridge novels popped up in quick succession, as if they had been stored from time immemorial in some sealed compartment in her brain, waiting for the right moment. *Glamorous Powers* was the second, followed by *Ultimate Prizes*, *Scandalous Risks*, *Mystical Paths* and *Absolute Truths*, six books in eight years. Each psychodrama is complete in itself and can be read on its own. Together they provide a sweeping, panoramic overview of the struggles and crises in the Church of England between 1937 and 1968, told through the fictionalised dramas of her three major characters and their families, representing the three major strands in the Church at the time. Charles Ashworth, who narrates the first and last of the series, is the conservative, middle-churchman, theologically sound and safe; Jon Darrow, describing his downfall induced by those oh-so-seductive, glamorous powers, is the Anglo-Catholic mystic; and Neville Aysgarth, recounting his all-consuming pursuit of the ultimate prizes, is the liberal, low Protestant.

To their chagrin she sacked her regular publishers, Hamish Hamilton, and opted instead for HarperCollins. The managing director of Penguin, which had published her earlier novels in paperback, was convinced that stories about the Church wouldn't sell nearly as well. 'Susan,' he said, 'no one's interested in religion these days.' Months later, when the publication of Salman Rushdie's *Satanic Verses* and Iran's pronouncement of a death sentence on the author meant that he was obliged to turn up for an official dinner in an armoured car with blacked-out windows, under heavy escort, she assumed the director had changed his mind.

But the books sold – about 200,000 copies each – because at the end of the day they are ripping good, read-until-morning yarns. They are not works of Christian polemics, she explained in a lecture in 1994, they simply pose those tricky questions we all prefer to dodge, such as, 'What makes for lasting happiness? How can we stop getting into messes and making ourselves miserable? How do we forgive someone rather than just going through the motions? [This, she admits, is "a tough one".] How do we live in harmony with a spouse or parent who drives us up the wall? And, most important – how do we live harmoniously with ourselves, when our unresolved problems push us in the opposite direction?'

'I don't write autobiography; I get my kicks from being someone else,' she said, when I went back to see her in what she calls her 'minimalist' flat in London seven years later to find out how it felt to be hailed at last as a modern-day Trollope (only now the flat was starker than ever as she was in the process of moving back to her roots in Surrey). 'But inevitably I draw on experience. There is something of me on every page.' As I suspected, although it is impossible to paint a clear biographical portrait of Susan Howatch from her books, her fingerprints are nonetheless there for all to see, as surely as any creation bears the hallmark of its creator. With each book they seemed firmer, surer, for as the years passed her faith deepened and her grasp of theology became a more powerful tool in the execution of her plot.

She does not, she insists, write 'vicars and knickers' novels, though she is often asked why her clergy are such emotional wrecks, drinking too much and having affairs. 'My books are about spiritual journeys. I think it's very hard for clergymen because they are the recipients of all our projections. Women especially project on to them their need for the father or husband they've never had, the superman of their dreams. We all want them to be the holy person we know we're not – the stainless-steel saint. I was very keen to draw them as real people, neither the wimps portrayed on TV, nor the stereotypes who are virtuous without effort, because it's only when we see them as ordinary human beings that their true heroism becomes apparent. Sweating blood to live up to your beliefs can be very heroic. Yes, they get into messes, as we all do, when they're cut off from God and deeply unhappy. Booze and sex are an attempt to fill the void, artificial ways of anaesthetising the pain. But when they sin they repent, and are forgiven, redeemed, reprieved, renewed. They serve the community better than before.'

Each Starbridge hero hurtles his way to the inevitable clerical breakdown and ultimate repair at the hands of a spiritual adviser. These characters are popular with the clergy, who have never seen themselves so passionately, dynamically or empathetically portrayed before. They are red-blooded heroes, not slimy, sexless, Trollopian schemers. Howatch is quite obviously very committed to her men, not in a maudlin way like Dorothy Sayers, who, she maintains, fell in love with her fictional detective, Lord Peter Wimsey, and sacrificed objectivity to sentimentality. In Starbridge she is God, a pale and feeble reflection of the Creator, admittedly, but a benevolent and compassionate deity all the same, who understands why her creatures behave as they do, and still believes in their potential without being soft on their sin.

When I tried to suggest that Neville Aysgarth had taken advantage of his privileged position as Archdeacon of Starbridge to seduce a naive and much younger woman, using his power inappropriately, as certain church ministers have been known to do, and that it therefore constituted a form of abuse, she became very defensive. 'It could certainly be construed as abuse, but it's much more complicated than that. There was no series of "other women". He loved Venetia. Look at his desperate home situation, caught in a relationship he had outgrown. Venetia is his grand illusion, his escape. Infatuation turns to obsessive love, which is destructive, but that's another matter. Call it the aberration of a middle-aged man, if you like, but not abuse.'

'But he abandons her.'

'He takes the difficult option. Stays and cares for a wife he no longer really loves – because he feels responsible for her. Isn't that heroic, self-sacrificial? Doesn't it contradict the self-indulgence around today?'

The story is based on a historical event: Prime Minister Asquith's doomed and tragic infatuation with the daughter of his closest friend. Susan had wanted to write it for years, recasting Asquith as a clergyman, but it was only after her own religious conversion that she had the confidence to do it.

Of her three major characters I like Aysgarth least, but remain extremely fond of Jon Darrow. She has been struck by the way different people develop their own particular favourites. She finds Darrow the most complex of her characters: almost superhuman in *Glittering Images*, confused and muddled when he tells his own story in *Glamorous Powers*, an aggravating buccaneer in *Ultimate Prizes*, Venetia's 'fabulous old pet' in *Scandalous Risks*, an inadequate elderly parent in *Mystical Paths*, and a wise and valued friend to Charles Ashworth in the final book. 'No one portrait is complete in itself,' she explains. 'Truth has many sides, and each is one aspect of the whole truth about the person. Only the creator has access to the full picture. Which side we see depends on our human perspective, which goes to show how little we really know people. With every new book I simply shake the kaleidoscope and present the reader with a new facet of reality.'

Her male readers feel that for a woman she writes very convincingly as a man. She manages to get beneath a skin that is neither as thick nor as protective as the owner would have others believe. She suspects her skill probably comes from the close study of masculinity she made during 11 years of marriage. Her powers of observation, I reflect with considerable admiration, must be far more finely tuned than mine, for I have been married twice as long as that and still find it hard to work out what makes a man tick. 'A competent novelist should transcend gender,' she responds dismissively. 'People are people, not male or female. Some men are much less complex than women.'

She has, she says with undisguised admiration, met many deeply spiritual men, not afraid of their feminine side. Given the pressures they face, and others' expectations of them, that is no mean achievement. 'Our highly competitive society isn't kind to men, especially men who are predisposed to a more reflective kind of life. Hensley Henson, Bishop of Durham in the 1930s, refused to have a telephone. He spent every morning alone in his study, praying, reading, writing. Bishops today are like cats on a hot tin roof, pulled in every direction, responding to ceaseless demand, expected to be all things to all people. It must put their marriages under severe strain.'

Like Charles Ashworth in *Absolute Truths* when he becomes Bishop of Starbridge, men's careers make them lose touch with their true selves. They become the victims both of a forceful masculine culture and their own biological drives. 'Men compete with each other instinctively. They are driven by the urge for power. By nature, they have to achieve, have to be on top. Everything about them must go up. They can't even fake sex. A woman can. We have much more scope to be ourselves,' Susan says.

Although Ashworth loves his wife, Lyle, he loses sight of her. She becomes a mere prop, albeit a crucial one, in the advancement of his career. 'What does he think I am, a robot who does all the chores at the touch of a button? I clean his shoes, fill his cigarette case, organise his wardrobe, run his house, control that trout, Peabody, protect him from all the church women who adore him passionately, make sure he has nourishing meals at the correct times, listen to his moans and groans – and provide sex on demand. Do I ever get any thanks? No, he takes me for granted. It's not right, Charles, it's not right!' writes Lyle. Theirs is the classic breakdown in communication between spouses, where the woman feels she has become little more than a convenience.

Lyle's response is to set up a prayer meeting for clergy wives in the cathedral close. Although at first they have little in common, the women discover a comforting sisterhood as they share their deepest fears and longings, for themselves, their men and their children. Charles is bemused, indulgent, but so busy playing at bishop that it is not until he stumbles across Lyle's diary that the terrible realisation dawns that she, not he, has been in touch with God, and therefore reality.

Lyle Ashworth, the perfect bishop's wife, is aware that the role is not enough. Her prayer meeting is an attempt to beat a system which tries to force her too into a stereotype of perfect composure and control. 'Women are more adept at circum-navigating,' says Susan. 'They have an easier time than men. They don't have the same social demands to be the breadwinner, to aim for a mega job. When I was in my early twenties I was able to throw in my boring job at a solicitor's firm so that I could write. I would have broken out in the end, even if I had been a man, but it would have been much later and much messier. Women have far greater opportunity to explore their potential.'

'But your women have little opportunity to fulfil that potential,' I argue.

'Ah', she says, 'but you have to project yourself into the 1930s, 1940s and 1960s, to see things from their perspective. Their horizons were fairly narrow. Today we're frustrated by their passivity, but marriage was the only expectation of a well-brought-up middle-class woman. Just think – there were no washing machines or mixers, no helpful gadgets in those days, and they were expected to wait on their men hand and foot. I think women then were much tougher than we assume.'

I find some of her lesser women are quite weak, I say, and suffer meekly and maddeningly when put upon.

She balks at the idea.

'People usually say they find my women very powerful.'

The Wagnerian-style heroines like Aysgarth's wife, Dido, I agree, but what about those simple, little first wives who die quickly and whose misery casts a giant shadow over their husbands for the rest of the book – the ones called Jane or Betty or Grace, for example? 'They cry a lot,' I say to her.

'So do the men!' she retorts. She won't be pushed into any suggestion that she portrays the downtrodden woman as a feminist gesture. 'It was marriage to the particular man, not men in general, that was the problem. Betty was sweet, talkative and brainless. With any spouse other than the highly intense Jon

Darrow she would have been perfectly happy.'

At this point I play my trump card. 'What about Emily, Aysgarth's sister?' She is a secondary heroine with a great deal to say about a woman's lot. 'A feminist?' she says to her brother in *Ultimate Prizes*, 'I'm no such thing. No woman in her right mind would be a feminist. Feminism encourages men to kick you in the teeth and trample on you. No man likes a feminist, just as no man likes a woman who's clever. Think of Mother – kicked in the teeth by three men and left to die in misery.'

'Men did hate feminists 50 years ago,' Susan admits. 'Emily is based on an unmarried aunt of mine who had four good-looking brothers, but was plain herself. It was very unjust. A plain woman was nothing unless she got herself a man.'

'"My sex alone classified me as inferior to you and Willy,"' I quote at her. '"It's such a novelty having a man ask my opinion, that it's hardly surprising if I get carried away."'

'That's right. Men were awfully bitchy. They thought women with opinions were aggressive.'

I wonder whether there isn't a great deal of Susan Howatch, the frustrated serious writer, condemned in the UK to the Mills and Boon shelves, in women like Emily.

'Are things really very different today?'

'There's a bit of that in the way they reacted to Mrs Thatcher,' she says, to my surprise. 'There are still a few battles to be won. Women are underpaid compared to men. But gender isn't really a big issue for me.'

Even she admits that it's only when she leaves the great metropolis for the more suburban backwater of Surrey that she realises how little has changed, how a woman at home is still the badge of a successful middle-class man, and a devoted, self-sacrificial clergy wife the secret of the successful parson. On the other hand, the gracious and kindly clerics who inhabit the lofty halls of academia, like one of her gurus, the priest and physicist Dr John Polkinghorne, openly admire her books, and bend over backwards to be attentive, proving that even the oldest institutions, fossilised as they are, can be coaxed out of their misogyny.

'Those old public schoolboys who run the Church of England would never permit a woman to play cricket on their hallowed turf,' says a sarcastic Venetia in *Scandalous Risks* about the possibility of women priests. In November 1992 the last great institution to impose professional limits on women finally conceded defeat. Susan Howatch had gone on record in 1986 saying she felt that leadership in the Church was a male charism, and that she was therefore opposed to the idea of women priests. She has no such objections today. 'I met some wonderful women deacons and it suddenly seemed incredibly silly that they were not allowed to say the magic words. John Baker, the ex-Bishop of Salisbury, also helped me to see that in the Church of England Eucharist the priest is not an icon or representative of Christ. Christ is represented by the bread and wine. The priest represents humanity, so gender is irrelevant. I know there are those who disagree and are leaving the church, but in 20 years' time we'll wonder what the fuss was all about.'

That assertion is based on her uncontestable knowledge of recent church history. She tells me with glee that the great cleric and preacher Charles Raven, who died in 1964, and whose writings were the basis for Neville Aysgarth's religious thought, thoroughly enjoyed the company of women, spoke out in favour of their ordination and, probably as a result, was never made a bishop. 'The Church couldn't go on as it was. It had become stuffy. The 1960s were the watershed, and it has never really recovered from the fall-out. In our thrusting macho society, where pulling the birds is what counts and church-going is seen as effeminate, men are not encouraged to develop their spiritual side. The Anglo-Catholic wing must seem a bit limp. The evangelicals are more robust. They attract more men. I'm fond of the Church. It is a dynamic, exciting place. It's important to me to show those outside that there are attractive, intelligent men in it wrestling with the implications of their faith.'

But is God good for women? 'Well, I've been very blessed,' she says, laughing, 'though it took me a long time to give Him the credit. I think a lot of people are negative about religion because there's a lot of bad religion about, which is repressive and oppressing. Good religion allows you to be fully human and happy, to realise your full potential.'

The icing on Susan's cake was the return of her daughter, Antonia, to England in 1986, giving her a chance to redeem the relationship. Motherhood obviously matters to her. She claims it was a formative, broadening experience. Although she has never explored her personal situation in her books, unsatisfactory parenting is a major theme in her writing. Caught up in a hormonal maelstrom of personal ambition, all of her leading men fail as fathers, as they have been failed. Significantly fewer of her women make inadequate mothers. Venetia is largely ignored by both her parents, Susan points out to me. Although it is not spelt out in the text, their neglect predisposes her to having an affair with an older man. But there is a way of breaking free from the negative patterns we inherit. Susan has discovered what she was looking for when she wrote *The Wheel of Fortune*. Only when we come to terms with our past, only when we lay it to rest by understanding and forgiving those who have hurt us, do we become fully healed, fully whole. That is the essence of redemption.

Reflected in another human being who fails her, God is not good news for Venetia. 'He ruined me,' she says of Dean Aysgarth, years after their affair. In *Mystical Paths* Jon Darrow's son, Nick, a young ordinand, out of kilter with his self and his sexuality, has sex with the widow he is trying to comfort and heal. At a particularly traumatic time in his own life, looking for comfort, Charles Ashworth seduces a divorcee. While both the latter two characters are horrified by their actions, they do tend to be rather ruinous for women. Susan is not convinced that this is entirely the case. 'Of course, if a man is particularly magnetic like Bishop Alex Jardine, there is a danger of abusing his privileged position, as there is for a doctor or a politician or any man with power.' Unlike the powerful men whose sorry stories hit the newspaper headlines, her characters admit the self-seeking nature of their ways, repent of them and endeavour to do better in the future.

'For all the problems in their marriages, Dido, with her

upwardly mobile husband, beautiful house and lavish dinner parties, and Lyle, the clever manager, with her successful bishop of a husband, would have thought God had been very good to them. They didn't question God as a male archetype the way we do now. They didn't have any concept of God as mother. I had a great-aunt who had a book on Mother Julian on her shelf. That was terribly avant-garde. Women tended to accept the patriarchal view of things. Besides, Lyle was intelligent enough to know God was beyond gender. How do you measure whether God is good to you? It all depends on where you stand. Since we are unique we all view things from our own perspective and within our own limitations, as they did.'

Watching today's career women, with all their so-called freedoms, Susan Howatch wonders whether they aren't in danger of ending up like men, under pressure and out of touch with what matters most. 'When I see women who appear to have it all – and some of them are priests – a high-powered career, success, marriage, and a family, I don't know how they manage to keep all the plates spinning, and think that one day they're going to have to make some very difficult choices.'

Her own choice has been to remain celibate because she feels that too much energy is expended on sex. 'Being celibate gives me the time to concentrate on other things. Thank God, we're beginning to realise that you don't have to be married or in a relationship to be normal. People are more than their genitals. Some, like Jon Darrow, shouldn't marry at all if it's merely to satisfy their own needs. Life isn't about self-fulfilment in the New Age sense of the word, all me, me, me. The mystical Christian view is that we need to line up our ego, our true self, with God, so that we can become the person He intended us to be, and serve others the way He intended us to do.'

Small wonder, therefore, that, in true mystical tradition, she is wary of the those three great enemies of the spirit: sex, money and power. In an era when amassing money is the ultimate middle-class virtue, she remains convinced that financial dilemmas are a sure sign of materialism laying siege to the soul. 'Money is neutral. It's what you do with it that counts. I feel sorry for the lottery-winners. It's hard to keep it as your servant, not your master. The best thing is to give as much of it away as you can.'

She did exactly that. But the endowment of £1 million by a self-confessed scientific illiterate to fund the Starbridge lectureship in theology and natural science at Cambridge University was, for some, the ultimate injury, elevating religion to a level where it suddenly had to be taken seriously by dozens of embarrassed journalists and angry atheists. The latter wrote to the newspapers. Of what use was theology? Should not this money have been given to the poor? This very criticism was levelled at Mary Magdalene when she poured an alabaster-boxful of expensive perfume over the Christ she loved.

The irony was not lost on Susan Howatch, who was none-theless surprised at the fury she provoked. 'I suppose the decision not to believe is as much a spiritual decision as to believe, and somehow they felt threatened.' She was amused that they were as blissfully unaware of the fact that science and theology were no longer at loggerheads as they were of parroting the New Testament they despised. In a letter to the *Independent* in March 1993, responding to Larry Adler, she wrote, 'Why does it never occur to him that if you nurture people's souls in addition to their brains, these people *will* give to the starving millions in Somalia – and to the destitute in British inner cities – and indeed, to every other place where there is a need to love thy neighbour as thyself?'

Of course, if she had replaced the Volkswagen she uses to run around London with a Porsche, no one would have batted an eyelid. To most people, particularly those outside the Church, she will always be an enigma – the millionairess writer who made a packet out of tales of love and luxury, but lives a simple, celibate life, defying all the usual stereotypes of success. No journalist ever appears to write about her without reference to money, as if there has to be some obvious explanation for her behaviour other than religion – but they can't quite put their finger on it.

To those inside the Church her actions are a little more comprehensible – though not all enjoy her books, or are comfortable watching the clergy lose their dignity and self-control. Some vehemently dismiss such embarrassing display as unrealistic. They tend to be men. A few of them, strangely enough, seem to bear an uncanny resemblance to her more confused, emotionally constipated characters.

For those with stomach enough to stand seeing the dirt wrung from their clerical smalls, for her thousands of other, avid readers, there has been a slow realisation, during the unfolding of the Starbridge saga, which has felt like a 50-year pilgrimage, that for good or ill one woman with no episcopal clout, who is not and is never likely to be a priest, has changed the Church's image forever. However uncomfortable, it is a shrewd, more honest, portrait – exposing temptation, weakness and failure, issues normally hushed, hard for all humans to admit, doubly difficult for men. The fact that they survive, chastised, but stronger, saner, more sensitive, must mean God is good for men, and for the women who love them.

No church-centred fiction writer since Trollope has been as widely read as Susan Howatch. But to say she has popularised the clergy is to trivialise her achievement, particularly in the light of the publicity that surrounds all tales of clerical misdemeanours. I have known and know of many clergymen, and the occasional rabbi, who could not handle his own sexuality, who got a buzz from the power invested in the clerical persona and saw no relation between the public role and personal holiness or any discrepancy when the two didn't match. All ended by causing immense pain for themselves, their spouses and their victims, not to mention the havoc they loosed in their churches and the bewilderment they left behind. In some cases the church hierarchy had been informed of their difficulties but could not, or would not, believe what they were told, and allowed the hypocrisy to continue. Would that they had read and digested their Starbridge. As any writer knows, fiction is a pale reflection of real life.

If the demand for a more authentic lifestyle is the domain of prophecy, Susan Howatch is without doubt a modern prophet. In both her life and her books, she challenges the false and illusory gods of contemporary society – money, power, status, sex and glamour – and calls on all human beings to live their lives aligned with the one true God, which alone is the key to real integration, satisfaction and happiness. When asked by one rather cynical journalist whether she seriously believed God knew she was writing books for Him, she said in her usual no-nonsense way, 'Don't be funny, of course He does.'

After completing the six Starbridge books about the Church of England, Susan has now written a trilogy of novels about the Christian ministry of healing (A Question of Integrity – *1997,* The High Flyer – *1999,* The Heartbreaker – *2003). She has also acquired a son-in-law, two grandsons, and a fellowship (King's College, London)*

CHAPTER 4

The Fashion Consultant:
Nellie Thornton

'I'd like to dress the entire government in tracksuit bottoms and ill-fitting tops, and see what it does to *their* social life', she says as we hurtle at breakneck speed from one destination to the next in Nellie Thornton's hectic schedule, through some of the loveliest scenery in Yorkshire.

This novel picture of our parliamentarians temporarily distracts me from the view, as well as bringing a huge grin to Nellie's face. It's an honest, open sort of face, crinkling round the eyes and mouth, full of life and determination. I look and listen for the tiniest trace of bitterness. There is none. Bitterness is born of defeat, and defeat is a word that doesn't exist in her vocabulary. Anger does. And there are times when Nellie Thornton is very angry indeed; angry that thousands of people are denied access to the clothing market for no other reason than by birth or misfortune they happen to be the wrong shape; even more angry at the loss of dignity and ostracism that causes.

Her solution was to set up the first fashion consultancy in the country for disabled people.

I first heard of Nellie's work from mutual acquaintances and, being a bit of a fashion victim, was intrigued. Being 'small, but perfectly proportioned', as the petite ranges patronisingly call it, (or are those the clothes they're describing?), caused me problems from the moment my age made it a bit of a joke to go on shopping in the children's department. It is no joke to be non-standard. Jackets hang off my shoulders, sleeves trail on the ground, and I can almost take enough off trousers to make myself a pair of shorts as well. It never occurred to me that illness or accident could rob me of the little choice I had, cutting me off, not only from one of life's basic pleasures but ultimately from career and company. BBC's *The Clothes Show* had featured Nellie's work, I was told. I made up my mind to go and see it for myself.

'Nellie's changed my life,' says Mrs Holdsworth. We have pulled up outside a sheltered housing complex, unloaded skeins, bobbins, patterns, fabric and an overlocker from the boot. Mrs Holdsworth had a stroke two years ago. Since then, until Nellie came on the scene, she was relegated to a life in jumper, skirt and unmanageable zips. Not any longer. Nellie is now showing her how to adapt a basic sewing pattern to her own needs, and how to sew on a machine using only her right arm. This is the highlight of her week. Her daughter is on hand with hot coffee, home-made cake and biscuits.

'I've a dress now, and a posh suit,' she tells me proudly, temporarily looking up from a seam. 'Thanks to Nellie I can go out again with my head held high.'

Nellie's distracted, matching up pieces of fabric.

'If you feel good, you'll tackle anything,' she says, through teeth bristling with pins, a throw-away remark, easily missed, philosophy Yorkshire-style, plain, straightforward and face-smackingly obvious. Then why did no one else see its potential to open up the world to thousands of people who rarely felt good enough to venture beyond their own front door?

'Ah,' she says, (whenever you ask her about herself, she has a disarming way of pointing you somewhere else), 'because I saw what it could do. I have Marion to thank for that.'

Marion was a stroke patient in the Airedale Hospital when she caught Nellie's attention. Nellie, on placement from Ilkley College where she was studying for a diploma in higher education, was intrigued by a very dejected-looking figure who never smiled, was barely able to communicate and was lost in clothing a great deal too big for her. 'I would have said she was severely depressed. She cried a lot, and looked much older than she actually was. In fact it was a shock to find out she was only in her fifties. One day I said to her, "Do you need to wear clothes as big as that so that you can manoeuvre a wheelchair?" Her reply took me aback. All she said was, "You wear what you can get into." The next day I brought back swatches of fabric and a selection of patterns from home, and told her to choose herself an outfit. I'd adapt it to whatever her needs were.'

The day the dress was finished was a day Nellie will never forget. 'I laid it out in front of her and her whole face lit up. "Just give me half an hour, Nellie," she said, so I went out into the garden to wait. When she appeared I could hardly believe my eyes. It was like a vision. This was an entirely different person – a total transformation. She looked wonderful. She'd done her hair, put her make-up on, and she was out of the wheelchair, walking for the first time, albeit with a Zimmer frame. Then, once she got out into the garden, she threw the frame away too. "Stuff this," she said, "it'll ruin the photograph." I'll never forget the joy, the look of sheer triumph on her face. I knew in that moment what I had to do. What worked for Marion would work for countless others too.'

One year later, in 1980, Nellie applied to the local authorities for a grant for a dressmaking training centre and workshop and found herself with £35,000. 'Nellie Thornton who'd never had more than £35 in her pocket! I was terrified. I'd never set up anything in my life.' She rented rooms in a listed mill building in scenic Baildon, perched on the edge of the Yorkshire Dales, and Fashion Services for Disabled People was born.

Visitors converged from far and wide to watch her at work and learn her methods. Twenty-four workshops modelled on Nellie's prototype were set up all over the British Isles. Her influence began to spread abroad. Nothing, it appeared, could hinder the spectacular growth of this neglected, humanitarian aspect of the fashion market. But a mere eight years later, a change in government policy and the whole scheme began to tumble around her ears.

The blow would have irreparably beaten most mortals. It merely stunned Nellie. 'Finding the Solutions' is a chapter heading in her book, *Fashion for Disabled People*. It could just as well be a chapter heading in the story of her life.

'There's no such thing as impossible,' she says, with a dismissive wave of the hand, as we repack the boot of the car and take our leave of Mrs Holdsworth. 'If I've learned anything from disabled people, it's that.'

And so we 'pop home' for a quick bite – to a standard 1930s house, on one of the least interesting streets of Ilkley, blackened with honest Yorkshire grime. The main railway line to Bradford and Leeds runs within six metres of the front door. Husband John sits in his favourite armchair by a gas convector fire in the small room next to the kitchen, reading the daily paper. Unlike Nellie, he is enjoying a tranquil, traditional retirement. He stretches, gets up and puts fresh cloth, cutlery and paper serviettes on the table. Lunch is Nellie's home-made tomato soup and plum pie.

'He makes me take a day off every week now that I'm retired,' she says.

I ask her whether she didn't feel totally disheartened by the threat to all she had worked for.

'A problem is a challenge, not an obstacle. There has to be a way round it.'

Even when the 'challenge' all but destroys the dream?

She turns to her husband who has been watching her with quiet admiration. 'Was I disheartened, John?'

'Nellie, disheartened?' He smiles and shakes his head.

'I might have been,' she admits grudgingly, 'if Baildon had closed. But it couldn't fold, could it?'

She holds out the palms of her hands to me. It's a disarming gesture, open, trusting. This is after all a rhetorical question.

'Good must somehow win in the end. What we're doing is just. It's right. I met a woman once – do you remember her, John? – so large she had no underwear. Her only nightie was two sheets sewn together, leaving holes for the neck and arms. Can you imagine? And you wonder why I couldn't give up? The harder it gets the harder I fight. The day I watched Marion dancing in the garden I knew there'd be no turning back. I'd witnessed a minor miracle.'

Is it the Marions of this world that transform an ordinary dressmaking teacher into a pioneer and campaigner for thousands of voiceless, powerless citizens against a government impervious to their basic human needs? Would she have had such a dramatic affect on anyone other than Nellie, on a man for example? Or does it require some extraordinary combination of qualities, which include not only basic fashion awareness and tailoring skills but above all an instinctive ability to identify with the pain of other people, and the will, the energy, the passion to do something about it? What made her do what she did?

She reaches for the coffee pot, fills a china cup and, looking past me, journeys back to the beginning of the story.

'Of course, it was a surprise. Life began for me at 49. That was the day we opened Fashion Services, and I knew that everything that had ever happened to me up till then had been leading to this moment.'

～

'You are what you're raised with.'

You learn not to argue with Nellie's northern wisdom.

The formative influences that shaped her destiny were an integral part of the Yorkshire Dales in the days when the old stone towns belonged to a warm, tough, industrious working class, dependent on the mills for their livelihood, long before a well-to-do, professional class exploited their charm and turned them into commuter dormitories. Her father, an office manager, was crippled with polio. Nellie accompanied him to London every year where he was fitted for a new boot. 'I never thought of him as disabled. He ran faster than we did.' He was also the organist and a very committed member of the local Methodist church. Attendance for his children was compulsory – three times on a Sunday. 'And woe betide us if we tried to do anything other than read on the Sabbath. We weren't even allowed to knit. Mother did

– behind his back. But people can change. He was a loving man and mellowed as the years went by.'

Her mother cared for the world. 'There wasn't a single member of the family didn't live with us at some time or another. And if there was no family to look after, she was out in the community, visiting the shut-ins, too frail to go out, or the local retirement home.'

As a child Nellie never gave the future a thought. There wasn't much in the way of choice for a girl from her background in rural Yorkshire. It had to be the mill, office work or nursing. Her mother thought nursing the best possibility and sent her off with a group of other would-be nurses to look round Leeds Infirmary. She passed out at the first bed and had to be collected on the way out; an inauspicious and ironic beginning to a career which would involve spending a great deal of her working life in a variety of nursing homes, albeit in a very different capacity.

In the end, the mill it had to be. 'When I was 15 Mother announced she'd fixed me up with a job as a textile designer at Driver Brothers, the weavers. I was to start the following Monday. Fortunately, I loved it.'

Seven years of creating material for Jacqmar, of working with one of the first companies to use a new fabric called nylon, of training in wool and worsted weaving at night school came to an end when Nellie was pregnant with her first son. She had met John, an office manager like her father, on a coach outing. He was tall, as she was, and she found his quiet, dignified manner attractive from the start. Unlike many of her contemporaries, who felt forced for financial reasons to return to work while their children were small, she had made up her mind to stay at home. One particular childhood experience remained vivid in her memory. 'I must have been about 13. Mother wanted to do something for the war effort and got a job as a railway porter two days a week. I came home to an empty house for the first time. There was no one there to ask me about my day, and I hated it. I think it was my first experience of what it must be like to live alone. I vowed there and then I'd always be at home when my children came in from school.'

This was no conventional, stay-at-home housewifery. Seminal forces were already at work. She volunteered to drive disabled children to the local playgroup and joined a Good Neighbour scheme. 'I used to visit the local retirement homes. They were unsupervised in those days, unchecked, awful. One day I watched two intelligent women sitting on the floor of their bedroom with a mountain of shoes between them, trying to find a matching pair each. I walked out and wept.'

Her determination to stay at home was put to the test when John was made redundant. 'The children were eight and five. I could have got a job. But what would that have done to John's pride? In those days the man was the breadwinner. You can't do worse than take away a person's dignity. So I took in sewing. There were times when the pressure of it nearly drove me to a breakdown.'

It was a client, seeing how run-down she was, who suggested teaching as an alternative. While John in desperation took a junior office job, Nellie completed a City and Guilds dressmaking course, and started teaching evening classes at Craven College in Skipton.

Advertised on the college board one day was a seminar at Keele University on the therapeutic use of art and craft with the elderly. Nellie could not know that that seminar was to change the course of her life. 'I came back bursting with enthusiasm, rushed to the college principal and told him I had found the way of the future. Rather than waiting for the retired, the elderly or the lonely to come to us for classes, we should be taking art and craft out into the community to them.'

The concept, which had a futuristic ring to it in the light of more recent developments in health and social care, appealed to the principal, and he gave Nellie the go-ahead to start what she affectionately calls her 'outreach'. Within weeks she had managed to set up courses in Skipton in two old people's homes and a hospital. 'I didn't really appreciate what I was taking on, which is just as well, as I would probably never have done it. Upholstery, collage, joinery, woodwork, I responded to every demand, and had to teach myself as I went along.'

The greatest challenge to her patience and commitment came

from what was the Burley Hall Social Services Nursing Home in Burley-in-Wharfedale. 'On my first morning I was welcomed with, "We've had five therapists before you. None of them lasted more than six months." I went into a large sitting-room. Armchairs lined the room. In them drooped 20 or so elderly people with vacant expressions on their faces. I said in my most jolly voice, "Let's make some Christmas decorations." An eye opened. A head moved. Someone groaned. "We've getten enough," shouted one old boy. But when the coffee bell rang, you couldn't see any of them for dust. There was life there all right. But I had to learn an invaluable lesson: not to patronise people because they're old and tired. I had to earn their respect, and the right to be there. We had to get to know each other.'

After months of patient Tuesday mornings Nellie eventually discovered who could do what. 'There was a 90-year-old wizard of a four-pin knitter. I remembered from my playgroup driving days that children with spina bifida needed socks without seams because they have little feeling below the waist and are prone to pressure sores, so I encouraged her to knit for one particular little girl I knew. The child was delighted with her socks, and wrote to thank the old lady. That was the beginning of a very special relationship, which meant a great deal to them both.'

And then there was Harry, the joiner, who had had a stroke. Nellie asked him if he would make a train for a disabled child. He carved and sanded and painted for days. 'What a labour of love. It was entirely his project. He was the professional, I was the amateur, remember.'

Nellie recalls with sadness the sequel to this story. Seven years later she went to visit her father in hospital; and who, to her surprise, should be in the next bed, but Harry? It was obvious he was dying. 'I went over and whispered to him, "Harry, do you remember me?" He reached out and took my hand. "Oh yes," he said, "I remember you. We made a train together."' No one, says Nellie, had done anything with him since.

In 1976 Nellie, already in her mid-forties, felt immensely frustrated. There were so many elderly people condemned to living half a life, so much more she could do, if only she knew how.

Her decision to take a diploma in higher education led to the placement at the Airedale Hospital and the fertile meeting with Marion. Her other placement, as a dressmaking teacher at the Whetley Hill Disablement Centre, was equally formative, but in a very different way.

The permanent dressmaking teacher was leaving. Nellie was asked to take over and given a half-day introduction to the class, which amounted to, 'This one falls over, so watch the flex. That one fits, don't let her use the iron. The one over there is incontinent.' Left on her own, she was almost paralysed with fear. She felt totally inadequate, but unwilling to abandon a group of students who so obviously needed the best she could give them. There was only one thing to do – take another course, this time in palsy, fits and incontinence. 'It's fear that keeps most of us from relating to disabled people. Once you understand what's going on, when you know what to do, the fear is removed, and when there's no fear you see the person, not the disability.'

In Whetley Hill there were other seriously disabled people and their carers who forced Nellie to face her prejudices, and challenged her to see their God-given value as human beings. One was an ex-master baker with a muscle-wasting disease that had reduced his body to jelly. He could still speak, but everything else had to be done for him by his wife, who went on caring for him at home. Yet every day he arrived immaculate, his shirt ironed, trousers pressed, hair brushed. It left a lasting impression on her. 'Even his serviette was spotless. It was a privilege to feed him. He was such a wise man. He once said to me, "The first thing you learn when you're disabled, Nellie, is patience. Everything you do is in someone else's time." Everyone respected him and went to him with their problems, because he listened and he cared. He brightened the lives of so many people. That man achieved more in the eight months of his illness than some of us do in a lifetime.'

Marion, Harry, the four-pin knitter, the master baker, the members of her classes in homes, hospitals and day centres, all contributed in their own way to Nellie's growing frustration and indignation. How could society ignore, disown or discard such a wealth of broken yet beautiful humanity? If God cared for all the creatures He had made, who were we to discriminate, to say implicitly that only one kind was entitled to enjoy the world, while the rest should be shut away and forgotten? Fortunately, she had a firm and far-sighted ally in her boss, the principal of Ilkley College, where she now worked. 'Apart from all the other problems they have to contend with,' she stormed at him one day, 'do you realise how difficult it is for disabled people to find decent clothes? How can you go out if you literally have nothing to wear? And what can be done about it?'

'What do you want to do?' he asked her.

'Me? What am I supposed to do?'

The question merely compounded her sense of ignorance and uselessness. How could one middle-aged dressmaking teacher make any difference to what was a problem of national, if not international, proportions?

'No, seriously, Nellie,' he said, 'suppose I had access to a certain amount of funding, what would you do with it?'

It didn't take long to describe the dream. It had been taking shape in her mind for some time, now that she stopped to acknowledge the fact.

'Create some kind of workshop, I suppose,' she said, 'so that those who would like to make their own clothes have the training to adapt patterns to suit their needs, and those who can't or won't have someone to make them for them.'

She gave their conversation little thought over the next weeks. Forming the dream into a concrete shape had been a particularly effective way of letting off steam, nothing more. Until the principal rang her. 'Do you know what next year happens to be, Nellie? The Year of the Disabled. I think I may have got you some money, so get up here fast, and fill in the forms.'

'I still don't know how we did it,' she says, looking back at the fraught beginnings of Fashion Services for Disabled People. The arrangement was extremely complex. For funding purposes the business was divided into two, the training side requiring a secretary, researcher and technician whose wages were provided by the Community Programme, and the workshop employing a manager and ten machinists paid for by Manpower Services, with a budget controlled by Ilkley College. The college refused to release any money until they saw receipts. Nellie, who had no cash of her own, and a workshop to build, ran up huge debts. Job Creation scheme workers poured their left-over concrete down the gents' toilets and put Baildon mill's entire plumbing system for over a dozen workshops out of action. But in February 1982 the training side of the project opened, with Nellie as director, and the first disabled young people began their course.

'No tracksuit bottoms' might have been their motto. 'Imagine being condemned to wear nothing but tracksuit bottoms for the rest of your life when your peers are wearing jeans and jackets! Disabled young people want to wear denim, not clothes that mark them out as different. But where do they find fashion garments if they're not a standard shape, if they have a parent or carer who has to help them in and out of them a dozen times a day?'

Nellie remembers how all the members of that first course brought their own particular problems. 'One girl had severe spasms, but we managed to find her a hand-held machine. One was blind, and we learned ways of attaching a matchbox with Sellotape to the machine so that she could feel her way along a seam. Another had no arms. She made herself a lovely dress, holding the needle between her teeth, and flicking the fabric over with her nose so that she could pull the needle out the other side. They learned to work together in pairs or as a team, each making up for what the other lacked. They had such guts, such determination. The excitement and satisfaction on their faces whenever they finished a garment made every ounce of sweat, theirs and ours, worthwhile. We had such a strong sense that we were breaking new ground. I learned then that no obstacle was insurmountable. It was an invaluable lesson in the light of what was to come.'

The fashion consultancy side of the business was ready to

open in January 1983, and experienced protracted teething problems. For the first three years, under Manpower Services' rules, the ten machinists sent by the Job Centre were untrained, not the professional dressmakers Nellie had in mind. She and her manager seemed to spend more time as agony aunts, sorting out the workers' complex love lives, than they did their sewing. Eventually, when the source of funding changed, Nellie was able to employ four professional garment-makers, and at long last the fashion service she had seen in her dreams became a reality.

The customer, she says, was king. Each was to be consulted in full about style, colour and fabric. Individual taste and choice, denied them for so long, were to be respected. Any hint of patronising was a contradiction of the entire process, which was meant to be as pleasurable and as confidence-boosting an exercise as it was for any able-bodied person. Clients could choose to make an appointment for a consultation at Baildon, or receive a visit in a hospital, a day centre, a school or in the privacy and comfort of their own home.

The four professional dressmakers found their creative ingenuity tested to the limit by the unusual demands of the job. Garments had to disguise feeding tubes, keep hyperactive toddlers warm, cover a wheelchair, cope with callipers, metal braces, incontinence – and still look attractive and fashionable. Each piece of clothing told its own story. There was the paraplegic young man, paralysed from the neck down, who refused to be best man at his brother's wedding – until Fashion Services promised him his first formal suit; the schoolteacher with a curvature of the spine due to severe osteoporosis, for whom crossing any room was becoming an increasing nightmare, who sat in a corner at any function because she knew her clothes didn't hang correctly, and whose new clothes enabled her to face the classroom with confidence again; Samantha, the teenager with spina bifida whose great ambition was to have a pair of jeans, but could never find any to fit. Her mother, seeing her face the first time she put on the denims that had been specially made for her, broke down.

For Nellie it was all she had ever hoped, Marion's story

repeated over and over again, not only in Yorkshire but throughout the UK, as others heard about her work, and set up similar fashion consultancies based upon what they had seen at Baildon. The better known her work became the more she was in demand as a speaker and trainer, and not just in the UK. The Cerebral Palsy Society invited her to Rome and Athens. If the UK was insensitive to the needs of disabled people, she says, then Greece was in the Dark Ages. Wheelchairs were not allowed in the Athens streets. Disabled young people tended to be hidden from view and were bussed from home every day to specialist centres. Nellie was given seven dressmakers to train. Not one spoke a word of English. 'My antics to make them understand what I was saying had them in stitches (pardon the pun!). It's always difficult to make dressmakers see why, when you sew for disabled people, the first thing you have to do is disobey all the traditional rules of dressmaking. Professionals hate that. It's quite an adjustment. But with a great deal of miming and persuasion, we got there in the end.'

To her surprise, Nellie found herself forced to justify her work to the parents too, who couldn't understand why it was important to make a disabled child look nice. 'Nothing would convince them – until they saw the transformation. Then they were delighted. Some were overwhelmed. It was as if they were seeing their child for the first time.'

Despite mounting international success, funding for each of the 24 UK workshops was precarious. When Manpower Services withdrew its support after only three years, Fashion Services lurched from year to year, spared by Nellie's constant badgering of the authorities, by local media support, the feature on *The Clothes Show* or a visit from the Princess of Wales. 'The only charge we passed on to the customer was for materials and making-up. What else could they afford? A disabled person's clothing allowance is barely enough to cover their absolute basic needs, let alone pay for a tailor-made garment. Any allowance had to be applied for anyway, which makes many disabled people feel as if they're begging. It puts them in the charity bracket and destroys their self-esteem. Some will go without clothes rather than fill in yet more forms. There was no way we were ever going to be profitable in the traditional business sense. But how do you explain that to government leaders preconditioned to thinking in terms of financial, rather than human gain? It's a matter of radically altering the way our society thinks, and you can't do it overnight.'

1988 was the watershed. The government replaced the Manpower Services Community Programme with a new employment training scheme, more rigidly linked to the requirements of UK industry. On that basis most of the workshops were no longer eligible for funding. A young woman without arms pushing a needle through fabric with her nose, pulling it out of the back with her teeth, was hardly what a would-be industrial magnate, bent on satisfying the shareholders, would regard as the ideal employee.

Overnight, Nellie the project director became Nellie the campaigner. The survival of her dreams depended on it. But the opposition was far too powerful for a lone woman, even a woman of Nellie's determination. Like Helen Taylor-Thompson, what she needed was a lobbying force behind her. Hazel Howard, Nellie's researcher, banded the 20 surviving projects into the National Association of Clothing Workshops, and the two women led them into battle. Soon they had an army of college councils, social services and voluntary organisations on their side.

There were casualties. During the campaign, many of the workshops were forced to close. It was immensely frustrating, bitterly disappointing, but no deterrent. In fact it had the opposite effect on Nellie. She suddenly realised that in many ways she had reached the culmination of all she had hoped to achieve. Instead of pursuing her goals quietly in the back streets, the issue had been forced out into the marketplace. Here was the opportunity to make the government aware of the special needs of disabled people, to challenge society's money-led philosophy, to tackle national ignorance and indifference at its very heart.

If Marcus Fox, MP for Shipley, Chairman of the 1922 Committee, that bastion of traditional Tory policy-making, had ever thought that no earth-disturbing scheme would emerge from his tranquil neck of the Yorkshire woods, he was quickly disabused. Nellie set about him like a virago. She was a familiar figure on his doorstep. She soon knew her way around the House of Commons. She succeeded in raising questions in both Houses of Parliament. There were visits to the workshops from ministers and, eventually, in 1991, the commissioning of a government report. 'I think it was a sop,' Nellie says with glee, 'anything to get us off their backs. I think they thought they would lose us in copious research. Or that the project would finally prove to be unfeasible, uneconomical. How wrong they were.'

In fact Sally Guthrie of the Social Policy Unit at York University urged immediate funding for the 11 remaining projects. But three years of further stalling passed and more workshops came to a standstill before the Department of Health finally awarded the National Association of Clothing Workshops the funding for a research and development worker, to establish a country-wide network of community-based clothing services and promote the awareness of the clothing needs of disabled people. Thanks to the work of Lynn Purcell, some of the workshops are once more showing signs of life.

With her project receiving national recognition at last, Nellie felt she could retire – from her work in Baildon at least. Local authority and charitable funding had enabled it to survive. The training side was taken over by Bradford and Ilkley Adult Education College and now offers nationally recognised certificated courses in a range of subjects for disabled people, their relatives and carers. The nature of the funding now means that these are predominantly young people with learning difficulties who are taught personal presentation, how to prepare a CV and interview techniques to help them with their job prospects. 'The problem with that,' sighs Nellie, 'is that because of their limited abilities, there is little room for individuality. They do some garment-making. But given the circumstances, what do you think they make? Tracksuits!'

⌒

She sits now staring reflectively into her cup of coffee, the dregs long since cold, pleased or pained, I cannot really tell. A mixture of both, I suspect, given the ups and downs of her story.

'Was it hard to say goodbye to your baby?' I prompt her.

She starts.

'You have to let go and walk away. Others have taken over now. It's only fair on them. Besides, I'd had enough of fighting, enough of the politics. I'm grass-roots, not academic. All I ever wanted to do was right a few wrongs.'

I am more convinced than ever that Nellie Thornton, mill girl turned amazon, is one of the many unsung heroines of the twentieth century. Typically, there has been no MBE or OBE, little public recognition of her efforts. But then, we live in a society with fixed ideas of achievement, dismissing anyone who seeks to improve the lot of the elderly or the disabled as 'worthy'. To be called worthy is to be damned with faint praise indeed. It doesn't earn anyone a spot on the *Good Morning* show, one ITV researcher told me. The yawn factor is just too high. Or perhaps, more truthfully, it is the ostrich-with-head-in-the-sand factor, the pretence that we will never be a deserving recipient of Nellie's attentions. But who is to know? That is what really frightens us.

Nellie had the courage to lift up her head and look, and what she saw made her so angry that her life would never be the same again. In her own quiet way, confronting us with our deepest fears and prejudices, she is an uncomfortable person to know. But then, campaigners such as Octavia Hill and Josephine Butler can't have been easy company either. 'I never thought about what Fashion Services might become,' she says, 'I just can't stand injustice.' The Victorians set out to conquer mountains and claim new territory. Today's pioneering women seem to fall into pioneering against the odds and their own best intentions, but for all that, their energy and determination are no less than those of their nineteenth-century sisters. It has the same source – a refusal to accept what is. 'The fact that many people miss out on life and don't get their fair share of the cake, for reasons beyond their control, makes me blaze with fury. The way it happens automatically when we get old. We seem to assume that if someone has food and a roof over their head, that's all they need. We've done our bit. But I guarantee you this – put them in an institution without stimulation, without offering them any sense of worth and they'll join the gang in depression and inertia within three weeks.'

She pauses for breath, but the passion in her eyes, her voice, in the clenching and unclenching of her hands, criss-crossed with blue veins, is undiminished. I suspect that many of the unacceptable sights she has seen over the years are being replayed in her mind by some internal video machine. 'What's the use of seeing?' she demands, looking me straight in the face, 'if you don't do anything about it?'

Many of us do just that, I remind her, we see and do precisely nothing. We don't become pioneers.

'The course of our lives is mapped out for us. We're all given opportunities. It's up to us to take them or leave them. If we take them, God gives us the strength and help we need.'

Would Nellie have done what she did without her faith to propel her? She thinks for a while, but cannot say. Her faith and compassion for all human beings are so inextricably bound they cannot be unravelled and examined separately. That's the way she was raised, she would tell you, and it makes her unbearably sad that it isn't the same today. That isn't a criticism of young people. Some are wonderful. The middle-aged, the well-heeled successful executives, are all guilty of disposing of an unwanted parent or a has-been of a spouse. 'They put them in a home, forget about them and get on with their own selfish lives. It breaks my heart.'

For many years she cared for her own mother, who lived a few yards down the road in her own house, and died only months ago. 'Mother struggled with immense frustration in old age. I realised that she had needed to be needed. That's why she did so much for others. It's a terrible snare. It left her feeling useless.'

'Is that not you?' I ask, determined to find a speck of anything other than pure altruism.

She thinks not, but it's hard to be sure. How do we know how we will feel when it's our turn to be incapacitated, vulnerable and dependent on others?

Being a regular member of her local Methodist church, and a Sunday-school teacher for many years, has she then, I wonder, been inspired by the words of Jesus in the Gospels, 'I was naked and you clothed me. If you did that for the least of my brothers or sisters, you did it for me'?

'Goodness no,' she says dismissively, 'I'm much more Mrs Do-As-You-Would-Be-Done-By in *The Water Babies*. Doing what you feel God wants you to do is ...' – she pauses to find the word – 'instinctive. The Church can't be in the community and not serve the community. That's what the Wharfe Valley Community Project is all about.'

This, I realise with a shock, is the name of yet another of Nellie's amazing schemes, her latest. This 'little retirement project' was what the flying visit to Mrs Holdsworth and all the other weekly entries in her diary are all about. Shortly after her retirement from Fashion Services, she attended a meeting at Ilkley Age Concern and mooted an imaginative, ambitious idea, which already had the support of her local Soroptimists. She would travel the Wharfe Valley area and discover how many housebound people, alone, or in residential care, would like to be involved in what she called 'skill sharing'. Well over a hundred expressed a longing to feel useful and wanted again. Next she provided social services with a bank of volunteers who would share their respective skills with an elderly or housebound person for one hour a week over a ten-week period. There are, of course, no limits to Nellie's hours. She also manages training the volunteers. Her 'outreach' has been reborn.

'If you're disabled round these parts and they see you in a new dress,' Mrs Holdsworth whispered to me as we took our leave, 'they say, "You've been to see Nellie Thornton."'

And still Nellie's fertile mind conjures up bigger and better dreams: of a time when measurements will be fed into a computer, which will design dress patterns accordingly, making any shape standard; of the day when Marks & Spencer and other major department stores will have a designated fashion adviser for disabled people, so that they don't have to fight their way through the masses for clothes which are totally unsuitable in any case. She has made enquiries about both. In fact she has positively pestered Marks & Spencer, only to be told she is simply, 'a woman before her time'.

'A visionary, then?' I ask her.

'No, no, no, not a visionary,' she says modestly, 'an idealist perhaps.'

In our present, highly ambivalent society, where success is alternately feted and spurned, where compassion is dismissed as weak-mindedness and religion is condemned for its hypocrisy, Nellie stands out as someone who typifies the essence of true religion as defined in the Old Testament: 'And what does the Lord require of you but to love mercy, do justice and walk humbly with your God.' In other words she is one of those rare commodities: a totally unself-conscious Christian.

'What do I get out of going to church? I suppose it's like everything else, you get out what you put in. If all you do when you get there is worry about whether you remembered to put the joint in the oven, or turn it down so the meat isn't burnt to a cinder, you'll get nothing. I once saw a poster on my way to the Blind Centre.'

Another of her port of calls, I assume. It's hard to keep up with Nellie.

'It said, "Stop, listen, and await further directions", and I thought, yes, that's it, that's what church is, a chance to stop, leave our problems in God's hands, and listen to what He wants us to do next, through hymns, readings, sermons or simply through an unintentional comment made by a member of the congregation. Sometimes,' she admits a little sheepishly, 'the silliest things give you the courage to go on. I was driving towards Addingham one day, at the height of the struggle, and consumed with self-doubt as I suppose most of us are from time to time, and suddenly, on a small stretch of road, the tyres seemed to start singing the tune of "Knock and the door shall be opened unto you, seek, and ye shall find." It was a rather novel way for God to tell me I was on the right track, not to give up now.'

And how has John coped with her work?, I ask her, as he gets up and quietly leaves the room. I remember how important it was to her that her husband should have his sense of dignity intact.

'He's the cornerstone,' she says of him, 'I couldn't have done it without his support.'

Was he threatened by her success, its demands upon her time, the lecturing trips abroad?

'No, not John. He always said, "If this is what makes you happy, do it, only don't expect me to live at your speed."'

If there are any regrets it's that she hasn't the same amount of time that he has to spend with the grandchildren.

Would she have achieved what she achieved had she been a man? Hasn't the struggle been harder because she's a woman?

On the contrary, laughs Nellie, you learn to milk your femininity for all its worth. 'It was a positive advantage when I set up the business. I was an innocent female in a world of men, and the bureaucratic red tape melted before me. "That poor helpless woman," they said. I could see it in their faces. Yes, there were times when they patronised me, but being an innocent abroad was useful. I did what I needed to do, and found out later there were rules I should have followed.'

She would be the first to admit that the support and encouragement of her husband and male colleagues have been invaluable, given her propensity for the usual female sense of inadequacy and timidity, taken with a large dose of nonconformist unworthiness. But perhaps the founder of Fashion Services had to be female. In a world exploiting the basic biological instincts of men, only a woman can be fully aware of the importance of body image. Only a woman can understand the pain of not fulfilling the accepted norms of sexual attractiveness, of becoming one of society's faceless, invisible masses. Yes, Nellie says, God is good for women, of every shape, size and age, not just for the Linda Evangelistas and Helena Christensens of this world, with their perfect youthful faces and bodies. But society is not. It is downright cruel. That was the basic injustice that made Nellie rage. With God's help that rage was turned from a destructive into an unstoppable force, which enabled countless women and men to know, and even feel for the first time, the goodness of a God who loved them exactly as they were. 'There are no limits to what a woman can achieve today. I think I've proved that. But then,' she pauses and thinks for a while, 'it all depends what we mean by achievement. If one person says she feels good, confident, valued, if I've restored someone's dignity, that's achievement enough for me.'

Nellie was sadly widowed in 2001. She is very grateful for the tremendous support she receives from her two sons.

The machinery is now in place at Baildon to produce computer patterns for people with disabilities, and the software is being developed. Wharfe Valley Community Project is moving premises into a large care complex built by Abbeyfield Society as a millennium project, where they will provide activities for the new day centre, including cookery. Nellie will be working full time, and acknowledges that retirement seems remote – and rather boring!

CHAPTER 5

The Army Officer: Lieutenant-Colonel Jan Ransom, MBE

'It's for you,' my husband calls up the stairs.

'Who?'

'A woman. Jan something, I think she said.'

'Oh, that'll be my lieutenant-colonel,' I shout, on my way to the phone.

'She didn't sound much like a lieutenant-colonel to me,' I hear him mutter, as he heads back to his study.

She didn't look much like a lieutenant-colonel either as she walked towards me on a glorious June day across the car park of the Medical Services and Adjutant-General's Corps Manning and Record Office in Chester. The building looks as it sounds, austere, redbrick, unremarkable, surrounded by high fences and gardens designed for their manageability rather than aesthetic pleasure, closely clipped lawns and shrubs, concrete walkways. It couldn't have looked more obviously army had MoD been emblazoned in neon lights on the front – a stark contrast to the famous timbered houses, colourful gift-shops, quaint bridges and tree-lined river banks of this picturesque city, shimmering in the sun as I drove through.

Security was genial, jokey and thorough.

'Some of the black and tan?' ask the guards as I drive up to the gates and roll down my window.

'Sorry?'

'Guinness?'

'Oh, yes – but only a half pint'.

Before the words are out, a lurid yellow block with the number six marked on it is attached magnetically to my bonnet, I'm ticked off the list and a visitor's label is hung around my neck.

'Park over there – and we'll let the Colonel know you're here.'

In seconds, as I get out of the car, she appears before me – an impressive figure in silvery floral dress and bold fuschia jacket.

'You thought I'd be in uniform,' she smiles, holding out a hand, noting with evident pleasure my failed attempt to conceal my surprise. I am still registering the short, very blond hair, a hint of make-up, the stronger, southern, slightly more nasal accent than I had consciously noticed when we spoke on the phone, and an instinctive sense that here is someone who, despite the care taken with her appearance, would feel equally if not more comfortable in trousers.

'I don't really know what I expected,' I tell her in all honesty, 'but my husband doesn't think you sound like a lieutenant-colonel.'

She throws back her head and laughs uproariously.

'He expected me to bark my orders at him, did he?'

'Well, he was in the cadets at school – bad memories of bossy sergeants, I'm afraid.'

'Not my style,' she says, as we walk up the drive, 'at least, it isn't now.'

It is quiet. There is little sign of movement or of any activity. She too seems aware of how lacking in the usual army energy it seems. 'Sorry, I can't offer you soldiers marching, training or doing drill duty, none of the typical scenes of army life. We're administrative here, very dull.'

Life at the Adjutant-General's Corps Manning and Records Office may sound, and even appear, dull at first glance, as one walks up the stone stairs and down the bare linoleum corridors, punctuated with green gloss doors marked with a strange coded jumble of numbers and letters like OIC/SO1 AG Corps, 2.34

(standing apparently for Officer in Charge/Staff Officer 1, second floor, room 34), but inside Lieutenant-Colonel Ransom's office, a light, pleasant upstairs room, I soon discover there is nothing dull about the work they do. The destiny of 7,000 men, their wives and children, is decided here. 'We handle postings and careers,' she explains, while an assistant hands me a cup of coffee. 'We can send soldiers to the Gulf, to Bosnia, to Northern Ireland, anywhere in the world.'

'A giant-sized game of chess?' I have my own preconceptions about the army.

'No,' she says firmly, 'These are real people with real lives. It's a huge responsibility. I try to give my staff the support they need because they have some very difficult decisions to make.'

She suddenly jumps up, deciding I need to see what she means for myself, and carries me on a wave of enthusiasm down to the other end of the corridor, through a large open-plan area where eight administrative staff, most of them female, are engrossed in telephone conversations, to a small office, which is Major Mick Cotton's centre of command. 'If you'd been here yesterday,' she says, 'there would have been a map of the world spread out in the middle of the room with the eight of them round it, wouldn't there, Mick? Today they're following up the consequences of yesterday's decisions.'

He smiles in agreement, a man who evidently relishes the challenges of this particular job. 'Each soldier has a 22-year career, which we try and map out for him. It's a tough assignment. There's the wife's job to consider, or the children's education, or ageing parents. Some just want the sun. One soldier married a Bulgarian girl and bought a house in Sofia. We hadn't a suitable posting for him there. That was a real brain-teaser. Then we realised there was a regular flight to Sofia from Stansted Airport and posted him nearby. The Channel Tunnel has made commuting a great deal easier.'

'But in the end these are secondary factors,' Jan chips in, lest I should be in any doubt about the real nature of what goes on here. Life in the army is beginning to sound like a globetrotter's paradise. 'Our prime goal is to man the service. And we are chronically short of manpower. The crisis in Bosnia has lasted longer than any of us expected. It increases our commitments, and stretches our resources to the limit. I can't let the army send a unit to a dangerous area like Bosnia with gaps in it. Nor can I hire untrained casual labour or temporary staff.'

Mick agrees. 'A husband may have to take a posting alone for two years.'

'Isn't that risky?' I ask. 'What with HIV and all?'

'We encourage accompanied service whenever possible,' Jan says. 'As you say, it makes sense. A soldier gives his best when he has his family with him. It just isn't always possible – but it's a lot better than it used to be. We're growing up, aren't we?'

She turns to Mick Cotton for affirmation, and he nods enthusiastically.

'We allow for personal choice if we can. Compassion demands we at least try to fit the difficult bits of the jigsaw together.'

As we walk back down the corridor she stresses again what a difficult job her staff have, how hard they work. 'You can please some of the soldiers some of the time, but never all of them all of the time. If we move them around without sufficient warning they become insecure. Morale matters and depends upon us getting it right. Our work may well be administrative – but it is crucial.'

Back in her office she reflects on the fact that from her own experience you have good postings and bad postings. They seem to even out. None of course, including her own, lasts much longer than two years – just as well, I imagine, if it's a bad posting. But before I can ask her to comment there is a knock at the door and the head of the other major in her command, Paul Burns, appears.

'Come in, come in,' she says to him. 'Just the man. Take a seat.'

As he settles she tells him I have come to find out more about the place of women in the army. 'I thought you could tell her more about what it's like to have a woman in command than I could.'

Major Burns, she explains to me, is in charge of soldiers' careers and promotions. 'A man who entered the army uncommissioned himself and has risen through the ranks. A meteor. One of our "tipped to go far".

He demurs good-humouredly, as she gets up. 'I'll leave you to it and you can tell her whatever you want.'

There's a pause as he decides what to say. No one in this institution ever speaks, I'm beginning to realise, without thinking carefully about it first. Words after all are powerful weapons.

'As the colonel says ...'

Colonel! I am still struggling to marry up the concept with the rather jolly vision in shocking pink, who has just left the room.

'... I started army life as a private, and all my commanding officers up to now have been male. But I think the female commanding officers here can hold their heads high beside any of them.'

He is an attractive young man in casual jacket and tie, with a shock of curly brown hair and gentle Northern Irish voice, not army-brusque nor brash, but dependable, utterly reliable, I imagine, in a crisis.

'Is it hard for women officers?' I probe.

'Yes. There is jealousy of women who progress through the ranks. I don't have any problems myself. If they have the gifts to get there, if they get the high grades in staff reports, good luck to them, I say. I think they have to work doubly hard to prove they are equal in every way to the men. So they more than deserve promotion when it comes.'

Is it different, I wonder, working for a woman, after working for a man?

He doesn't appear to have thought about that, I notice with interest, and there is a lengthy pause.

'There are strengths and weaknesses in both the sexes.'

'But are women more ... sensitive?'

I'm pressing a point. He isn't very sure. I feel the question is probably unfair. I feel he wants to say that a man can be sensitive too. But he is, after all, a soldier.

'Perhaps. In this department a slightly greater awareness of the personal-problems implications of the decisions we make is an advantage. Speaking for myself, it's just nice to have a change. Women do have a different perspective.'

Even if he isn't very sure what that difference is, instinct tells him it's healthy for all the staff.

'I like gentlemen,' Jan says appreciatively, as she returns to her desk and the major leaves the room. There is a short pause while we both savour the pleasures of meeting such a member of the species, not so far removed from savouring a good wine or a decent cheese.

'You've come across quite a few who are not, I take it?'

'Paul is very forward-thinking. Not all men are comfortable having a woman in command. If a man has a negative experience of a female officer it seems to cloud his judgment of them for the rest of his career. Some say to me, "Oh, you're all right, Jan. You're not like the rest." They relate to the person, you see, but struggle with the idea.'

But bigotry, she admits, is not a male prerogative. 'The thing about personal prejudice is that none of us recognise it for what it is. For quite a long time I was wearing blinkers too. I was ferociously opposed to the ordination of women. I would openly say it was wrong for a woman to have authority over men, without the slightest awareness that that was exactly what I had. It was all right for me, but wrong for a woman who wanted to be a priest. How blind can you be? I've softened. Recognised my double standards. Thank God, He never leaves you standing still.'

In the army, she says, male chauvinism is so deeply and historically ingrained that it can't be avoided to a certain extent. 'The men don't realise they're putting women down. But it's how you as a woman respond to it that counts. A couple of summers ago I was out walking with a male friend and we were having quite a heated debate. "You're a man," I said to him. "What's the male viewpoint on this?" He stopped, looked me straight in the eye and said, "Jan, do you have a problem with men?" I laughed and said, "Of course not, I love men, I work with them all the time," but the truth was that resentment had been building up for some time, and I wasn't prepared to own the anger I felt. I had been very hurt and women who have been hurt become defensive. They can be unpleasantly aggressive and that only compounds the problem. I know, I've done it. Learning to forgive, not hanging on to the hurt, is the key. It's the only way to make lasting, positive relationships.'

'Does that mean you don't challenge chauvinism when you see it?'

She thinks for a moment.

'Usually, I ignore it. That's how I choose to handle it. Or I may try and use humour or a mild rebuke. I prefer the gentle approach. I'm not a confrontational sort of person – unless pushed too far. Anyway, chauvinism is never quite direct enough for you to tackle it when it's happening. It's only afterwards you say to yourself, "Hang on a minute, I know what that was."'

I tell her Paul Burns thinks a woman is probably more sensitive to the emotional implications of a posting. Yes, she agrees, you have to understand the impact of sending a man as target practice for a few invisible Serbs. But, just in case I'm under any illusion, 'I'm here first and foremost because I'm a soldier, because I know what's needed in Bosnia. This job requires a military eye. It couldn't be done by just any civil servant.'

It's time to go for lunch. 'This book you're writing,' Jan asks with curiosity, getting up from her desk, 'Are there any particular themes emerging?'

Thinking particularly of Superintendent Ruth Clark, I tell her it seems women are bringing a new dimension to the concept of leadership, that they're not prepared to become men, but opt for a more uniquely female approach. Is that possible in the army, or does it undermine a woman's authority?

'It probably is different from anywhere else. In the army women have to conform to a certain extent. If you don't play men at their own games you don't even get into the competition. Take, for example, physical fitness. To do as well as the men, the women have to make half the effort again. They push themselves so hard they often end up with injuries. On the other hand, if we make allowances, adjust the timings for women, they don't get the same sense of achievement, and the men say they haven't really proved they deserve promotion. They haven't got there on their own merits. We're working on it – but there are no easy solutions.'

'And as you climb the ranks,' I ask her, 'Do you still have to play the game a man's way?'

'I think women can be as ambitious as men, but I don't think we're as prepared to play dirty to get to the top. That could simply be because we're more devious. They tend to use brawn, while we use our brains – or possibly our more intuitive female gifts.'

I study her face for a moment.

'No, not charm, we don't flirt,' she adds firmly, in case there should be any doubt. 'It's just that while they tend to confront, we look for the way round a situation.'

It strikes me, if that is the case, that in not promoting women sooner, the army made a major tactical error.

As we walk out into the sunshine, down the road, and across the footbridge over the river into the town, Jan explains that she is unusual for the army, and not just because she is a high-ranking woman officer. Her background is working-class.

I suddenly realise why the voice with its southern accent had taken me and my husband by surprise. Not just because it was softer, more hesitant than we expected. But because, subconsciously, we anticipated hearing the jolly, upper-crust tones of the stereotypical army officer.

We pause on the bridge for a moment and lean over the rails, watching the dozens of boats, some for work, many for pleasure, bobbing merrily on the sparkling water below. The river stretches out for miles, a broad, glistening silver band disappearing far away in the distance behind a mass of lush greenery. All along its banks Lowry-like figures sit in groups, lie stretched out or meander along hand in hand, eating ice cream. Chester is almost in carnival mood.

'Isn't it lovely?' I say to her. Worlds apart from the one we have left behind.

'Isn't it.'

She seems to be drinking the entire scene in, her face suffused with pleasure.

'Do you allow it to get to you, knowing it's for such a short time?'

She inhales deeply.

'No, I've come to accept it. I've learned to enjoy now, this moment – before it's gone. I'll be in Glasgow in a few months time. I knew that when I was posted to this job. Eighteen months here. Eighteen months there.'

Is it my imagination, or do I detect a certain wistfulness in her voice?

'Glasgow's a lovely city too,' I say encouragingly.

'Yes, so I've heard.'

We find a table under a gaudy umbrella at one of the riverside cafés. 'I hope the food is okay,' she says anxiously. 'The officers' mess is really very good. I'm so sorry it's closed.'

I'm not. It's great to be out of doors. Besides, at a time when many institutions are bridging the great divide between managers and workers by making them eat together in the staff canteen, the idea of an officers' mess seems a little archaic, a throw-back to a rigid class system of which Jan is evidently still conscious.

Her father was in the navy for 28 years – mostly in the ranks, though he was commissioned for the last five years, and no, she says quickly, since he left when she was five, it wasn't his influence that made her decide on a career in the armed forces. An electronics engineer, he was made redundant when she was 13, and thereafter, with her mother, ran a small guest house in Portsmouth. There was little traditional family life.

'I was very independent. I had to be – an only child raised in a working environment. My mother is the sort of woman who rolls up her sleeves and gets stuck in. She's still running a small hotel at 73.'

Which of her two parents influenced her the most? I ask.

She reflects for a while. Her mother, she thinks, but then her father was older, she was only 20 when he died, and she is very close to her mother now. It's difficult to remember how she felt as a child. She does remember how hard her mother always worked.

She failed the eleven-plus, left Southsea Modern School for Girls with one A level, and went on to take a diploma in home economics at Sheffield Polytechnic. 'So I'm a qualified housewife,' she says with a grin, watching for my reaction. She has a way of catching a listener off guard by lobbing the occasional unexpected remark, and is highly amused when it hits the wicket.

'Then why the army?' I ask.

She had, she explains, already joined the Officers' Training Corps and the pleasures of domesticity began to pale by comparison with the excitement of the outdoor life. 'I thought I might become a probation officer one day. I'd always wanted to help the under-privileged.'

She suddenly sees how her remark might be misinterpreted, and adds quickly, 'Soldiers aren't under-privileged. But I wasn't really serious about the army. It was just a short-term opportunity to have fun before I settled down to do something useful.' After two months at the WRAC College in Camberley she was commissioned into the WRAC in 1975, commanding both men and women, and there followed 'three wonderful years, mountain-climbing, orienteering, parachuting, canoeing and breaking my pelvis'.

She loved army life, not just the adventure and the great outdoors, but the rough-and-readiness, the comradeship, the professionalism and the opportunity for travel. 'The army moves you around very quickly. It offers variety, and a great deal of responsibility at a very early age – more than in most other jobs. The late 1970s were great years. I was young, in charge, and having all the fun I could ever want.'

As staff officer for physical training at Bulford, administering the sports programme for a year – ironic, she says, for an outdoor rather than a sporty type – she discovered that when it came to the exercise of power, there was a fine line between responsibility and tyranny. 'If I decided we were going to win a canoe race, we were going to win it, even if it meant turfing the men out of bed to train at some unearthly hour morning after morning. I could be very assertive. Well, I could be more than that.'

As she talks, she gesticulates with gusto. Had I been younger, and a great deal more energetic, I might almost have been tempted to join up at this point. But then, she is enormously enthusiastic about everything – except the food in Chester cafés – biting off life in more than the average-sized chunks.

'Are you happy here? I've no idea what the pâté will be like.'

I assure her I'm bound to have eaten far worse, wondering whether I might have indeed missed something at the officers' mess, and encourage her to go on with the story.

In 1980 life began to change. A posting to Munster to the 4th Armoured Brigade proved a turning point. This was a busy administrative job overseeing discipline and courts-martial, introducing her to a shadowy side of army life. There was a great deal less time for fun. She was 26, and began to have serious thoughts about her future. If she intended pursuing a different career, or had any thoughts of getting married, now was the time to do it.

She shared some of her anxieties with her superior officer, Major Ian Durie and his wife, Janie. Major-General Durie, as he later became, would be a familiar face on British television screens during his command in the Gulf War. 'They were a lovely couple,' she says. 'They gave me time, listened to my worries, and then prayed for me, which was a new experience. They just loved me.' In the end she decided to press on with her army career, to take the exams which would enable her to become a captain, or even a major.

In 1983, two weeks before her twenty-ninth birthday, at the RAC Centre in Bovington where she was now stationed, a 12-page letter arrived from Ian Durie. She took it to her room in the officers' mess and sat in the silence, reading it slowly from beginning to end. 'He explained that Jesus had died for me so that my sins could be forgiven. I was utterly broken, and just sat there, crying. I remember wondering why no one had ever told me that before. I'd been christened, confirmed. I'd always believed in

God, though I didn't go to church regularly until I was in Munster. No one could say I "needed" Jesus. I was perceived as being extremely successful, a captain in the British army in line for further promotion, on a very good salary, running a sports car with a sailboard on the roof. I had plenty of boyfriends. Life was good. But everything I had seemed frivolous and superficial compared with what was on offer. "Life in all its fullness," Jesus said. Whatever that was, I wanted it. I've never been one for half measures.'

Within weeks she was sent to the Falklands. The war had been over for two years, but living conditions for the military were still extremely difficult. Jan, for whom the world was suddenly a bluer blue and greener green, was aware of little but the beauty of the islands. 'They were breathtaking. And the wildlife was thrilling. I couldn't get over the rare birds and the seals. There we were in very trying circumstances, living in makeshift Portakabins without any of the basic creature comforts, driving round the utter desolation in vehicles the Argentinians had left behind, and all I could say, over and over again, was, "It's such a privilege to be here." Soldiers would stare at me open-mouthed. I was nauseating.'

She had been put in charge of visits – organising the itineraries of an array of senior officials and politicians, who came to the Falklands as part of a profile-raising exercise. The army still segregated the sexes at that late stage. Labour was rigidly divided, roles carefully prescribed. While the men were building a new airport, the 30 girls Jan commanded acted as their clerks, cooks and drivers. But, for good or ill, war changes people. Female soldiers who endured the same dangers, the same dire conditions as the men, were hardly going to be satisfied with back-up jobs in peacetime. They had, after all, proved they were equal to the men in every way. The dividing wall was beginning to crumble.

For Jan, another, more personal barrier was about to be breached. For her next assignment she was sent as an instructor to that bastion of upper-class, male conservatism: the Royal Military Academy at Sandhurst.

Sandhurst had just become co-educational. It was not the easiest time to be there. Captain Ransom had the task of transforming two platoons of raw young women, straight from school, into second-lieutenants, just at the time when, after hundreds of years, a military education for a woman was beginning to resemble a man's.

She thoroughly enjoyed getting to know the girls, training them in leadership skills, military life, and how to dress and behave as officers and ladies. That included the social graces and basic good manners often overlooked by a non-public-school education. Some didn't even know how to hold a knife and fork. Setting them up for their future careers gave her a great sense of satisfaction. But there were difficulties. The collapse of ancient structures may bruise a few supporting egos. Whereas before, the girls had been trained for clerical or administrative jobs, now they were taught military tactics and how to handle weapons. They marched in the same parades as the men. The men, Jan thinks, were bound to be threatened.

'Afraid of competition for their jobs?' I ask.

'No, I don't think you can always rationalise these things. They just felt as if women were encroaching on their territory. It had been an exclusively male environment since time immemorial. In a group men are more comfortable with other men. Women make them feel vulnerable. They're afraid of being shown up, of having their weaknesses and failures made public. You can't change a culture overnight.'

But if the new Sandhurst was hard for the men, it was extremely difficult for the women too, trying to bring their essentially female perspective into situations hitherto viewed unthinkingly and exclusively through male eyes. 'Fighting had always been a man's game. The women had a male tactics teacher for example, who didn't see things the way they did. Relations could be severely strained.' Caught in the middle, Jan found it a very painful experience. She was glad, at that stage, not to be the female major and chief negotiator.

She pauses as a waitress arrives balancing two large plates of toast, pâté and salad.

'Now, a mere ten years later, co-education is taken for granted, of course,' she says, inspecting the plates carefully as they are placed in front of us, to ensure what's on them is fit for consumption. 'Those were teething troubles, but what happened at Sandhurst shouldn't be underestimated. It changed the entire army culture. Until then the WRAC College had been a bit like a finishing school for women who aimed to get to the top and behaved with the authoritarianism of a public-school headmistress when they got there. But they couldn't get away with treating men like that, any more than a male officer could bark his orders out at a woman. Because of integration, there's a much more professional, less archaic approach to leadership. We try to encourage respect and trust, not rule by fear. Both male and female staff come to me with all kinds of problems, including their marital difficulties. I suspect they feel less inhibited with a woman.'

She evidently decides the food is all it ought to be, and tucks in with relish.

~

'I'm a trained killer.'

We have just pushed away two empty plates and sit sipping the remains of our Diet Cokes, lethargically watching the world pass by.

'Pardon?'

At the next table two middle-aged women are spooning food into the mouths of toddlers, thoroughly enjoying playing grandma for the day.

'I've never killed anyone, actually, but I would if I had to – in obedience, not because I wanted to.'

We decide not to get into the subject of the ethics of war, in case we are still sitting here this time next year. Suffice to say she believes that for the sake of peace a just war may be necessary.

'"Blessed are the peacemakers." That's largely what we are. In Bosnia. In Northern Ireland. I didn't even carry a gun when I was in Northern Ireland. But I can shoot straight. I have my annual personal weapons test next week to make sure I can.'

'Tell me about Northern Ireland,' I prompt. 'Were you ever frightened?'

'No. Professionalism takes over. There's a job to be done, so you get on and do it. Checking under your car before you drive off becomes second nature.'

'What was the most difficult thing about life there?'

'Seeing the Irish tear each other apart. I just loved them – Catholic and Protestant. They're a warm, generous-hearted people with a rich history and culture which we English never fully understand or appreciate until we live with them.'

It was as Major Ransom that she went in 1984 to command the Women's Ulster Defence Regiment, known as the Greenfinches. Her role was to encourage and support female soldiers who went on patrol with the men and carried out searches of women suspects. 'Those girls had been in the UDR all their lives. I don't know how they coped. But then, it's only when you leave that you realise how tense life is. Everybody seems to talk about guns, bombs, terrorists and security virtually all the time. They're the main subjects of conversation. You forget what normal chit-chat is.'

For her services she was awarded an MBE. She is not sure why, and doesn't think she was any more conscientious than her colleagues. 'I was absolutely astounded. I thought I had done the job as I always do – to the best of my ability. Those girls deserved my 100 per cent commitment. All feared for their families. Every one of them had suffered in some way. They lived with pain and loss on a daily basis, which was more than I had ever done. Perhaps, because of that, I did give more than 100 per cent. Anyway, I don't want to sound ungrateful. I'm not. It was an immense honour to meet the Queen.'

If she wasn't afraid in Ireland, has she ever been afraid, I ask.

'Yes, in England. When I told a group of male colleagues that I found it offensive when they blasphemed. I told you I don't like confrontation. I felt very shaky.'

'What did they say?'

'Not a lot. I think they were very surprised. But one of them said afterwards he thought I had guts.'

It reminds me of John Wesley's challenge to every Christian to be willing to preach a sermon or die at a moment's notice. Dying, said a friend to me once, could be the easier option.

In Ireland, living in the Lisburn mess, attending a home group at Lisburn Cathedral, she began to appreciate for the first time the importance of being a part of the local community. 'A single woman can't exist in isolation. But if you're in the army you don't have the time to build a community around yourself in the normal way. Fortunately, getting involved in a church enables you to make deeper relationships faster. You can get very close to people quickly if you're prepared to take the risk. That was something I had to learn. It was completely contrary to the army culture.'

The words 'army culture' appear to come into our conversation a great deal. I ask her to explain what she means. She struggles a little, plays with her straw. Generally speaking, she says, it's the pervading atmosphere that requires a stiff British upper lip in all circumstances. An officer is expected to have integrity, honesty, a high moral code in all relationships, to behave like a gentleman – or the female equivalent – at least in public. Stealing or cheating on someone else's wife, for example, is unacceptable. It's all about building trust, teamwork and comradeship. But not about vulnerability. 'Vulnerability is different. That's about admitting your weakness, not majoring on your strengths. It comes from within. It's human rather than professional. It seems to me to be the Christian way, and I've had to make a conscious decision to let it be a part of my life both inside and outside the army.'

'Is that easier for a woman, than for a man?'

'Oh yes. Men are much more defensive. Their male ego gets in the way. I think that's why there are more women than men in the churches in this country. Old British pride keeps the men out.'

I suggest that this suspicion of emotion, this insistence on a rather macho approach, is perhaps the downside of what she calls the 'army culture'. She admits that once it becomes a way of life it can be a very hard pattern to break. Losing sight of the real person inside is one of the greatest threats the culture can impose. 'There are very rigid, set ways of doing things. You're expected to perform and conform. To a certain extent, I don't see how you can run an army in any other way. The bottom line is that we are preparing for war. Discipline is crucial. If people don't use the correct channels, the lines of communication break down. You can't have a few wild cards when a person's life is at stake. On the other hand, you don't need to let it manipulate you into fulfilling every expectation, or con you into thinking that you are making deep and meaningful friendships. It's important to go on being yourself – in and outside the system. When I go to a new church I don't tell people my rank. I say "I'm Jan, I work for the army." Otherwise you have to carry their preconceptions before they have the chance to get to know the real you.'

I suspect that resisting the prevailing culture takes a great deal more courage than Jan is prepared to admit, particularly for a lone, high-ranking female officer. Being real, being vulnerable, allowing yourself to love, is, as she says, a risky business in an environment where openness can be a sign of weakness and relationships are transitory. There are few risks without price, and the price has been a great deal of pain. It was in Brunei she learned that if you are prepared to give away your heart, it may end up in pieces.

In 1988 the British army sent her on 'loan service' to the Sultan to train his Women's Company Royal Armed Forces. She was a big fish in a small pond, answerable only to the colonel, who happened to be the Sultan's second wife. Anyone else might have been tempted to take advantage of her extremely powerful, privileged position. Even the girls she trained were expecting the major to give them a hard time, but it was no longer Jan's way. 'In a society where men have priority, they were not used to being treated with dignity, justice and fairness. No one had ever given them the right to speak before. They were lovely – hard-working and honourable, so easy to teach, with everything to strive for, so much more than in our society. I wanted them to have every opportunity I could give them.' Not surprisingly, there developed between Jan and her girls a deep and lasting bond.

She loved everything about life in Brunei, the conditions, the climate, but most of all, the diversity of cultures. At work in the Sultan's palace she was mixing with people steeped in all the luxury great riches could afford. By way of contrast, at the ex-pat Chinese church she attended, her closest friends were the poorest of the poor, Filipinos and Malaysians who had come to Brunei as servants to escape a life of destitution in the overcrowded long-houses at home. With their warmth and openness and simplicity of faith they found a niche in her heart no one had found before. 'Far Eastern food became my favourite. It still is.'

There were times when she balked at the way women were treated, when she was forbidden to drive in the same car as a man, when, inadvertently, she held out a hand to a man in greeting and he refused to shake it, but, gradually, she began to feel that there was actually an integrity about the Muslim culture that the British culture lacked. 'There weren't the dual standards. In this country we make a pretence of equal opportunities. We pretend chauvinism doesn't exist. After all, where's the man who will admit to it? In Brunei a woman knows exactly where she stands. Because I knew what the opposition was, I learned to find my way round it.'

'But is there is a way round it?' I ask in surprise.

'Brunei isn't Saudi Arabia. It's more tolerant. The main thing is to make sure a man never loses face.'

'That never stuck in your throat?'

'Oh yes, sometimes. It riled me when I saw men and women in totally separate groups. I used to tell myself it was stupid. How naive can you be? In time I learned that they were more comfortable in their separate groups, as we often are in Britain. Brunei wasn't all that different from Sandhurst. You can't change long-held patterns of behaviour overnight. But you can begin to scratch at some of the less acceptable ones, and that was what I tried to do with my girls, give them new possibilities, new horizons.'

Leaving her girls and her church after three years, her longest and happiest posting, was like severing the umbilical cord. Seventy friends came to the airport to wave her off. The pain of parting was worse than any she had ever known before. As the plane left the tarmac she felt as if she had left a part of herself in Brunei. 'Every time I leave a church it's like losing an arm or a leg. But that day, knowing I might never see those wonderful people again, I felt as if my heart had been wrenched out. It was terrible.'

Life at the headquarters of the British Army of the Rhine in Germany was insipid, colourless by comparison. One grey day seemed to drag into another. She had missed the action in the Gulf War – but not the consequences. The vast expenditure necessitated major cuts in the government's defence budget. The time for rewards was over, the time for redundancies had come. 'Options for Change' the package was called, euphemistically. It seemed ungrateful to say the least. Morale in the army was at an all-time low. It reflected her own mood. No one explained about the bereavement process, that she might feel depressed or irrationally angry for at least 18 months. She didn't even make allowances for herself. 'I said to myself, "You're a big girl, Jan. You know what the army's like. Forget Brunei. Get on with life." So I did. I worked and I worked. But I had shut down my emotions. I wasn't prepared to be hurt like that again.'

This seems the appropriate moment to ask her whether she thinks God is good for women.

'He is if they let Him. Well, that's my experience at any rate. I wouldn't let Him be good to me when I was in the Rhine. Army life can be unbearably lonely at times. It seemed as if He had taken away the only real brothers and sisters I had ever had, and I was furious. I held Him at arm's length, like a resentful child. But then I moved to Nottingham, and in a different environment, one step and two years further away from Brunei, I began to understand. God isn't being deliberately obtuse or mean. He isn't an ogre. He loves me. I know that now in my innermost being, and it makes me feel I can cope with almost anything. That's what gives me my confidence – to be an army officer and a woman.'

God wants women to fulfil their full potential, she says, but they don't always want it for themselves. 'They're afraid of men, afraid of other women, they can be afraid of their own shadow if they have been constantly put down. Christian women can be frumpy, old before their time. Their faith seems to shrivel, not free them. They think they have to become shy, shrinking little violets.'

I look at her out of the corner of my eyes, and she laughs.

'I see you've noticed I'm not exactly a quiet individual – with my up-front leadership style, bleached-blond hair and loud jacket. But that's me. I'm not afraid of showing my vulnerability any more, of taking risks, because I'm not afraid of rejection. God's love can make women a success.'

I wonder, after Nellie Thornton's very touching and rather radical definition of achievement, how Jan Ransom sees it.

'To be the best you can be,' she says quite simply. 'I'm not overly ambitious. I didn't plan to become a lieutenant-colonel, I just wanted to be of service. I knew my confidential staff reports were good, but I was utterly amazed when it happened.'

Service. It's an old-fashioned word which seemed to have disappeared from the British vocabulary with maids, butlers and the world of upstairs-downstairs.

'What does service mean?'

'Putting other people before yourself,' she says.

'In the army sense? Active service, for example?'

'No, in the Christian sense. Not counting the cost. Like Jesus. I love that verse in the Bible where he says, "I did not come to be served but to serve and to give my life as a ransom for many." It has my name in it,' she points out, in case I hadn't noticed, and laughs again. 'That's the antithesis of power. Power is a drug. It worries me. I got high on it once. You say, "Go, soldier," and he goes. "Come, soldier," and he comes. You can bring him to heel with one word. And it can go to your head. You become domineering, unpleasant – whether you're a man or a woman. In my position I may well have to tell a soldier something he or she doesn't want to hear. I've had to learn that there's a way of communicating unpalatable truths without destroying people. Always try to leave a person's dignity and self-worth intact.'

If a woman can be seduced into playing the power game as easily as a man, I'm wondering whether women have any particular contribution to make to army life.

'Oh yes, by resisting willco,' Jan says confidently.

'Willco?'

'Yes, the male work ethic. Will co-operate. Will do. Will work every hour God gives. From 6am to 7pm as I did in the Rhine. That driving, achieving, competitive male ethos can suck you in before you know it. Come in early to get things done. Stay on late until they're finished. But on the whole women have other priorities – relationships, for example.'

'Godchildren?' I ask.

'Yes, nine of them,' she says ruefully. 'And no, I don't manage to keep up with them all. When I went to Nottingham inspecting financial and administrative systems – not very exciting – I suddenly realised what madness it all was. I began to learn to keep work in perspective. And still managed promotion and a transfer to glorious Chester.'

She stretches. A clock somewhere chimes three. I apologise for keeping her from her work.

'I've left the day free for you,' she stresses, snatching up the bill and disappearing to pay it, before I register what she is doing.

The two grandmothers at the next table have finished feeding their grandchildren and push them in their buggies backwards and forwards, to get them to sleep. It seems incongruous somehow. Our lives are in proximity for an hour or two in the same café, but their world and Jan's have so very little in common.

'Were you ever tempted to leave the army?' I ask her, as we wander slowly back over the bridge.

'Several times. After the Falkland Islands. I was full of missionary zeal. I was offered a job as a church administrator. Some of my friends were very excited about it. Funny how everyone else seems to know better than you do what's right for your life. But I knew then I was meant to stay in the army.'

'Could you have stayed on if you had married?'

'I would have left. I'm old-fashioned about things like that. I would have put my family first rather than face divided loyalties. But the truth is that from the age of ten I never really wanted children. It may have something to do with being an only child. I can see the joy they bring, I just knew it wasn't for me. I did want to get married though. I asked God to give me a husband or make me content as I was. I got the latter. It wasn't what I expected, but I'm perfectly happy with it now. The trying bit is when people feel sorry for you and say, "What's a nice girl like you doing on the shelf?", as if marriage is the be-all and end-all of existence.'

No one, I reflect, as we walk back into the august offices of the Adjutant General (who is the Adjutant General anyway?), could think that Jan Ransom hasn't lived. I look for the Ladies. There isn't one – not downstairs anyway, only a Gents. Typical. One last little reminder that as a woman I am still here under suffrance. After a hurried trip upstairs, we return to my car in the car park. Like an excited schoolgirl she tells me she is going back to Brunei in a few weeks' time for the first time in five years. She can hardly wait. I suddenly wonder about the pain she must have left behind and always leaves behind every time she moves on. Does she ever think about it?

'I'm very aware of it. But I've come to see that close relationships are worth the pain. I suppose I handle mine by suppressing it, and I expect others to do the same. That's the army for you. But if it hadn't been for my faith I wouldn't even have thought about it. That must be some improvement.

'I must remember to give them that thing back', I say, pointing to the lurid yellow magnet on my car bonnet.

She nods.

'They tried to attach one of those things to me when I first arrived, but my estate car is made of fibreglass. That foxed them.'

I drive off, leaving her guffawing loudly.

On the other side of Chester, heading for the motorway, I feel I am awaking from a dream. The river, the boats, the fiesta colours and soporific afternoon heat haze, they were all part of my imagination, weren't they? It strikes me that soon it may seem like that to Jan. There must be times when she feels that all the places she has ever been to, Germany, the Falklands, Ireland and Brunei, she only actually visited in her dreams. They have come and gone, turning her life into a fascinating but fairly meaningless kaleidoscopic whirl of impressions. It is her faith that enables her to see shapes and patterns, to make some kind of sense of it all, to grasp and hold on to an illusive reality.

In one way, a soldier faces the reality of events that we civilians only ever see as the horror on our television screens. In another, he or she is cushioned from the real world by the army environment, the mess, simply putting on the uniform or being constantly on the move. It is without doubt a difficult choice for women, who have a more highly developed nesting instinct than men. But Jan's lifestyle would be little different if she were a top executive for Marks & Spencer, obedient, mobile and transitory. There would be the same temptation to resist any real attachments, to remain rootless. But she steadfastly refuses that particular self-protection, making a life for herself outside as well as inside the army. But then, those who get to the top are those strong enough to conform to company requirements, while keeping their individuality intact. And Jan is a strong individual, swimming with and against the tide with similar ease, surviving and challenging the system by dint of who, not what she is. That, she would say, is the goodness of God, His intention for every woman.

In the Spring of 2002 Jan retired from the army after 26 years service, having reached the pinnacle of her career as Commanding Officer of The School of Employment Training. She left to fulfil her lifelong ambition to be involved in full-time Christian ministry and is now working part time for the Officers' Christian Union. Jan has set up a charity called 'Flame International' which will facilitate running conferences for women in Africa, Borneo and Eastern Europe or wherever the Lord opens the door. She has a heart for ministry to women, wanting to see them set free to become the women God intended them to be.

CHAPTER 6

The Rabbi: Julia Neuberger

She was the second woman rabbi in Britain, the first in the world to have her own congregation. And no one could have been more surprised than she was – except perhaps her parents. Her mother had a horror of institutionalised religion. Her father was against the idea of women rabbis. And as for Julia herself, she more or less fell into her profession as a third-year student of Assyriology and Hebrew at Newnham College, Cambridge, when the doors of her chosen career – in archaeology – slammed firmly shut in her face. In 1971 a dig in Iraq was out for a Jew; and for diplomatic reasons a Turkish dig was out for a Brit. It was then that one of her tutors, Nicholas de Lange, suggested she think about becoming a rabbi. Until that moment, the idea had never crossed her mind. There were, of course, no precedents, no all-important role models. The whole thing, says Julia, was decidedly bizarre.

She would never have called herself religious. Her immediate family was not particularly devout. There were aunts, uncles and cousins who adhered fairly strictly to the orthodox rules and regulations, but Julia's father had started attending the West London Reform Synagogue, and she accompanied him every Saturday – after they had done the weekend shopping together at Camden market. Reform Judaism had little time for what were deemed the culturally outdated minutiae of the law, such as not travelling on the bus, or handling money on the Sabbath.

Nonetheless, Friday nights in the home of her paternal grandmother, Anna Schwab, instilled an appreciation, deeper than childish reason or logic, of what it meant to be Jewish. Twenty, or even 30 relatives and friends congregated around the table with its flickering Sabbath candles, to say kiddush, the blessings for bread and wine, to eat until they could barely move and to talk and talk long into the night. At Passover, when special crockery was required, there would be such a large gathering that dishes would have to be washed halfway through the meal to ensure there were enough for the pudding. Julia knew that her non-Jewish friends did not have regular family get-togethers like this, that their lives seemed to lack a sense of occasion. But it was only later she grasped the full significance of the fact that she actually preferred being at her grandmother's than out with her school friends. Rushing back from school on a Friday to change out of her messy, dinner-stained school uniform, hopelessly creased from the week's battles, into something more special, was 'a sign of a weekly sense of the holy, a true sense of the importance of the Sabbath, even though I could not have put it into words when I was a child. I knew only that that is what we did, that it made us different from others, that I liked it, that there was something special, separate, about Friday evening en famille that made me respond both to my close family and to the wider net. It is a sense I have never lost, a sense of wonder at the end of the week, at the day of rest, that is, I believe, quintessentially Jewish.'[1]

The future chair of the Camden and Islington Community Health Trust grew up with an abiding passion for community, long before the word or even the concept passed, in a reduced state, into NHS vocabulary. The Hampstead of her childhood, home to many Jewish fugitives from the Nazis, had its own distinctive character. Post-war it was less posh than it is now, a colourful, continental world of hand-made Viennese chocolate shops, delicatessens selling sauerkraut and pickled herrings, and ladies in faded Persian-lamb coats drinking bitter coffee and talking in heavily accented voices in the Dorice Restaurant on Finchley Road. Some, desperately poor, lived alone in rooms in other people's rented flats, surrounded by the bits of bric-a-brac they had managed to bring with them, poignant little pieces of Meissen china, the treasured detritus of former genteel lives, cruelly uprooted and smashed apart.

From almost the moment of her birth, the Holocaust cast its malevolent shadow across Julia's path. She lived and breathed in the painful, rather disoriented atmosphere of the refugee. Her mother, Liesel, narrowly escaped from Germany in 1937, and managed to get her brother and parents out just before the war began. But many aunts and uncles disappeared without trace or explanation, apart from the occasional, harrowing rumour of a suicide leap from a train bound for the death camps. Most of the adults she knew had lost someone near or dear. Her maternal grandfather, who spoke little English, sunk slowly into his own private hell, and spent his last years in the safety of London, 'escaping' from the Nazis, shouting, 'They're after me,' mistrusting even his old drinking partners and friends. There was no way of protecting the child from the trauma and terror of what had happened, should her parents have wanted to do so. At an early age she was forced to face the terrible reality that 'by an accident of time I was not there'.[2]

Yet there were many who bore no bitterness for their difficult, disrupted lives, who rarely complained, whose experiences made them warmer, kinder, more giving. Their example was the subconscious challenge that would push her, throughout her life, to look for ways of sublimating the anger simmering away gently beneath the surface of her psyche, by using it positively to build a fairer, better world. Only then could there be an end to the appalling damage that was inflicted on the innocent and was passed, with highly destructive potential, from one generation to the next, as apparently normal, civilised human beings descended into grossly subnormal, subhuman behaviour.

Ironically, it was from her mother that Julia inherited her fair, Aryan prettiness and pink-and-white, fine-porcelain complexion. Where stereotypes are concerned, she is the classic British rose, whose delicate looks and dulcet voice belie the force and determination within. Nor was Liesel Schwab the stereotypical Jewish mother with a neurotic obsession for housework and chopped liver. To survive in Britain she worked first as a domestic, then as a counter hand in Marks & Spencer in East Ham, where she had to work on Saturdays. She was quickly promoted to manageress but left in 1949 before the birth of her daughter. After Julia was born she went on working for various Jewish refugee organisations and found more fulfilment, Julia suspects, than that other powerful female force in the Schwab dynasty, Julia's indomitable paternal grandmother.

It is to Anna Schwab that Julia owes her combative flair, her pleasure in a good verbal sparring. Like Julia, Anna, whose husband had come to England to work for the London branch of a family merchant bank, would have also held her own on the BBC's *Question Time, Any Questions?* or *The Moral Maze*, given half a chance. But between the wars there were few if any outlets for a woman of her energy and spirit. In 1933, for a few brief years, she found her destiny, staging one-woman sit-ins on the Home Office steps, resolutely refusing to budge until the government issued visas for any Jewish child she managed to house.

Julia never found her grandmother easy, but admired her battling spirit and feisty determination nonetheless. The argumentative family matriarch had a profound influence on the woman she would become. In February 1995 in *The Times* she described to journalist Judy Goodkin how she used to call on Anna on her way home from primary school. 'Ours was very much a relationship of equals; she would scoff at my music theory homework, and I would tell her without hesitation I thought she was being ridiculous. It strikes me as incredible now that a woman of her age would allow a child to be so outspoken.'

Anna did not approve of the Reform Judaism of Julia's parents and would say so but, having seen how schisms divided the Jewish community in Frankfurt when she was a girl, felt that the unity of the family was more important than religious considerations. 'The marvellous thing about her was that she was always willing to argue the toss.'

Born in Britain, Anna's son Walter, Julia's father, was a quiet, unassuming man, a civil servant who had sacrificed academic qualifications to work on a kibbutz in Palestine. His parents, who had sent him to a British public school and were delighted when he won a place at Cambridge University, didn't speak to him for three years. He had committed the cardinal Jewish sin of failing to live up to parental expectations. With his upper-crust accent he was supposed to be the perfect English gentleman, not a romantic adventurer pursuing wild Zionist dreams in some God-forsaken wilderness. Zionism seemed little short of madness – until the extent of the Nazi threat became clear. 'You were right,' Anna wrote to him in 1938, 'I was wrong. Come back and help us with the refugees.'

Julia thinks it is significant she was an only child. Walter expected as much of her as he would of a son. It was he, and later an Israeli tutor, who taught her Hebrew. 'In fact all his hopes for the next generation were wrapped up in me. Which is why education was so important, as it is in many Jewish homes.'

A hive of hyperactivity, with boundless expectations of its pupils, South Hampstead High School for Girls provided the perfect academic environment for a highly intelligent, questioning young woman. Julia suspects she was seen as a bit of a bluestocking because she was more interested in her books than in the Swinging Sixties pop-and-fashion scene. She played her Beatles records like any other teenager, but couldn't identify with the paroxysm of emotion they seemed to provoke. She bought a concessionary pair of impractical white Courrèges moonboots with holes in the toes, which left more than just her feet cold. 'You had to talk about pop music and clothes because that's what everybody talked about, but it wasn't what I really wanted to talk about – I still don't.'

About a third of her fellow pupils were Jewish. They held their own separate prayers at the beginning of the day, except on Wednesdays, when Christian and Jewish girls joined together for an act of worship. As a senior prefect Julia was responsible for vetting the hymns for unacceptable references to Jesus or the Trinity. 'It's only now I realise that apart from the psalms, no hymn is really safe, but I thought they were wonderful and the other side definitely had all the best tunes.'

There was no noticeable anti-Semitism in those years after the war. The Holocaust had aroused strong British sympathy. The only difference being Jewish made to the non-Jewish girls, or rather to their mothers, was that they had to consider what to give their friends to eat when they took them home for tea. It was very confusing for anyone who wasn't Jewish. Jewish families, who appeared on the face of it to be very similar in their religious observance, varied enormously in the degree to which they adhered to the dietary laws.

The lack of enforced conformity, an environment where being different was commonplace and acceptable, provided, Julia believes, an essential foundation for young girls who would grow up to take their places in a more hostile world. 'The early recognition that the school would have to adapt to its Jewish pupils, rather than the Jewish pupils adapt to the school, was, I suspect, critical in shaping the way we thought, and in making us assume we would be offered equality wherever we went.'[3]

She is now an avid supporter of single-sex education. In a mixed-gender context, boys take the initiative, girls learn to follow. And this does little for the girls' fragile self-confidence. Girls, she feels, are more likely to blossom and find their real selves in an environment that doesn't commit them to an instinctive deference to men. They need to be infused with extra derring-do. Her experience as an employer tells her, 'Men plot their careers. Women tend to fall into theirs. They need the leadership opportunities that an all-girls education offers. Mine gave me a great start.' The heady mix of a private-school education, forceful women in the family, and a father who believed in her led Julia to believe there was nothing a woman could not do – except perhaps become a rabbi.

In her late teens she began to think deeply about the meaning of life, and the significance of being Jewish. There were intense and lengthy discussions with her mother well into the night. For a while she toyed with the idea of becoming orthodox – until her two orthodox female cousins celebrated bat chayil (daughter of valour), a reluctant concession to increasing pressure from orthodox Jewish women for a female equivalent of bar mitzvah, the ceremony at 13 that marks a boy's passage into religious manhood. It took place on a Sunday afternoon, not, like a bar mitzvah, in the Saturday Sabbath service. Even so, one member of the congregation walked out. He didn't approve of girls reading the Hebrew scriptures. Nor would her cousins ever have the opportunity of reading them in public again. It was, Julia felt, a waste of a ceremony. What she saw she recognised as tokenism. Women were not going to be treated as equals within Jewish orthodoxy. She decided she was better suited where she was.

Her own bat mitzvah (daughter of the Commandment), in the West London Reform Synagogue – in the Reform rather than orthodox tradition – was a different matter, a genuine opportunity for a young woman to become a full member of the adult congregation. Post-bat mitzvah classes were taken by a new and very junior young rabbi called Hugo Gryn. They were inspirational. A Holocaust survivor himself, he encouraged her to explore a Jewish approach to the great moral and ethical debates of the day. Not that there was one single Jewish line or view. Jews rarely agree about anything. But he showed her how a working knowledge of Jewish law, history, theology and experience could cast light on the most perplexing and confusing of human dilemmas. Most important of all, while many Jews tended to channel their intellects into legal, medical or financial outlets, he taught her that spirituality also merits a person's academic best. He not only whetted her intellectual appetite, he opened her eyes to the richness of her inheritance in a way no one else could have done. Her Judaism became a deep and vast resource waiting to be tapped. Today, even after years of study, she feels she is only just dipping in a toe, and making ripples on the surface.

'Is God good for women? I don't think he sees us as men or women – just as human beings. Spirituality has therefore always been good for women. But religions, the man-made structures, have been historically bad for women. Women can change those.'

Julia did not become a rabbi with the express intention of changing the structures. It wasn't until she started training at the

Leo Baeck College that she saw the real face of antagonism and prejudice towards women for the first time. Newnham, where she had taken her degree, was an all-women's college. At Cambridge University in the early 1970s there were ten men for every woman. 'We were in demand.' True, in many intellectual circles these were the heady years of feminism, but books such as *The Female Eunuch*, by fellow Newnham graduate, Germaine Greer, published in 1971, seemed a bit of an irrelevance. Julia and her cronies didn't believe men were deliberately trying to keep women down, she wrote later, because 'as soon as the error of their ways was pointed out to them, they would all move up and make room for us'.[4] Equality, for what she now sees as a rather naive group of undergraduates, meant campaigning for mixed colleges. Trinity, the most prestigious of the male colleges, she remembers vaguely, had some major debate with Newnham students about whether female students should be admitted to the Junior Common Room, because there would be a problem over the use of the bathrooms and loos. Looking back, 'It all seems terribly absurd. I didn't take it seriously.' She was, in fact, finally quite grateful for a single-sex environment where a woman could work without the distraction of being lured into washing and mending for a man.

At the time she started attending the Leo Baeck College, she simply didn't believe discrimination existed. No one had ever said 'no' to her before. 'I thought they were potty thinking there were things a woman couldn't do.' That strong, defiant streak of hers, nurtured not repressed by an awfully un-English childhood, where children were not only seen and heard but expected to have an opinion, would never suffer fools gladly or allow them to curb her style. 'I must have been born bloody-minded; if someone tells me an idea is impossible, I simply have to do it to prove them wrong'.

In time, however, she understood. Some of the misogyny was not as unthinking as it appeared. It was very important for a Liberal college to be seen to be authentically Jewish. Liberal Judaism prided itself on pushing the religious boundaries – too far, said its critics. Training women as rabbis was further than too far. It was a threat to that most sacred of Jewish institutions, the family. A woman's place was in the home, not the pulpit, 'being a nice *little* Jewish wife', preoccupied with household duties.

There were deliberate attempts, largely from fellow students, to make her feel extremely uncomfortable; more, she now reflects, than at any other time in her life. Bowing with meek submission to their superior judgment was not in her nature, and that compounded the problem. They made it clear they found her up-front, argumentative style aggressive. 'I was assertive, I admit, but not nearly as aggressive as they were. It's all right for a man to be forceful, to have strong opinions, but not a woman.' It was a no-win situation. Their bigotry made her angry but, she maintains, anger was not and still is not an acceptably feminine emotion. It simply isn't 'nice'.

On the whole, the college, especially the older members of staff, treated her with respect and courtesy, refusing to allow synagogues to be choosy about having a female student on placement. Bertram Jacobs, the administrator, was a saintly man and a wonderful support. Lionel Blue taught her down-to-earth rabbinical practice such as not leaving your prayer-book on the coffin during a cremation, because when you pressed the button it would disappear. She studied Talmud with the great theologian Louis Jacobs, and spiritual poetry with mediaeval scholar David Goldstein. It was a highly intensive period of study but she thrived on it.

Julia was the college's second female student to qualify as a rabbi. The first, Jackie Tabick, was sensitive and pastoral, and appeared content at that time to accept an educational post, a chaplaincy, rather than force herself on what might have been an unwilling congregation. (Later she went on to become associate rabbi to Hugo Gryn at the West London Synagogue.) Julia, on the other hand, abounding in confidence, felt a growing determination to be a trailblazer. 'For a time I really did think Jackie would get all the publicity, take all the flak. But then I realised I wasn't prepared to be denied the most senior posts simply because I was a woman. When the heads of the college leant across the rather large conference table and said, "You're not going to want to lead a congregation, are you?" my first thought was, "Well, now that you come to mention it ...'"

She did have to take her share of the flak, and some of it came from a source very close to home. After all, within her own family some were orthodox, and even those who weren't were far from convinced that becoming a rabbi was an acceptable thing for a woman to do. One cousin thought she was far too bright to waste it on religion. 'I think it was further evidence of my not behaving well, not knowing my place. But then, I've never known my place.' Yet when, after five years of serving congregations in Bristol, Liverpool and Nottingham as a student or trainee, she finally became the fully-fledged rabbi of the South London Liberal Synagogue, and stood at her induction to preach her first sermon, her parents, like so many others, overwhelmed at the historical significance of the occasion, were filled with pride.

Women, she says, have no intention of staying in a male-defined place. The major monotheistic religions, Judaism, Christianity and Islam, all revolve around an essentially male view of God and the world. The Hebrew Bible may well be divinely inspired, but it was written down by men wearing their inevitable male blinkers. But for those with the will and the eyes to see it, woman's story is there, hidden behind the text.

For example, when Abraham sends his servant to find his son, Isaac, a wife, who made the original decision? Sarah, of course. She always makes all the major decisions. It is Sarah who gives Abraham her servant girl, Hagar; Sarah who drives Hagar out, with her son, Ishmael, when Hagar's superciliousness becomes too much for her. Within an apparently male-dominated story, here is a woman who gets her own way. 'And the old rabbis just couldn't hack it,' says the expert in Hebrew and Babylonian languages. 'They began to doctor the texts a little. They couldn't believe, for example, that Miriam, sister of Moses and a mere woman, would lead a rebellion against him. So they added Aaron to the story for good measure.'

The other three matriarchs, Rebecca, Leah and Rachel, were equally decisive, determined and forceful. In fact they were so given to underhanded scheming that Julia wonders whether, at kiddush, when a mother prays that her daughter will grow up to be like them, it wouldn't be a better idea to substitute, 'May you be like Ruth, strong, sensible and spiritual, or the daughters of Zelophehad, a model of modern assertiveness, who, having no brothers, negotiated their way into inheriting their father's property.'

'Women's studies of the Bible and other texts have to be such that there seems to be some point for young girls, inspired by their innate spirituality, to explore that side of themselves and see it not only in terms of religion, as hitherto organised by men, but in terms of women's lives, women's experience, women's spirituality, women's capacity to serve God and humanity.'[5] The intention in reinterpreting the biblical stories was not to denigrate men, but to stimulate and inspire the next generation of women into fulfilling their rightful, God-ordained place in the scheme of things.

Apart from notable exceptions, such as the great Beruriah, reputed in the Talmud to be even wiser than her husband, the famous Rabbi Meir, and despite the quality of the education they received, women were gradually written out of Jewish history and discouraged from taking part in the religious life of the local synagogue. Julia believes their exclusion began as a special exemption from religious duties when they had unweaned babies and small children. But in the early centuries what was meant to be liberating gradually became restrictive, as men went on limiting their wives to domestic duties long after the children were out of infancy. Some learned rabbis suggested that woman was created with a special capacity for privacy. She didn't need to be a part of the congregation. She could have a perfectly satisfactory, even superior, spiritual life to the men, at home. Julia's response to that? 'Nice try! It's good to read that women are superior to men in something – even if it was an attempt to maintain the status quo.'

By the Middle Ages, the perfect wife of the book of Proverbs had become something of a prototype. Women did not only cook the food. They provided it. They took care of all the practicalities involved in running a home, while the men devoted themselves to study. The great Jewish mother was born. She had power, she had dignity, she was head of the family, but she took her status from her husband – by extension.

It is, says Julia, an extremely limited, and limiting view of woman's potential, an excuse for males to cover their threatened feelings, a means of keeping their own territory intact. If a Jewish woman is capable of running a home and the family business, then why is she not also capable of taking on religious duties? That is the issue that the great protagonists of the Jewish mother duck, and it annoys her intensely. 'Human beings create inequality, not God. Nature gives women things to do like having children, but that doesn't mean we can't do anything else. What about when the children grow up? Or if a woman is single? Or childless?'

Here, Julia admits, Christianity had the edge. Its monastic tradition enabled many a single Christian woman to be considered a spiritual person in their own right. A nun had status. A mother superior had immense power in the church. But then celibacy was regarded as a virtue in a way it never was in Judaism. In the *Guardian* in November 1995 she wrote, 'Judaism is positive about many aspects of women's lives; it celebrates the strength of mothers, and has always emphasised the education of girls (if not to the level of boys). In particular, it is positive about female sexuality – to the surprise of non-Jews. This is not to suggest there is adulation of any kind of female raunchy behaviour, or of women behaving in anything other than a modest fashion. But, nevertheless, alongside the second-class legal status of women sits a belief dating from early rabbinic times that it is a husband's duty to give his wife sexual pleasure. This is a far cry from Christianity's general difficulty in regarding sex as anything but sinful, even if essential, for most people.'

Nonetheless, in religious institutions women have long been relied upon, exploited and unthanked, so that, 'uncomplaining, they have carried out tasks men have not wanted to do'.[6] The time has come, she says tartly, when that must change. Women should refuse to carry out these tasks unless they are recognised as essential, not 'the icing on the cake'. If they move into pastoral jobs they must demand appropriate training and support. A certain degree of 'polite toughness', a sacrifice of 'niceness' not very familiar in religious circles, are required, if it is to be understood that women mean business.

Despite their chequered, rather restricted history, Julia believes women have always found ways of breaking out of the system and expressing their spirituality. The role models she missed as a child, both historic and contemporary, were there all the time, had she but known it. Becoming the rabbi of the South London Synagogue may have seemed very radical to the Jewish community, but its founder president had been a woman. 'We tend to think of Lily Montagu now as a sweet little old lady, but she was a feisty pioneer in the great tradition of the nineteenth-century female social reformers, Octavia Hill and Josephine Butler, and their more openly feminist Jewish counterparts, Bertha Pappenheim and Rosa Luxemburg. She had a great passion to make Judaism accessible, especially to shop-girls who worked on Saturday mornings, and started her own Saturday afternoon services.'

Bertha Pappenheim was the heroine of her grandmother, Anna Schwab. Bertha's head was depicted on a framed block of German stamps hanging beside Anna's chair and, on reflection, it now surprises Julia that she told her very little about this extraordinary unpaid social worker, who worked with prostitutes, campaigned for an end to the white slave market and was Freud's disturbed yet talented Anna O.

Julia's favourite is Ernestine Rose, daughter of a Polish rabbi, who contested an arranged marriage and the confiscation of property inherited from her mother, rightfully hers under Jewish law. She won her case, married a follower of Robert Owen (the English socialist and inspiration for the co-operative movement) and sailed to America, to become a leading early American feminist.

There was in fact a small band of radical, reforming Jewish feminists, whose revolutionary zeal must have terrified most of the men in their orbit. Was theirs a double rebellion, Julia wonders, a fight, not only against the conventions of the day, but also against the limitations of being a Jewish woman?

For Julia in the 1990s there have been few, if any, obvious limitations to what she has wanted to do. She manages to combine chairing a Community Health Trust with a host of other commitments, including being vice-president of the Royal College of Nursing and of the Patients Association, a member of the Medical Research Council and the General Medical Council, taking on various school governorships and charities, and patronages, lecturing at the Leo Baeck College, running training courses for the King's Fund College, broadcasting, writing books and, last but not least, becoming Chancellor of the University of Ulster.

The list would be exhausting for someone with less energy or a less multi-track approach to her work. But Julia juggles all the plates with an acrobatic dexterity that leaves colleagues, friends and even her administrative back-up with a slightly breathless combination of admiration and irritation. She hardly ever says no, a weakness she owns with little hope of a solution. This is the contemporary version of the Proverbial wife – who not only has it all, but loves it all. For let no one be deceived into thinking that husband and children are simply one commitment among many. Her face lights up when she talks about them. Home is the epicentre of her life. A safe haven. A gift she never takes for granted. 'Knowing your place in the family structure makes you feel secure. That's been very important for me. Having a refugee mother made me very insecure.'

Her role as wife and mother is a stark and liberating contrast to the hyper-efficient, super-professional image she carries with her almost everywhere else. It's the ordinariness of family life she appreciates the most, the rows of boots in the hall that tell her Matthew has brought his friends home, the noise when Harriet is entertaining hers. She loves having teenagers. She finds them such fun. The house is perpetually in chaos, the fridge permanently empty – and it really doesn't matter. 'Family life has its own order,' she says. 'You can't stay on your dignity for long. They know you too well. They tease you and bring you down to size.'

Her husband, Anthony, whom she met in Cambridge, teaches finance at the London Business School, thoroughly enjoys her public persona, checks her copy for magazines and books, and tells her she 'doesn't think straight'. He's looking for logic, for categoric facts, while her style is personal and relational. That, she's convinced, is a sign of the different way men and women communicate, and a useful complementariness. Theirs is by no means a conventional marriage. When the children were small he took more care of them than she did. One or the other is often away, but that makes togetherness all the more special. 'We like family life – even the boring domestic bits, like cooking a meal together on a Friday evening.'

Jewish rituals are as important to her as they ever were, perhaps more so now that she has a home of her own. While never stopping her children from going out with their friends on a Friday evening, she hopes they will feel there is something more compelling at home. 'I'm not sure we've got the family right these days in our society – its too nuclear. We need to create opportunities for the extended family. We're usually about 25 at our Passover Seder. It's become quite a tradition.' Just as she did when she was a child, Matthew and Harriet have noticed how unusual it is for their non-Jewish school friends to have family gatherings like that. 'To sit and eat together, to pray together without prayers being a separate and solemn event, makes the family a wonderful focus. It becomes the heart of religious observance, and the home becomes the place of worship, suggesting that, while synagogue is important, that it is where you study and learn and go to pray in a congregation, it is not the heart of your Jewish being.'[7]

It was this tendency of women to make choices in favour of their homes, their children, their parents, their own personal needs, over and above their careers, that we discussed when I went to see her at the typically Victorian-hospital headquarters of the Camden and Islington Community Health Trust, a rather gloomy, silent and anachronistic oasis in the heart of London. Her father-in-law was very ill and she was clearly upset. But if she wished she were somewhere else, which I suspect she did, she tried not to show it, and answered my questions about the changes women were bringing to the workplace with equanimity and enthusiasm.

'I think women can challenge workaholism in a way men can't.' She has created her own bolt hole, a house in West Cork, cut off from the unreasonable demands of civilisation. As she leaves the ferry port and drives west along a glorious stretch of unspoiled Irish coastline, she begins to breathe again, to shake off the pressures which reduce her to a less than a truly human state. It's more than an escape, it's a lifeline. 'So I say to the board, "Sorry, I won't be at the next meeting, I'm having a holiday," and the men say, "But you've just had one." And I say, "So what? I'm having another." But it's hard for them. They live with the expectation of working ridiculous hours. Their jobs are threatened if they don't. Their whole world revolves around their work. I play a full part at board meetings, but then I switch off. Time to stop work, time for the family.'

She has noticed too that women have an entirely different, more collaborative style in the boardroom. 'Men score points. It's innate. You have to come back at them and argue with them. They find it hard to let their front down, to make real friends. Women can't survive without friendship. We're constantly making connections with each other. On the other hand, I do get impatient with groups of women who are so busy being nice to each other that they can't make a decision.'

She sits on her desk facing me, her legs swinging slightly from time to time. This is no high-powered executive, putting distance between us by desk or dress. Her skirts are full and flared, down to her ankles, covering what she claims, ruefully, is not the best of her features. She wears blazers and a hint of a ruffle, or long, floaty, feminine scarves. I tell her I have been to see Mary Spillane, the Colour-Me-Beautiful guru, an admirer of hers since her political campaign to win a seat for the Social Democratic Party during the 1983 election. Mary has asked me to offer her a free personal fashion consultation. She laughs dismissively. 'I can't bear these people who tell you what you should wear. I wear what I like, like this.' She throws an end of her rich, velvet wrap back over her shoulder, and we return to the subject that really matters.

'More women are taking a lead, more are becoming well known, and are breaking through the glass ceiling – in science, for example. But their contribution is largely unrecognised. We acknowledge the importance of the involvement of women in the business world, for example, but it's political rather than actual. There's still a lot of tokenism going on.'

In 1991, in her book, *Whatever's Happening to Women?*, she expressed her disappointment that so few of her Newnham contemporaries, who had shared their hopes and dreams together long into the night, had actually made it to the top. They vanished like meteors into the hidden depths of domesticity, while hordes of undistinguished, uninspiring men were running the country. Germaine Greer's angry 1970s feminism, she maintained, had led women up a blind alley rather than to the head of the boardroom table. The idea that a woman could do anything a man could do, and even do without a man, was interesting in theory, impossible in practice. Behaving like a man – even if you were Margaret Thatcher – was counter-productive. It antagonised men. It denied the world of work the socially sensitive changes inspired by a uniquely feminine approach. Everything was not always men's fault. 'The problem is not whether we (boys and girls) are different, as we clearly are, and have different interests and skills. The problem lies in accepting those differences, in dealing with them, in counteracting them when that seems socially useful, and in trying not to confuse biological and hormonal differences with social ones.'[8]

In denying the biological differences between the genders, radical feminism of the 1960s and 1970s ignored the fact that the nurturing side of women meant they instinctively took on most of the caring – both for children and elderly or other dependent adults. And in that it did a great deal of harm. Women were not prepared for the cost of 'having it all'. They didn't realise Shirley Conran's *Superwoman* was fictitious. They couldn't simultaneously be a brilliant cook, wonderful lover, superb mother and high-powered executive – and stay sane. Not while society was hostile and state provision grossly inadequate. We live, Julia said, in a state where 'caring is a private matter', where there are few nursery-school places, a rarity of after-school provision and disdain for women who resort to using a crèche or putting mother in a home. The result? Complete and utter exhaustion. Many women, if they were lucky enough to afford it, simply gave up the struggle. They weren't unhappy. Far from it. To her frustration, once the pressure was off, they blossomed. But the loss to society of all that female gift and talent was immense. They should have been able to keep the career – and still blossom.

Some of her female critics were none too happy with her upper-middle-class references to problems with nannies and housekeepers. 'Her problem is that she doesn't know how the other half lives,' smirked Conservative MP Edwina Currie. In fact, she knew a great deal better than Edwina Currie the strain of trying to live up to the expectations of being the good Jewish wife, mother and daughter, not to mention, rabbi. There was a day when even her legendary energy finally gave out, and she gave in to the torture known to every woman – guilt. 'Both my parents were ill and in different hospitals and I was trying to visit them both and carry on my pastoral work as a rabbi. I spent the entire time thinking I should be somewhere else. I burst into tears at the traffic lights in Sloane Square. It was not like me.'

She doesn't criticise women who give up their careers to stay at home, but she does believe it should be a genuine choice, not an assumption or an expectation or a survival mechanism. What worries her is that looking back she feels that some of the things she minded about most have changed very little since the 1975 Equal Opportunities Act. To counter this apparent failure she has made it her business to encourage women to aim high, to take assertiveness, self-presentation and voice-control classes. She runs a course called Leadership 2000 for female chief executives and senior women in the NHS. 'It is important to the future of the Health Service', says the King's Fund College pro-motional brochure, 'that women continue to contribute at very senior levels in an environment which requires organisations to make major shifts in culture and style of management.'

'Networks for women enable them to maximise their con-tribution to society.' That, she says, is an essential part of 1990s' moderate feminism. There's great mileage in the way women bond with one another, and learn from each other.' To pull up the ladder on another woman is unnatural, anathema to her. While she herself would always appoint the best person for the job, she believes it is important for women to give each other a leg up.

There are many men too, and not all new generation, raised in the school of fair-mindedness, who don't see gender as an issue, and instinctively encourage women to fulfil their potential. 'The congregation at the South London Synagogue is deeply egalitarian. They were lovely to me. They chose me as their rabbi rather than a man. Senior rabbis like Hugo Gryn and John Rayner have given me a great deal of support. So have politicians like Roy Jenkins and Anthony Lester.'

It is, however, a source of pain to her that orthodox Judaism's Chief Rabbi, Dr Jonathan Sachs, appears unwilling or unable to respond to the results of the report he initiated on the position of women in orthodox Anglo-Jewry. There is still no progress in establishing a liturgy for childbirth or the gift of a daughter, or in introducing a proper coming-of-age service for a 12-year-old girl. 'Feminism has done religious groups a great deal of good. It has made the most paternalistic men think again – or driven them further into fundamentalism. The backlash makes me very sad. All fundamentalism is frightening. It says, "I'm right, you're wrong." It uses religion as a stick to beat people with. It closes down all chance of debate.'

She was in Waterstone's bookshop in Hampstead signing copies of her autobiography, *On Being Jewish*, when a man stood up and said, 'You're dangerous.' Though she thrives on controversy, it's a clean fight she enjoys, not punches below the belt. Though she can laugh at the idea of being dangerous now, even take it as a compliment, it doesn't alter the underlying implication that while bigotry is about, her ideal world is a long way off. Those who fail to see women as equal are, she says, suffering from a form of colour-blindness. They are restricted to vision in muted shades of grey.

'I see myself as a pioneer. But for me pioneering was not about becoming a rabbi. That was simply a means to an end.'

In Judaism the role of the rabbi is not the same as the role of the church minister or priest. The word means 'teacher', not 'pastor'. It has academic, not hierarchical or managerial clout. It has to do with passing on Jewish history, thought and practice to later generations, not the administration of buildings or involvement in the complex minutiae of the lives of individual members of the congregation. Rabbis, however, are coming under increasing pressure to adopt a more culturally Christianised approach, involving counselling and pastoral care. Julia found visiting the bereaved and the dying surprisingly rewarding, an unexpected landmark in her own spiritual quest, conferring 'a sense of calm and resolution, which made me understand a little of what it is like to get nearer one's maker'. Up till then she had seen the moral and cultural rather than the spiritual benefits of Judaism. In *On Being Jewish* she makes it clear, however, that she believes religious ritual is meaningless without moral action. Her first commitment, her prime calling as a Jew, is to work for social justice. 'I've always used my novelty value as a woman rabbi to get my message across. When journalists ask me daft questions, about what I wear, for example, I answer them, then tell them what I really want to say.' And what she really has to say covers a wide range of issues from ethics to racism, sexuality to mental health, all part of a large human-rights package.

The determination to fight for a fairer, better world was fed almost by osmosis to the child who grew up in the bitter-sweet atmosphere of a post-war Jewish community, living under the shadow of the Holocaust. Apart from their refugee work, her family were not, in the political sense, particularly socially active. But she learned that if there was anything you could do to alleviate human suffering, you should do it. 'My passion for human rights tells you a lot about me. As the child of a refugee, growing up with the consequences of the most appalling inhumanity, knowing it could have been me, how could I not campaign on behalf of the exploited and oppressed?'

Judaism is the most humanistic of the monotheistic religions. Away with any notion that suffering may be good for the spirit. It is to be averted, combated, denounced. It says the bulk of human misery is caused by human action, and can be transformed only by human intervention. Religious duty requires giving large amounts to charity. Her congregation in South London was extremely generous – which compounds her anger with the erroneous stereotype of the mean Jew.

Liberal Judaism in particular has always seen itself as the inheritor of the great Hebrew prophetic tradition. The prophetic ideals, the great scholar Claude Montefiore, one of its founding fathers, wrote in 1902, were justice, mercy and loving kindness. The prophets had 'a passion for righteousness'. And that passion for righteousness, says Julia, is, at its best, what Judaism has to offer. What does it mean? 'Speaking out against policies that lead to poverty in big cities, against racial prejudice, against immigration controls operated by colour rather than by need or right.'[9] It means challenging the status quo.

It was a principle which led her to stand as an SDP candidate in the 1983 election – with encouragement from local Christian colleagues. To her huge amusement and delight, they wrote her little notes of support – 'We clergy must stick together ...' – as if balancing in the political middle was the natural and obvious stance of a minister. Three years later the political fence gave way. The Church of England published its *Faith in the City* report, demanding an urgent response to urban deprivation, and was dubbed, by certain Tories, a Marxist document. The Anglican Church, says Julia wryly, had resorted to the great Jewish prophetic tradition of denouncing human misery. Ironically, the report was not supported by the then Chief Rabbi Lord Jakobovits, a Thatcherite, who seemed to think the poor should pull themselves up by their own bootlaces. That was a view from which Julia and many of her fellow Jews loudly dissociated themselves.

Jewish people also find aligning themselves with one particular political party very uncomfortable, she says, with some frustration, which means they haven't always been as outspoken as their religion requires on issues such as race, in which, after all, they have a vested interest. Many of us, she is quick to point out, would not be here today if Britain had not offered the Jews asylum. 'Asylum is an important concept in the Hebrew Bible, which we appear to have lost today. We have lost all sense of the need for time and space. Not just for political fugitives. For those with mental health problems too.'

Mental health is part of her brief as chair of a Community Health Trust, along with the care of the elderly, and all community medical and nursing services for a large part of inner London. She had said a sad goodbye to the South London Liberal Synagogue in 1989, believing the time had come to devote herself to a wider, more amorphous congregation, one without a voice at the most vulnerable point of their lives: the thousands of people and their relatives annually at the mercy of the NHS. Her passion for patients' rights had crept up slowly, almost from behind, an unexpected consequence of involvement with the terminally ill. It shocked her that they appeared to have so little understanding of their condition and so little say in their treatment. The King's Fund, the medical research organisation, offered her a fellowship in their Policy Institute, to look at how research ethics committees worked – in other words, who decided what research on which patients was acceptable. Two years later she spent seven months as a Visiting Fellow at the Harvard Medical School, looking at ways of training young health professionals, so that their whole approach could be more 'user-friendly' from the patient's perspective.

When she starts talking about health issues, particularly the rights of patients, she becomes more animated than ever. The ideas come so thick and fast, like grapeshot, that it is difficult to catch them all as they hurtle past. She was quoted in the *Guardian* recently as saying she wanted to be remembered as someone who wasn't often boring. It's a risk she is obviously not prepared to take.

Her involvement in medical ethics grew to encompass almost every aspect of an increasingly complex side of medicine. Modern technology was filling the field with landmines.

Becoming a member of the Human Fertilisation and Embryology Authority was a challenging and awesome responsibility. She was painfully aware of the way the use of the human embryo in fertilisation techniques stirred up strong emotions and very conflicting views within the general public, but felt that, as a Jew and as a woman, she had a contribution to make to the debate. Judaism, always conscious of the hidden human factor in any moral issue, had a strong life-affirming tradition. And no woman blessed with children could deny another woman the right to a child. 'Jews must share in the debate, precisely because we feel differently about the unborn child. We respect children, we desire to have them, and we share sympathy, ages old, for women unable to conceive.'[10]

The first recorded case of 'assisted conception' took place almost at the beginning of Jewish history, when Sarah gave her maid to her husband Abraham and they produced Ishmael. It was a form of surrogacy. Throughout the Hebrew Bible childlessness was a source of enormous distress. There was Rachel who said to her husband, 'Give me children or I die,' and Hannah, who prayed and wept so hard that the temple priest thought she was drunk. The distress is no less today. But how far should medical science go in resolving the situation before it ends up playing God? This was the dilemma Julia and her colleagues faced. Judaism provided only clues, not answers.

In other words, no new scientific development should be rejected per se because of a set of rigid, preformed ideas, which fail to take account of personal anguish. That, as she learned as a girl at the feet of Hugo Gryn, is not the Jewish way. For every three Jews there will be at least four opinions. 'Modern science and modern medicine, however terrifying the speed of their discoveries, are simply using human intelligence which is divinely given. We have every right to expect that intelligence to be exercised by morally responsible people for the good of others. If it is not, then it is up to other humans to ensure that abuse does not take place.'[11]

Having always maintained that, if women wanted to change the system, they should aim for the top, she could hardly turn down the invitation to chair a Health Trust. This came in 1993. 'I had so many hopes and aspirations. Running a Community Health Trust seemed a brilliant opportunity to pilot all kinds of new ideas. I had a vision to bring mental health, housing and financial advice services under one NHS roof, for example, providing the broadest possible kind of community health care. But existing services in the inner cities were already stretched to breaking point, and it was impossible to gather the resources, energy and space to do most of the things I had planned. The truth was that the government had no intention of allowing Trusts to be truly radical anyway. In the end,' she says sadly, 'we have neither the resources nor the freedoms we were promised.'

Nonetheless, on a national level, many of the changes for which she has campaigned so vigorously are slowly becoming the warp and woof of the NHS. Some criticise her for not being sure of what she really wants, for not concentrating her pioneering energies quite enough. But it would be impossible for one person to follow so many radical concepts through. She is simply a sower of seeds. She plants one here, two there, and half a dozen somewhere else, then waits to see what will take root. In June 1995, in the *Health Service Journal*, a magazine for managers, she conceded with a certain amount of satisfaction that 'a quiet sort of revolution' was turning the NHS upside down. Only a few years ago, asking the 'users' what they wanted from the service would have been regarded as dangerously advanced, if not totally absurd. 'It is something to celebrate in health care generally – and in mental health in particular – users' voices are being heard, and are being taken seriously'.

There is still a long way to go – and while that is so, government ministers and health service managers can expect to be confronted, even affronted, by her challenging, slightly abrasive style. There is an ambivalence, she wrote in one column, in our attitudes to mental health. 'The problem lies not so much with NHS politics as with complicated cultural attitudes – and mixed feelings about whether mental illness is genuinely mental illness at all.'

British culture, she says, terrified of all emotion, but

particularly negative emotion, demands we pull ourselves together and simply cope, whatever the tragedy or trauma. The success of the hospice movement is largely due to our inability to cope with the dreadful sight of someone weeping with pain. We can't face up to our personal bereavements. We have forgotten how 'to ritualise death and make mourning a communal, supported activity which allows gradual recovery and normalisation', let alone cope with major disasters. So how will we ever de-stigmatise mental health problems? How will we ever get away from a desire to be punitive in our treatment?

He or she who thought the rabbi went underground when Julia took on the might of the NHS has been misled. Her distinctly Jewish view of life and death is the crucial backdrop to all she does and says, holding the many different-shaped pieces of her career together. Who else could see so clearly, and would get away with saying in public, that our public confusion stems not so much from policies, as our accursed 'stiff British upper lip'?

The reduction of residential mental health facilities without adequate community replacement and support is, she maintains, a worrying sacrifice to the god of expediency. 'We're getting to the point where short-term intervention is all we have to offer. We take people in as day cases and bung them out as quickly as possible, whether they feel able to cope or not. But people only want to be at home if there is someone there to care for them.'

The rights of the carer are now firmly on her agenda too. 'The majority of carers are women. That's what society expects – but it doesn't expect to support them financially. So they give up work to become a carer, then when the sick or elderly relative dies, find themselves too old to get a new job, and without a proper pension. I'm horrified by the poverty of many women in retirement. Why should they be deprived of basic necessities like heating, all because they have sacrificed themselves to care for someone else?'

She wishes she had more time to fight their cause. She wishes the women's movement would divert some of its campaigning for better child care to better resources for the carer, since more women are caring for an elderly relative than for a child, and it is a more long-term commitment. Why hasn't it done so? Because of an invidious discrimination called ageism. 'I see it in the NHS and it worries me. Subconsciously elderly women are potential patients, not employees. A woman's employment opportunities decrease with her physical attractions. From her mid-fifties onwards a woman becomes faceless. Little has been written about women and the ageing process.'

And yet one of the most significant role models in Julia's life, one of the most outstanding political figures of the twentieth century, was an elderly Jewish woman – Golda Meir – a brilliant speaker and stateswoman, the 'darling of the world', Julia calls her, in her ability to explain Israel's moral dilemmas to the nations. Yet, maddeningly, like so many women, she would insist on playing the socially acceptable part – the nice little Jewish grandmother. Julia thinks it led to a gross undervaluing of a razor-sharp intellect and strategic sense every bit as formidable as Moshe Dayan's.

These days there is the same ambivalence in her attitude to Israel as there is to Golda Meir. Her innate sense of justice will not allow her to be as proud of it as she would like to be. And yet she loves it. There is an indescribable bond between a Jew and their one safe haven, their asylum, should it ever again become a necessity.

Meanwhile she fights to ensure that it won't – by raising the profile of all human rights in the country that has given her nationality, citizenship and status. 'I see myself as fierce, for example, on the treatment of gays,' she says. Thousands died in concentration camps alongside the Jews, the inevitable consequence of homophobia. Looking back, learning the lessons of the past, are, for her, the building blocks of the future. 'The Holocaust is past. We have survived.' Now the Jews, with their rich heritage and tradition, have a special contribution to make to the world.

Her own contribution to British life and thought has already been recognised with seven honorary degrees. As Chancellor of Ulster University, she was the first non-royal, female chancellor of a UK university, pipping the front runner, the former Northern Ireland secretary, Lord Prior, at the post. And yet she says,

'In some senses I'll never be a total insider. Gender, religion and attitude have seen to that.' For a pioneer, this ability to stand back and be the independent observer may well be crucial. If working within one organisation such as a Health Trust, provides only limited opportunity to change the system, then perhaps the objective onlooker, sympathetic but detached, is far better placed to change the world. Being a rabbi has its advantages. But then, so does being a woman. Even she admits, 'It may not be the norm, but I have achieved so much more as a woman, than ever I could as a man.'

Julia is now Chief Executive of the King's Fund, a high-powered independent health care charity that carries out extensive research into the workings of the NHS, and strives to make our health and social care systems more patient-friendly.

Notes

1. Julia Neuberger, *On Being Jewish* (Heinemann, 1995), p. 21.
2. ibid., p. 35.
3. ibid., p. 3.
4. Julia Neuberger, *Whatever's Happening to Women?*
   (Kyle Cathie, 1991), p. 119.
5. ibid., p. 151.
6. ibid., p. 156.
7. *On Being Jewish*, p. 21.
8. *Whatever's Happening to Women?*, p. 136.
9. *On Being Jewish*, p. 152.
10. ibid., p. 120.
11. ibid., p. 118.

CHAPTER 7

The Health Trust Chairman: Carolyn Johnson

I've always wanted to sit behind a desk like Carolyn Johnson's. Possibly because it seems the ultimate symbol of archetypal male power. Probably because it reminds me of my headmistress's enormous desk at school, and how I stood on the wrong side of it, trembling and quaking in my shoes, knowing my destiny lay in her hands and feeling utterly powerless.

It's a large, elegant desk, repro Louis XV, with perfect curves and lines and a polished mahogany finish so deep that if you stop to admire it you catch a multiple image of yourself mirrored in its surface.

Carolyn loves it too. For an informal, friendly chat she comes out from behind it and sits in one of two comfortable armchairs at the other end of the room, an area filled with family photos and flowers. For those rather more difficult interviews and decisions, she stays firmly behind it. It is a reminder to all at the Royal Preston and Sharoe Green Hospitals that this delightfully bubbly woman, in short skirt, with flowing blond locks, eyes as blue as best Wedgwood, and a gurgling laugh that fills the room, is ultimately she-who-must-be-obeyed.

Carolyn Johnson is a startling change from the stuffed-shirt, besuited male stereotype of a hospital manager, out of touch with his own humanity, let alone that of the patients. Nor does she fit the tight-lipped, aggressive female version of the caricature. When her packed schedule permits, she loves walking around the wards chatting to patients and staff, finding out how everyone is. While the Chief Executive is 'Mr Ashcroft', most of the staff say 'Hi, Carolyn', as they pass her in the corridor. Because of the large gold cross she wears round her neck, one or two tease her, calling her 'Mother Carolyn' or 'ma'am', 'How's your Trust, ma'am?'

She doesn't object to the proprietorial implication of the question. 'The hospital is my family. It brings out all my maternal instincts.' For a mother of six boys it could be regarded as a professional hazard. Some say she has shares and not just an interest in the maternity department. 'I have tremendous pride in the staff when I see their skills and achievements. I'll defend them from every assault. I can cope with personal criticism. It gives me a chance to improve and grow. But if anyone attacks my hospital I'm like a tigress, fearsome. If the attack is unjustified, I hurt for weeks.'

Her 'family', the Preston Acute Hospitals NHS Trust, consists of two large hospital sites, 3,750 staff, 1.6 million potential patients, and a budget of £97 million. It is the largest employer in Preston, and woe betide those who, lulled by her natural warmth and friendliness into thinking she is tame and manipulatable, question her ability to run it. Her mind is as sharp as a razor. A trained barrister, she can slice through the political manoeuvrings of a Health Service bureaucrat or cut an overbearing clinical manager or an obnoxious patient down to size with a flash of the eyes and the shortest of sentences. But when a complaint is justified, on the other hand, complainants soon discover there could be no more formidable advocate on their behalf.

She chairs countless meetings with an extraordinary combination of rational and intuitive skills, drawing out a gem from the most hesitant contributor, usually female, silencing the more bombastic, usually male, ultimately pulling every argument together to give a sense of cohesion, personal satisfaction and team effort. Then rushes off to deliver the family laundry to the hospital dry cleaner's, or to buy a few home-made goodies for tea from the hospital caterer's, or to whizz a child to the dentist's, or to A and E to have a rugby injury reset.

'Every hospital has its own personality and character,' she says, 'As chairman you reflect it.' But the relationship between this chairman and her hospital is undoubtedly symbiotic. Four years ago, in its pre-Carolyn era, the Royal Preston was an architect-standard, purpose-built, modern hospital, functional but unimaginative, all straight lines and right angles, endless polished-linoleum corridors, unfriendly signs and arrows and chairs in rows. Today, courtesy of private investment, there is a large public restaurant, luxurious by any standards, with conservatory and patio, table-waiting or self-service and a wide variety of international, fast and whole foods. It is used by many local community groups such as Rotary, for dinner dances, parties, wedding receptions. The swish new outpatients' waiting area, her pride and joy, is a comfortable oasis in the middle of a busy shopping mall where there is a florist, newsagent, hairdresser and pharmacist and other boutiques selling gifts and toiletries. It looks, feels and even smells more like an airport lounge than a hospital. Following her lead, female staff in the Day Case Unit have created a haven in muted shades of pink, with soft music playing in the background. In Preston a visit to the hospital is fast turning into a grand day out.

'The community should be involved with their local hospital, see it as their own and love it,' she maintains. Not everyone agrees with her. Initially, some of the older members of the community were appalled at the changes. Instinctively they felt that to do you good, a hospital visit should include a long, uncomfortable wait in depressing, quasi-Dickensian surroundings, with gloomy corridors, tatty furnishings and the nauseating smell of disinfectant. It should not provide an opportunity for a quick cut and blow-dry, or to buy a dried flower arrangement or a new nightie and T-shirt, even if there were obvious benefits in shopping therapy. Carolyn rode, rather than sat out, the storm. She enthused, disputed with the critics who said patients would be sitting in the hairdresser's salon when their appointment came up and, in time, people began to appreciate the restorative nature of pleasant surroundings.

One afternoon, passing through the outpatients' waiting lounge, as she does several times a day, on her way to or from visits to various consultants and staff, Carolyn came across an elderly couple sitting alone, looking for all the world as if they had just missed the last plane to leave the concourse. Intrigued, she stopped and asked them if she could help. Clinics had long since finished, or so she hoped. If not, then which consultant was defying the Patients Charter by making his patients wait a great deal longer for an appointment than the statutory 30 minutes? They told her whom they were waiting to see, and he did appear to be running very late – until she examined their appointment card and discovered they had the right date, but the wrong year. 'They would have had a very long wait if I hadn't intervened,' she laughs, then adds reflectively, 'but waiting for more than a year for an appointment is equally unacceptable. I made a mental note to find out why.'

No detail, however small, escapes her attention for long. 'There's never any room for complacency, always room for improvement.' She expects of her staff a ruthless determination to eradicate any revealed imperfections. They accept her high standards because she abides by them herself.

Her husband Barry is her hardest critic. A moderate, balanced, very Lancashire man, he is, in every sense, like a rock. 'I'm imaginative, he's practical. I'm excitable, he's down-to-earth. He says I'm an extremist and tones me down a bit. He's a perfect foil.' A constant flow of ideas pop up from her mind like plastic balls in a jet stream in a fair sideshow. It's Barry who reaches out and catches the one he thinks she ought to run with. Invariably, he's right. She would be lost, she says, without his sound good sense. She would like some positive praise, as well as constructive criticism, from time to time, but it is not his way. He hides his pride in her behind a mass of teasing banter: 'You know I'd tell you if I thought you were wrong.'

He isn't the only man alarmed by her intensity. She has an honesty and vulnerability that some of her male colleagues find seriously disconcerting, particularly at public meetings as she fields questions from the floor. The public and the press could lob anything at her. And they do. She takes the genuine enquiries, however tricky, in her stride, hiding only what medical confidentiality requires. 'We must be as open as we can be in the NHS. We are accountable to the public. They have a right to know how we're managing the resources entrusted to us.' The deliberate brickbats and barbs, those she deems the unintelligent gripes, she handles with a mixture of dexterity and obvious annoyance. She hasn't the time to suffer fools gladly. Life is too short.

Caution is not her way. It hems her in, holds her back. 'There is no leadership without risk,' says the woman who, at 15, when her parents were away, drove around in the family car without as much as a provisional driving licence. 'My blood runs cold when I think about it. I'd die if my children had ever done that. They moan that I won't go away and leave them in the house, but I remember what I used to get up to.'

Most women are not instinctively risk takers. Why did she do it? 'I don't know. It wasn't genetic. I would never have taken risks with immorality or drugs. My conscience would have never allowed it.' She is quite simply a thoroughly *Boys' Own* girl, who gets her highs from adventure. That kind of energy, unrepressed, though harnessed by experience and maturity, can be a powerful, if occasionally overwhelming, life force in the traditionally cautious culture of the NHS.

It was her daring and drive, her irrepressible enthusiasm and altogether alternative style of chairmanship that made me grab the opportunity of working as her press officer for two years. We came from opposite ends of the political spectrum, yet discovered a sisterhood and meeting of hearts and minds that made political considerations irrelevant. I sensed that behind the bounce and bubble was a woman who knew real pain and had learned to put it to work, who understood its importance in making her a full human being, in touch with herself and the thousands of hurting people surrounding her every day. I knew that what I saw, like beaten gold, does not emerge overnight. The refining process had taken some time. The result was that here was a woman confident enough to resist the leadership stereotypes and be completely herself. It had a radical effect on her organisation. And I wanted to know her secret.

When asked what was the greatest influence in her formative years, Carolyn will say it was growing up in Blackpool. The area certainly has its own inimitable culture, an almost island quality, fostered not only by the attitudes of the natives but also by the flat and salty marshlands of rural Fylde, which separate its more garish attractions from the rest of Lancashire. The coastal road runs for several miles, from Fleetwood in the north to Lytham in the south, in tandem with the tram track, and is divided on the left into untamed dunes and pleasant promenades, on the right into nouveau riche dwellings, lavish casinos, splendid hotels, struggling boarding-houses, and squalid malls and arcades. The sound of the waves crashing against the sea wall is drowned by the distorted nasal blare from bingo halls, pedlars of tat, and the Pleasure Beach. This is a hedonistic, self-seeking sort of environment, where those who can, 'make it', and those who can't are left behind.

The Battersbys have lived in Blackpool for generations. Farmers in Longridge near Preston, they brought the stones that helped to build it. They were by nature entrepreneurs, and it appears to have remained in the genes. Like his great-grandfather before him, Carolyn's father was the mayor. From an early age she went with him to the Conservative Party Conference. His encouragement was a powerful force in her life.

Born in 1952, the eldest of four girls, she grew up a free spirit in the great outdoors, driving the tractors and combine harvesters of the family's agricultural contracting business, riding her horse down the beach or in Blackpool's wide open spaces before they became the zoo. Hers would have been an idyllic childhood, but for the fact that her youngest sister, a twin, had been born with hydrocephalus and died when she was seven.

'It gave me an understanding of disability from an early age. I have never had any fear of it.'

Her mother, after caring for her youngest daughter, worked as a dietician at the Victoria Hospital, and lectured at the local catering college. Grandma, who lived with them, was the matriarch, the stability in the home, and Carolyn vividly remembers her slow, sad descent into second childhood, and how hard that was for them all.

After a state primary education, she passed her eleven-plus and went to Elmslie, the only Church of England girls' grammar school in the country. It lived up to its unique status by being very churchy, an Anglican version of a convent school, with catechism classes and a barrage of formal services. 'We all knew that the worst possible offence we could commit was to upset the headmistress just before a visit from the Bishop of Blackburn. It was the highlight of her year. When he appeared in full ecclesiastical regalia at the top of the imposing central staircase, even the girls were impressed. We were all terribly in awe of him.'

Religion had no place in her family life. Her father was a Catholic, her mother a Congregationalist, and the family rift caused by the marriage was so acrimonious that the couple left their children to make up their own minds. They were neither baptised, nor encouraged to be confirmed. Carolyn decided on both when she was 14, more because of pressure at school than genuine commitment. She occasionally attended a Roman Catholic church with her friends, but went to an Anglican church most Sundays, out of fear of admitting her non-attendance to the school chaplain, who asked for a show of hands on Monday morning. School religion gave her a sense of order, security and tradition – but not a faith.

Unlike Julia Neuberger, Carolyn is not convinced that an all-girl education was crucial in developing her leadership expectation and confidence. 'It was a small school and the teachers were able to give time on an individual basis to finding out what you were good at, but my motivation didn't come from school or my parents, it came from within.'

It came from living in bold, brassy Blackpool, the garish,

luminous focal point for a go-getting, highly competitive breed of people, a total contrast to the rather stolid, mill-centred folk of other Lancashire towns. 'Yes, it was self-seeking, but it was vibrant too. It was fun for a teenager growing up in the 1960s. There was so much going on, such opportunity. The bright lights attracted lots of young people who made their fortune at a very early age. Our parents tried to protect us from its worst excesses, but you knew you had to make your own mark. No one worried about jobs. Everyone was self-made. Blackpool made you feel you could do anything.'

Even as a teenager there were no half-measures for Carolyn. A member of the Young Conservatives she had begun to feel passionate about social issues. In the sixth form, after years of planning to be a vet, she changed her mind and opted instead for a career in law. A hearing impediment meant she had a loud voice, which, in the days before compulsory PA systems, was in great demand for school debates or to read notices or lessons in services. She discovered she enjoyed the cut and thrust of a good debate, that she had the power to be fairly persuasive.

Though Manchester University has one of the most highly acclaimed law schools in the country, Carolyn now wonders whether she should have gone further afield, but Blackpool's social whirl and a developing love interest there were far too attractive to leave entirely behind. Nonetheless, she threw herself with her usual gusto into the politics of the Student Union, chairing what she calls 'very hairy' debates on apartheid and taking part in rallies against Vietnam and demonstrations on a variety of world issues. More formative was the sight of the poverty on her own doorstep. 'Walking through Rusholme, seeing people begging on the Union steps, was a shock. I wanted to know why people lived in such appalling conditions. There had to be a way out.'

A major diversion put a temporary halt to the development of her political career. In her final year at Manchester she married John, a chartered accountant from Lytham. They bought a gingerbread cottage on a hill in semi-rural Todmorden and for a short while, despite her finals, shared the perfect idyll.

Joining an Inn of Court so that she could qualify as a barrister meant living in London. Heavily pregnant by now, she stayed with her sister, while John came down at weekends. It was an incredibly demanding year. Thirty-six compulsory dinners are an integral part of being called to the Bar. 'The dinners are where you learn your trade – from listening to your peers and defending yourself.' It was, she admits, a very aggressive, male-dominated environment, but she thrived on it, and her 'interesting condition' didn't appear to earn her either preferential treatment or censure. In fact it made very little difference at all. Unfortunately, however, baby Robert's timing was less than perfect and he decided to make an appearance just before her exams. But Carolyn hadn't managed to get this far to give up at such a minor hurdle, sat the exams and achieved her goal nonetheless.

'I made a conscious decision to have my family when I was young, so that I would be free to follow my career when I was older. You couldn't start work as a barrister, then stop and go back to it. Solicitors would have forgotten you.' Instead, she took a part-time job lecturing at Manchester University, then moved to Preston Polytechnic to help set up their new law degree course. 'They couldn't decide between two female candidates and appointed us both. At the time it seemed a very strange thing to do. Now, of course, I can see the hand of providence. My colleague was a Christian, and that turned out to be very significant for me in the trauma ahead.'

Her domestic situation wasn't easy. Child care in the 1970s was almost unheard of. As if that were not enough, the couple bought a ramshackle property in Preston and, while they slowly and painstakingly refurbished it themselves, lived in a caravan in the garden with their new baby. Finally their new home was ready.

One morning John left for work as usual. Carolyn was supposed to go with him, but had woken up feeling very strange. 'It's hard to explain. I wasn't ill, but I couldn't physically get up. It was as if I were pinned to the bed by a great force.' A few weeks earlier the husband of a close friend had been killed in a car crash. 'It had a powerful affect on me. Till then I'd taken life for granted. Suddenly I realised how terribly afraid of death I was. How could someone so young and vital die? What would I feel if it happened to me?'

She was roused from a strange, dream-like, half-waking state by a light at the foot of the bed, which she felt was John. 'Goodbye, Carolyn,' he said. That was all. When the doorbell rang a little later, she knew, as she opened the front door and found a policeman standing on the doorstep, that John was dead. 'It was very odd. There was the most terrible pain – and anger, such anger, and yet, at the same time, the strangest sense, welling up from somewhere even deeper, of warmth and peace and protection. All those textbook Bible verses I'd learned at school suddenly started to come alive. I played Handel's *Messiah* over and over again. I had the overwhelming sense that God was trying to get through to me, but couldn't work out what He was saying. After all, both I and my baby could have been in that car. We must have been spared for something.'

In desperation she consulted one vicar after another, including her old school chaplain, but they merely said yes, yes, it was perfectly normal to feel as she felt after such a major bereavement. Susan Howatch would have been able to tell her that, in Jungian terms, God Himself was exerting pressure on her psyche. It was her colleague at the polytechnic who finally said, 'Carolyn, do you think, maybe, you're in the process of becoming a Christian?', and painstakingly sat down day after day to read the Bible with her.

'People used to avoid me. It's bad enough knowing what to say to someone who's been bereaved, let alone found God. I think I was a bit overpowering. But the "if only" and "why" questions everyone expected me to ask had no relevance for me. I had lived a totally selfish life. My marriage, my home, my career were all that counted. Now I wanted to know what God wanted me to do.'

The immediate reality was that she was a single parent with a child to support and a home to run. Being the sole breadwinner, having sole responsibility for sorting the child-minding arrangements gave her a special bond with her baby son, whom she renamed John, after his father. 'He was the impetus which kept me going. We survived together.'

In years to come, this would be one of the major influences on her approach to staffing policies at the Preston Hospital. Flexible working hours, job-sharing, a holiday play-scheme, paternity leave, and the possibility of a crèche are all due to the insight gained during the most difficult months of her life. 'I learned how important it was for the workplace to take the individual's personal and family circumstances into account. Being a mother is one of the most enriching experiences a woman can have. It helps you to sort out your priorities, to see what really matters in life, to care at the deepest possible level. That must surely enhance our professional lives. We need to recognise the skills that mothering involves, and invite women to bring them into the workplace, not expect them to segregate their home and working lives.'

She is impatient with the old attitudes and structures, which are rigid and inflexible and make life stressful for both mothers and fathers. She feels they are there by tradition, not necessity, often because no one has thought to question them. 'Just because the old ways have existed for 40 years or more doesn't mean they're still relevant. We need radical change. If we become more flexible, minimise the pressure on our staff, enable both men and women to be parents, it will mean a better work performance, and that can only be good for the patients.'

After she had been on her own for several months, Carolyn's next-door neighbour, a farmer, introduced her to his 30-year-old bachelor cousin, a vet, the career Carolyn had so nearly chosen for herself. 'I was coping fairly well as a single woman and hadn't planned to remarry. I never thought I'd find such happiness again. But Barry was so attractive, different, older, conscientious, and he had the most wonderful sense of humour. I fell in love with him almost at once.'

They married in 1976, when John was two. David was born the following year. 'Barry always says to John, "I chose you. I had no choice in the others."' The law degree course was by now fairly well established at Preston, so Carolyn decided to call a halt to her career in order to devote herself to caring for her two children and to helping Barry develop his veterinary practice.

One day, under 'bargain offers' she saw an advertisement for a rambling old house with character, set in its own grounds, which would perfectly suit their needs – 'for the practice,' she insists, 'not a large family. We never planned that.' The price was reduced because the previous owner had committed suicide. His slippers were still by the bed, his cigarette stub in the ashtray on the bedside table. But the great evangelist and founder of Methodism, John Wesley, had preached in the house twice and that made it the right place for Carolyn.

She moved her family in, and spent the next few years in an almost permanently pregnant state, helping Barry to build up one of the most successful veterinary practices in Lancashire. She made contact with local farmers, answered the phone, dealt with the clients, handed out the drugs, went out speaking about the life of a vet's wife and, in a strange way, learned a great deal that would one day stand her in good stead. 'I saw dramatic changes in the treatment of animals over the years. Take anaesthesia, for example. We used to walk horses around for hours to get them over an anaesthetic, now they're round in minutes. Ultrasound and modern X-ray techniques have transformed diagnosis. When it comes to human health care, there seems to be an attitude around that says that all changes in the NHS are money-driven, but medicine is in a permanent state of change and development. That's what science and technology are about. You cannot hold the clock back, even though it may mean some very difficult decisions.'

Barry and Carolyn had four more sons: Michael in 1979; Andrew in 1980; Paul in 1981; and Stephen in 1986. It was, she says, one of the hardest moments in her life when she finally came to terms with the fact that her childbearing years were over. 'I've always loved babies and could have gone on having them forever. Mind you, after growing up in an all-girl household and going to an all-girl school, it was a bit of a shock to have six boys. They're so blunt, so boisterous!'

It is the essentially male nature of the household which hits you when you first walk through the front door, and enter what feels like Carolyn's lone centre of command. There's the loud banter, the faintest whiff of the rugby field, rows of dirty boots along the kitchen wall, and the bits of kit left on the floor, vainly looking for the washing machine. The house is nonetheless amazingly well ordered. 'They all know how to cook,' she says proudly. Small wonder she makes running a hospital look remarkably effortless. After this, it probably is.

We settle down in two armchairs by a roaring open fire in the comfortable, oak-panelled hallway, supervised by the black, beady eyes of a stag's head. The two dogs sprawl at our feet, and Barry, who rushes through between visits on his way to find himself some lunch in the kitchen, says how nice it is to see four women stretched out happily in front of the fire. We shout a rude comment after him, and he shouts back, 'Don't believe a word she says. Remember she's a politician!'

And from the depths of my subconscious I suddenly dredge an event I seem to have missed. Was it true that she stood for Parliament while Michael was still being breast-fed?

〜

'It was much easier than it sounds. I carried him around in a Moses basket and everyone thought it was my shopping.'

Carolyn, it now seems, had been anything but the perfect stay-at-home wife. A bundle of frustrated energy, she had had an overwhelming urge to do something useful with her life. Smuggling Bibles into Russia was one possibility, but the ever-practical Barry put a stop to that, and she began to think again about the mission on her own doorstep. 'I saw that politics was a way of changing society from within. The decision-makers had the influence. Why shouldn't I be one of them?'

In 1976, newly married, she had been elected to the Preston Borough Council. On the face of it local politics can appear fairly innocuous – endless disputes between neighbours or with the council, over boundaries, dog mess and dustbins. But with her usual perception Carolyn saw that behind the most inconsequential injuries there often lay a hidden agenda. 'Scratch the surface and you find a deep spiritual malaise, people filled with anger, emptiness and resentment.'

One particular incident proved to be an interesting object lesson. She called to see one of her constituents, a woman whose son had been electrocuted at the local leisure centre. In law, as a parent rather than a spouse, the mother was entitled to compensation of only £500. 'I knew she would be furious with such a piffling amount. But I said to her, "Money won't ease your pain. Let's look at you, at what your real needs are." Because of what I had been through I was able to empathise, to help her face her anger, and diffuse some of the bitterness. A little while later she became a Christian. I can't help but feel she received more compensation than any amount of money could have given her.'

'Getting behind' a complaint is now an integral part of her approach to her work at the hospital. At a time when compensation claims against the NHS are spiralling out of control, when thousands of pounds are spent on insurance, draining the system of crucial resources, she believes legal redress should always be the last option. 'Litigation is a sure sign of failure in the relationship between the patient and the Health Trust. We need to look at why people sue – usually because no one has sat down and listened to their anger, or they haven't had an adequate explanation or apology, or any reassurance that what happened to them won't happen again. The NHS has always closed ranks on the public. We've seen the patient, rather than our structures, as the problem. Now we're having to relearn our approach.'

The years 1976–9 were disastrous years for a limping Labour government. As the unions flexed their political muscles, cemeteries were closed, rubbish was piled high in the streets, and the usual slough of despondency and gloom took hold of the British nation. 'As a Christian I couldn't come to terms with the socialist idealism of that time. It seemed to assume that human beings were perfect and all you needed was the right political system to achieve a kind of Utopia. Everything had to be nationalised, everything prescribed from above. It manifestly didn't work.'

By comparison, Conservatism seemed to offer freedom. Human beings were not and never would be perfect, but they could be helped to help themselves, to develop skills and talents, which would be used for the benefit of everyone. It was the party of opportunity, not state control.

At this crucial time, the Conservative Party elected its charismatic first female leader. For Carolyn Johnson that was extremely significant. 'I identified with Margaret Thatcher because she was a woman. Like many women, I lacked that extra confidence to aim a little bit higher. Whenever I had thought of standing for Parliament, though I knew I could speak, I was only aware of all the things I couldn't do. Margaret Thatcher believed she could do anything. She was inspirational. I got my name on to the candidates' list, and she came and spent time with all of us, explaining how we could implement new policies and change society.'

For all her enthusiasm, constituencies wanted candidates a little older than 27, and she spent many months appearing before endless, abortive selection panels, made up of older, hostile Tory ladies. 'It was bitterly frustrating. I could see straight away that the men weren't the problem. They would have given me a chance. It was the older women who held younger women back. They judged by the restrictions imposed on them. It was a form of jealousy. Most were non-professional women, and they said to themselves, "Well, I certainly couldn't have managed a home, babies and a political career, so why should she?" Perhaps they were afraid that if they took me on it would be an admission of unfulfilment or inadequacy in their own lives.'

She spoke at the Conservative Party Conference that year on law and order, and left the platform to rapturous applause. But in the light of her failure to be selected as a candidate, it had an empty, hollow ring. At West Houghton, near Bolton, convinced she would be turned down yet again, she ended her speech in desperation with a final, flourishing, 'If you think I'm young, Pitt the Younger became prime minister at 23.' She was duly selected.

West Houghton was a safe Labour seat, so 'any mistakes I made didn't really matter. When your favourite topics are religion and politics, the two great taboos, you can hardly avoid making a few gaffes.'

Michael was a mere six weeks old when the 1979 General Election was called. Everyone thought the timing disastrous, except Carolyn. 'It was perfect. I just carried him around with me. Perhaps that's why he's such an extrovert.' She was feeding him in a little back room the caretaker provided the night of the election, when everyone else was counting the votes. There was a huge national landslide to the Conservatives and at one point she and the Labour candidate appeared to be neck and neck. 'Barry,' she says, 'went white with shock.'

In the end she whittled away the majority from 26,000 to 5,000, one of the largest swings in the country, and retired happily to bring up her burgeoning family. 'I wouldn't have stood if I thought I'd win the seat. The guilt would have been too great. I wanted to make the most of my children while they were young, to be the major source of influence and discipline, to give them my best. Each child is unique, and they're with you for such a short time – especially boys. Boys leave you.'

She was, she maintains, a very ordinary kind of a mum, involved in the local playgroups and schools, 'well, a school governor, and member of the preschool playgroups' association – more at the policy than the practical end, really'. It was a very fulfilling time of her life. 'Having the children all together was a great idea. It gave me a chance to meet lots of other mums. I've never had so many close relationships since. The days were hectic, but at least the evenings were free.' She is, she confesses, remembering those days with the benefit of hindsight, but then Carolyn has the gift of entering fully into all she does, looking neither backwards with regret, nor forwards with too much anticipation. She never admits exhaustion. In fact she tries to pack so much into every moment that nothing irritates her as much as people, be they colleague or guest, who arrive early for an appointment. She, on the other hand, with over-bulging diary, is almost always running late – a constant source of irritation to Barry. Given the present demands on her time, she is glad, she says now, that for a while, she put her career on ice.

In 1989, as she began to emerge from the nappy bucket, a vacancy on the Lancashire County Council provided an opportunity to fight a marginal seat. Unable to resist the challenge, she took the seat and became the Council spokesperson, with inevitable typecasting, for child care and social services. It was her first opportunity to look at human health issues. 'It was there that I learned how artificial political boundaries can be. There was little antagonism between the parties. Behind the scenes we may have had a different approach, but by and large, we worked together to develop community care.'

When the post of chief administrator to the UK's 35 university management schools became vacant, it provided her with the perfect opportunity to pick up a career she could revolve around her children. It was based at the University of Lancaster's Business School. At the same time she accepted an invitation to become a non-executive director of the new Lancaster Acute Hospital Trust, one of the first Health Trusts in the country. Her love affair with the NHS had just begun.

Carolyn hotly disputes the notion that the Tories want to destroy the NHS. 'The NHS should always be financed with public money, not just because it's politically prudent, but because access to health care is the right of every human being in a civilised nation. But the financial pot isn't bottomless. We have to encourage a healthy mix of public, private, voluntary and charitable investment in the service.' As an afterthought she adds, 'Actually, if I were seriously ill, I'd be reluctant to go to a private hospital. They don't have the high-tech back-up. In a real emergency you'd be taken to your nearest NHS hospital anyway. If we can provide rooms or even wings for patients who can afford private care, their money would help provide extra resources for the NHS.'

The Royal Lancaster Infirmary was one of the first hospitals in the country to become a Trust, 'an ambitious move given the fact that most of us were still feeling our way around the system, but very exciting'. It was here that she cut her eye-teeth, learning the art of managing a hospital without having major responsibility.

She is hugely enthusiastic about the advantages of Trust status, and reels them off with satisfaction. 'As a small board, rather than a huge conglomerate, you feel responsible. You know the needs of your hospital and the local community. You can decide on your own priorities, influence the way the hospital should go. At the same time you can respond quickly to the demands of the local population. Resources are better targeted, (they'll always be limited – that's a fact of life). Waste is reduced. I remember years ago, when my mum was chairman of the Blackpool Community Health Council, how bitterly she used to complain about waste in the NHS. Now staff know the cost of every bandage. We have to be good stewards of public money.'

She also learned from Lancaster's mistakes. 'There was still a tendency, lingering from the old days, to mistrust the public and keep any failures very quiet. It really is counter-productive. The truth has a way of leaking out. How can we expect the public to trust us if we are less than honest?'

Ultimately, being a non-executive director didn't provide enough outlet for her pioneering energy. She wanted to be involved in health policy at a national level and, when Preston's name appeared among the fourth wave of hopeful Trust applicants, agreed to let her name go forward to the Secretary of State as a possible chairman.

Members of the public they might be, users of the health service, but there was tremendous suspicion of the non-medical people who were being introduced into the system. One of the Preston consultants looked her up and down and asked, 'What experience have you got?'

'Pockets of experience,' she replied, 'legal, children, management, veterinary, marketing.' In fact, as a vet's wife, she had learned a great deal about being on call, putting patients first, the cost of medical equipment and drugs, medical ethics. 'Strange how useful that experience was. Nothing is ever wasted.' She was still surprised to be chosen.

As chairman Carolyn has several abiding passions. One is to see the Preston Hospital become a specialist medical centre in densely populated Lancashire, so that the inhabitants don't have to travel to Manchester or Liverpool for specialist treatment. It appalled her that some cancer patients were having to make a 160-kilometre round trip for radiotherapy. She was delighted when Malcolm McIllmurray, one of the country's foremost oncologists, whose innovative work in Lancaster had earned him an entry in *Debrett's Peerage*, agreed to be involved in setting up a cancer unit with radiotherapy at Preston, the first of its kind in a district general hospital. A practising Catholic, McIllmurray believed in a holistic approach to the care of cancer patients. Medical staff were to help them live with, as well as die from, the disease. It was not enough, he maintained, to offer chemo- or radiotherapy. A patient's spiritual and emotional needs must be taken into account, and that would include the use of a wide range of complementary therapies such aromatherapy, massage and relaxation techniques. Woodwork, art, music and creative writing were offered at Lancaster's St John's Hospice where, at different times, a sculptor, poet or musician in residence enabled patients to express their deepest feelings.

The possibility of a cancer unit in Preston along these lines was the fulfilment of one of Carolyn's greatest personal ambitions. 'Designing a cancer service that would revolve around the needs of the patient and provide the fullest possible support for their families was a huge challenge. I was convinced Malcolm McIllmurray was the man to do it. It's so important to get medical staff who share in your vision.'

I hear echoes of Helen Taylor-Thompson, knowing instinctively which staff would be best for Mildmay, determined to get them if at all possible.

'We women can be so tenacious,' Carolyn says.

Her vision of holistic care extended beyond a cancer unit to the whole hospital, and was summed up in the words of Edward Livingstone Trudeau, 'To cure sometimes, to relieve often, to comfort always'. But it was underpinned by her own faith. 'Medicine is becoming so highly specialised that we are in great danger of losing the humane aspect of treatment, focussing on the disease rather than the whole person. That would turn doctors into technicians. But healing and cure are not the same. A patient is not just a body. Healing takes account of the whole person. We should be teaching that at medical school, and looking at ways to go on supporting our medical staff in the difficult moral decisions they have to make. Their pastoral needs are as great as the patients'.'

As far as Carolyn was concerned that meant a radical revision of the chaplaincy. The changes both in society and in the NHS, along with the huge increase in the number of day patients, meant that the traditional chaplain's role, wandering the wards and bobbing up at the bedside, was decidedly dated. Few chairmen would either desire or dare to touch such an established institution, let alone say openly that the role was an anachronism, belonging to a bygone age. But it was at the heart of everything she wanted to do. Trust status meant that she, rather than the Church of England, was responsible for the chaplain's salary, and that gave her exactly the leverage she needed.

Out of courtesy she went to see the Bishop of Blackburn and explained why she wanted to move away from the traditional idea of a chaplain to a pastoral care leader, who would organise a large chaplaincy team with representatives of all Christian denominations and of other major faiths. The chapel would be transformed into a haven for staff, where they could debate the difficult ethical issues they faced or simply come and share their feelings. This team leader, she said, watching the bishop's increasing discomfort, would not necessarily be an ordained minister, or Anglican, or even male.

'Ah,' said the bishop to the chairman of the Trust, 'but if you appoint a woman priest I would have to appoint a man over her. The patients might not take communion from a woman.'

It was rather like waving a red rag in front of a bull. Most of her patients didn't give a toss about the gender-based scruples of the Church of England. In the event, despite a barrage of local media attention raised by a small group of traditionalists, a Methodist minister – a man – was appointed to the job, joined several months later by an Anglican woman priest. 'My only goal was to ensure that pastoral care be given the same recognition as clinical care. And now,' Carolyn says wryly, 'the Church holds us up as an example to others.'

She is also committed to seeing more women in key posts throughout the hospital, particularly as consultants. Nationally 52 per cent of medical students are female, but only about 12 per cent go on to achieve consultant status, predominantly in non-surgical roles. It is difficult to find female gynaecologists, yet immensely important in an area with a large Muslim population. She is convinced that, with flexible training packages and working hours, the situation will improve. 'In my experience it's women with children who are discriminated against, not women per se,' as she discovered all those years ago when facing parliamentary selection panels. 'And older women are still more likely than a man to poison the career path of a young mother.'

But when they put their personal jealousy aside, she believes women make better interviewers. 'We instinctively interpret body language, penetrate the façade, judge on criteria other than what immediately presents itself. God is very good for women. He has made us unique, very different from men, and we need to recognise and appreciate those differences.'

I ask her what she thinks they are.

'On the whole we're more people-oriented. They are more focussed, while women, as mothers, are used to juggling all the issues, practical, emotional, mental and spiritual, never excluding one to concentrate on the others. I'm not saying that makes women better doctors or nurses or that we have more empathy with patients. But it does mean we often speak a more accessible language. We need consultants who will relate to the patients, never mind their research experience.'

She also thinks men tend more easily to pomposity. Women, she says, find it easier to laugh at themselves and make fools of themselves.

Laugh at themselves, possibly, make fools of themselves, that sounds particularly Carolyn rather than female. As she speaks, a picture forms in my mind, Carolyn in short skirt, leaping on a multiplicity of stress-testing machines at a 'Health at Work' day, observed at a safe distance by several uncertain, stiff, male managers. I wasn't there myself. The scene was described to me by one of the health promotion specialists, who kept repeating with a mixture of wonder and admiration, 'The chairman's wild. She's wild.'

It isn't difficult to conjure up the teenager who loved riding her horse along the beach, driving the combine harvesters and tractors, not to mention her parents' car. There's a freshness about her, which the weight of management cannot suppress. It's liberating for those who can stand it, exceedingly uncomfortable for those who can't. Nothing is beyond her dignity. 'I just want to be myself. It must be painful for the men. They're not as free to be themselves. That's why it's such a travesty for a woman to try and behave like a man.'

Variation is important to her. 'Women have so many different phases in their lives, childbirth, child-raising, work in and outside the home, while men's lives are much more restricted, boring and samey. We can wear lots of lovely clothes in wonderful colours, change our image every day if we want. In fact – I really can't see many advantages in being a man.'

Strong words from someone whose life revolves around seven members of a disadvantaged gender. There's the temptation to wonder whether the lack of a daughter hasn't been a disappointing divine oversight, until she appears on the sidelines of the rugby pitch, yelling and shouting for her boys, cheering them on to victory. Never was there such a proud mother of boys.

But this phase will soon be over too, she acknowledges sadly. It is the first time I have seen her looking wistful. Her boys are growing away from her. 'Puberty's horrendous, a ghastly stage. That's when I hand over to Barry. He wasn't really into nappies, but he's brilliant with them now, shares their love of sport. There's a comradeship between a father and his boys to which a woman has no access. I can't say I don't feel left out. But there are compensations. Now that the older boys are bringing their girlfriends home, there's the chance of an occasional shopping expedition.'

She gives many more than the chairman's statutory three days a week to the Trust, working virtually full-time, except during school holidays. Hers is a delicate balance between work and home, but no one is ever in any doubt about which takes precedence. Forget the archetypal sitcom scenario of man in office, bothered by wife on phone nagging about minor domestic arrangements. Never a day passes without at least one call from a son who needs help in making some life-shattering decision about his rugby kit, how to do his homework, what to have for tea, and each gets the same attention as the Health Service purchaser threatening to take his custom to another hospital.

Years ago, after her huge success at West Houghton, she could have gone for a safe parliamentary seat. She would have been in government, might have even had a place in the Cabinet by now. 'Once, when I was at the House of Commons, I remember thinking, could I have sat on the back benches mid-week, well into the night, knowing Barry and the boys were at home? Some women could, but I couldn't. Organisationally I would have managed it, but I would have also missed something far too precious. It was no sacrifice. I simply made what I thought was the best choice.'

Strident feminism is not her way. She is equally comfortable in a supportive as in a leading role. During her first year as chairman of the Trust, she played the part of wife to the President of the Royal College of Veterinary Surgeons with equal gusto. They had a flat in London, hosted magnificent banquets, hobnobbed with royalty, met national dignitaries and, according to Carolyn, had one of the most wonderful years of her life, culminating in an appearance on BBC TV's *Question Time* – the night John Major announced his resignation as head of the Conservative Party. As a Christian, she had, she admitted in private, certain qualms about innovations introduced during his leadership, particularly the National Lottery. But she still believed he was the best possible leader for a party committed to creating a more equitable society by offering individuals security and fulfilment, and said so on the programme, which unfortunately gave her little opportunity to share her real vision for health issues. Transforming Preston from an ordinary district general hospital into a specialist health-care centre, supporting Barry at a time of major responsibility and privilege, seeing to the needs of six small, adolescent or older teenage boys, made her life a whirl of meetings, social engagements, swimming lessons and, as an afterthought, finding the right thing to wear.

Hardly surprising, given the major part they play in her life, that, like Susan Howatch, Carolyn Johnson is enormously fond of men, and empathises with the strains they face living in such a competitive world. She would love to introduce all kinds of self-awareness exercises on Trust board away-days, to explore relationships in greater depth, but realises it could terrorise her male colleagues, forcing them to retreat into a cave, not emerge into the sunlight. Men, she thinks, need to be coaxed gently out of their self-imposed imprisonment, not boxed and beaten by a load of politically correct harpies. 'I think we've gone a bit overboard on women's issues, It's right to get the balance, but we mustn't neglect men's health, or discriminate against them. Antagonism won't help. We should lead by example, not legislation. I've no time for political correctness. I'm the chairman, not a chair – to be sat on. Equal opportunities must mean equal. Women are quite capable of getting to the top on our own merits. In fact, we are far more likely to become pioneers, once we get over our lack of confidence, because we're not as afraid of falling on our faces.'

No one could be more economic with their use of power. She's blunt and can be abrasive, and when she is, even the flies on the wall sit up and take notice. That's because it's rare. 'Being the chairman means being the servant of all. One day I'll have to give account for the responsibility I have been given. If things go wrong, the buck stops here. After all, there's no one else to blame. But God isn't a hard taskmaster. I may flounder from time to time. It isn't comfortable, but there's no shame in admitting you were wrong. The important thing is to get up, and start again.'

Her motto is: 'Never do what's been done before – unless there's a very good reason.' It is the challenge to be original and creative that keeps her going when staff criticise her, when patients complain, when certain officials in the higher echelons of power patronise and underestimate her because she refuses to play the stereotype. Nothing deters her, not the pain, nor personal doubts to which, she says, every human being is subject, not even the added problem of her hearing impediment, which can turn a public meeting into a ordeal of lip-reading and guesswork. What she wants to achieve is too important to be held back by such minor obstacles. 'The NHS is the largest employer in Europe. What an opportunity to lead the way in developing good working practices, and a totally new approach to pastoral care.'

The Labour Government did not reappoint Carolyn to the Chairmanship of the Trust. She is now a grandmother and practises full time as a barrister in chambers in Manchester, specialising in family and child-care law. The changes she brought to the Royal Preston Hospital are still reaping benefits for patients and staff.

CHAPTER 8

The Politician: Hilary Armstrong, MP

Of 659 Members of Parliament, 120 are women. Prior to the 1997 General Election, there were only 61. It was obvious from the deep-throated braying, the 'haw-haws' and 'hear, hears', that accompanied every broadcast government debate. It is hardly fair representation, and it begs the question, if the genders were balanced the other way, in favour of women, how different might the country be?

Why do so few women become MPs? Both Julia Neuberger and Carolyn Johnson stood for Parliament, one for the Liberal Democrats, one for the Conservatives. Both did well, substantially increasing their party's votes, but neither was elected. It left me wondering how and what kind of woman does succeed in a political career, and whether, in the post-Thatcher era, women still have a uniquely female contribution to make. If God is good for women, there must be a better way for women to have a positive influence on government policy than vicariously, through her man, as a good little political wife.

Of the 61 female MPs there were, it was Hilary Armstrong, now Government Chief Whip, I chose to go and see, because I was fascinated to discover that she had had a moment of great power – as Parliamentary Private Secretary to John Smith, Leader of the Opposition. With him she was responsible for the extraordinary revival of Christian socialism that is at the heart of New Labour and is dear to Tony Blair. And, like me, her roots are buried in the deep, rich soil of the North-east.

The Honourable Member for Durham North-west is as north-eastern as Newcastle Brown and stottie cake. One grandfather was a boiler stoker in the shipyards, the other was an itinerant miner. The latter, abandoned as a lad by a drunken father, converted to Methodism, took the temperance pledge, and ended his life a highly respected county councillor and community leader. It was at chapel he acquired the basic literacy and the organisational and public-speaking skills that equipped him for these roles. He died before Hilary was born, but his legacy to his granddaughter was an instinctive, unshakeable belief in the power of Christian socialism.

His son, Hilary's father, a local preacher since boyhood, lived the same mix of faith and public spirit, equally comfortable as a Methodist circuit steward, recruiting new ministers to the area, or fulfilling his responsibilities in local government. On Saturdays Hilary accompanied him to political meetings at Sunderland Town Hall, on Sundays to chapel for all three services. Later, when she was old enough to decide for herself, she and her brother attended a different chapel with their friends. Although they were a close family they didn't live in each other's pockets. The children were given a great deal of independence.

I met her for the first time at 7 Millbank, the sleek New Labour headquarters in Westminster, having been meticulously checked and frisked before I was released to sink into the opulent velour armchairs in a plush waiting area, separated from the major part of the building by a wall of darkened glass. A steady stream of expressionless men in pin-striped suits with heavy briefcases stride past me, holding up ID cards, swing a glass door almost off its hinges and, on the other side of reality, pull a newspaper off a stand, scan the headlines briefly, put it back without a flicker of emotion and disappear down one of the many thickly carpeted corridors. In that other tinted world two brisk, industrious-looking young men in uniform at a large reception desk nod deferentially at their backs. Harassed-looking secretaries scurry past with mountainous armfuls of files. A television screen keeps me informed about what is being debated in the House.

Slightly to one side, facing me, the 'exit' to make-believe consists not of a door, but of a row of three human-size glass capsules, like revolving rockets in a fairground ride, only these remain stationary, while leavers press a button, climb in, then press another button to let them out again. This security device must be torture for the claustrophobic or the faint-hearted. Next to me, oblivious to the toing and froing, blasé about the goings-on in that other existence, a tousled-haired man in a grubby beige mac is absorbed in the *Red Star*.

Hilary appears at the glass door, late, apologetic and out of breath. She beckons me through and, like Alice in Wonderland, I trot after her down the corridors – until we end up in a canteen, much like a British Home Stores or Littlewoods café – drinking coffee out of mass-produced china at a Formica table. The mystique is beginning to wane.

She is, I reckon, in her late forties, tallish, with soft, brown hair framing her face, soft-spoken with an attractive north-eastern lilt. She weighs you up carefully behind her glasses. She is refreshingly un-men-in-uniform-brigade, wears mix-and-match rather than a suit, combines quiet competence with warmth, a sense of efficiency with an easy, straightforward manner. She has no side to her, makes no obvious attempt to create an impression. I know my time with her is strictly limited but she manages to make me feel it has no bounds, that she is entirely at my disposal.

The first thing I need to know about her, she says, is that for her there is no artificial divide between faith and politics. There was never any dramatic conversion to either camp. The two strands were an interwoven thread running through her childhood. Margaret Thatcher said something very similar in her autobiography, *The Path to Power*. Her childhood revolved around Methodism. She went to church two or three times on Sundays. Home was, 'practical, serious and intensely religious'. But there any resemblance in the upbringing of the two women appears to cease. The daughter of the successful grocer and mayor of Grantham was taught that Christianity was the source of personal achievement rather than social justice. All hangs, it appears, on the interpretation.

One of Hilary's earliest political memories was campaigning against apartheid in South Africa. 'My father, my brother and I demonstrated with placards in Sunderland town centre for a month, which wasn't something we usually did. We boycotted South African goods. Even my mother, who was not a political animal, harangued local shopkeepers.'

Both her parents were teachers in poorer parts of the town. 'Fighting poverty and inequality was instinctive. Although it was never spelled out, never preached at us, we knew we had been born to serve others, not to please ourselves. You couldn't just sit back. You had to get involved. Whether that was Christianity or socialism I can't say. The two were indistinguishable.'

Her father also taught her to hold her own in an argument. As chairman of the Council's education committee, he was responsible for implementing government policy to turn the town's schools comprehensive, including the grammar school where Hilary was a pupil. For an adolescent, defending her father to a critical, angry band of teachers was a tough but useful introduction to political conflict.

In the end, distracting outside interests spoilt her chances of the A-level grades she needed for the university of her choice. She opted instead for a brand new course in sociology at West Ham College of Technology, and left for London in October 1963, at the same time as Ernie Armstrong, her father, who had been elected Member of Parliament for Durham North-west. 'I used to come up to London once a week to sit in the gallery at the House of Commons and watch Dad – and to get a decent meal afterwards.'

These were the years of intense right-wing activism. Enoch Powell was in his heyday. The National Front coined the phrase, 'If you want a nigger for a neighbour, vote Labour', and Patrick Gordon Walker, the Labour politician, fought and lost the historic by-election in Smethwick, where racial tension had reached unbearable proportions. This was her first experience of racism at close quarters, and she found it deeply shocking. 'I'd been involved in election campaigns since the year dot and went to support Patrick Gordon Walker. I didn't realise Dad's campaign organiser, Geoff Foster, was in charge. His face dropped when he saw me. He knew I was stroppy and a bit of a heckler. He drew me on one side and said, "Hilary, it's not like at home. This is nasty stuff. Keep your head down and say nothing." I did as I was told, and he was right. The right wing started throwing smoke bombs. It was frightening. I'd never seen naked aggression like it, didn't think such bigotry was possible.'

West Ham College's Methodist Society was, however, more refined and middle-class than the chapel community she was used to, more intimidating than political brickbats for the Sunderland lass. Nonetheless, when they went painting and decorating down the Edgware Road as part of a community work project, Hilary was as horrified as the rest by the poverty they saw. 'The flats were rented, mainly by the elderly. There had been no attempt to modernise whatsoever. They were in a terrible state, dilapidated and freezing cold. Most still had gas mantles rather than electric lights. Public service in the North-east had tried to eradicate that kind of basic deprivation years ago. I realised then how forward-thinking men like my father had been.'

Looking back, she now sees that the most formative experience of all was two postgraduate years with VSO, teaching in a remote village school in Kenya. For the first time in her life she was completely alone. There was no popping to the House to get a meal out of Dad, or ringing home and reversing the charges to pour out her heart to Mum. All her securities were gone. In an alien culture everything she thought she believed was brought into question, and she began to have serious doubts.

Her head teacher, an African from a poor family, a deeply religious man and a great and visionary thinker whom she admired enormously, died very suddenly. It was more than a personal blow. It was a tragedy for the school. And then one of her brightest pupils was converted to Christianity by American missionaries. 'They told her she had to shun all her tribal traditions and cultural patterns of behaviour, she had to cut herself off from her people. She could have been one of the great intellectual powers in the country, but they destroyed her pride in the African way of life. She had a complete breakdown.'

Hilary became increasingly enraged with what the fundamentalists were doing in Kenya. The religion they imposed appeared to be white and Western, unable to embrace, or even affirm the riches of another culture. 'This wasn't real faith. It was a shrivelled, fossilised set of rules and regulations. They reduced Christianity to one particular way of doing things because they were too terrified to question or explore it for themselves. When tragedy came and God didn't intervene the way He was expected to, they too were lost.'

In time she came to see that God wasn't the problem. It was how people interpreted Him for their own purposes, using Him to reinforce their particular prejudices. 'The Methodism I grew up with was totally integrated in how the people lived, never separated from the trials and tribulations of ordinary life.' The interaction between Christianity and culture became one of her greatest passions. Few things make her as angry today as people who want to narrow religion down to a few rigid, unadaptable certainties. 'Christianity is about changing our patterns of behaviour, of course it is, but it isn't about losing who and what we essentially are. I have to work out what my faith means for me now in the society in which I live. Christ himself worked within the norms and restrictions of His society, without being subservient to them. In fact He used them to challenge the rules and regulations which determined how people were valued. Christianity lets women down, is poor on gender issues – when, unlike Christ, it fails to recognise the equality and value of every human being.'

Her socialism was also called into question. 'You learn about power when you're white in an ex-colonial country.' By the time Hilary left Kenya, she knew beyond any shadow of doubt that she wanted to be in politics. She would have liked to have stayed in Africa to fight for justice there, but reluctantly gave up the idea, feeling she had no right.

It was then she first realised that her own roots were deeply embedded in the tribal culture of North-east England, abandoned by countless of its own visionaries, whose dreams could not be contained within such apparently narrow boundaries. The obvious alternative was to return to familiar soil. After a variety of social work posts, she taught community work at Sunderland Polytechnic, and won a seat on the Durham County Council. To an objective onlooker, slotting back into the world of her childhood haunts may have seemed an easy option, but life almost anywhere else, says Hilary, would have been easier. Being Ernie Armstrong's daughter was a distinct disadvantage for such a headstrong independent thinker. 'It was not that I wasn't proud of Dad. I just wanted to be my own person, not come pre-packaged in a box. I wanted to live what I had learned in Africa – that you can't pretend you're any other than what you are.'

She refused every career opportunity, even those she most wanted, if they weren't obviously won on her own merits. On one occasion, after a particularly tough interview with the County Council for a social work post, one of the panel said, 'You knew we'd take you on anyway for your father's sake.' Hilary turned the job down.

In the early 1980s she put her name forward for several parliamentary seats. 'Proportionately, there were very few women MPs. Selectors always complained it was because women never put themselves forward as candidates. I wasn't going to let them get away with that excuse.' She was still turned down. The 'hard left' was making a deliberate and organised bid to gain the heart of the party, and Hilary was just not hard enough.

The family was thrown when Ernie Armstrong was invited to be Deputy Speaker of the House, and Durham North-west became vacant. Hilary, with her usual resistance to following in her father's footsteps, decided not to go for it. Then she discovered that many of her father's supporters were also opposed to her standing for election, and thought, 'How daft!' This was the challenge she had been waiting for – to convince the 'anti-dynasty' brigade that she wasn't simply a chip off the old block, but had her own ideas and policies.

At home tension mounted. For Ernie Armstrong it was an extremely difficult time. He badly wanted his daughter to have the opportunity she deserved, but was so terrified of any accusation of nepotism that he refused to discuss the campaign, never went to party meetings and hadn't a clue what was going on. 'The atmosphere was very strained. He had to cut himself off from all that mattered to him the most. I knew beyond any shadow of doubt how much he wanted it for me, but he was terribly anxious he would get in the way.'

She won the seat in 1987 by the narrowest of margins, increasing her majority substantially in the next election. Ernie didn't go to Westminster for a year, to give his daughter the time she needed to make her own way in the House.

It is 10.30 am, and a very busy day in the constituency is well under way by the time I have completed my journey east across the glorious North York Moors to a part of the world that is strangely familiar, yet so different from when I was a child.

This is Crook in County Durham. My mother owned a pram shop here in the High Street in the 1960s. I used to come with her and take the money for dummies, rattles and small toys. Prams and cots and larger items were paid for on the 'never-never'. Times were hard even then. Work at the pit shaft had ground to an irrevocable halt. Alternative industry was slow in coming. When it finally arrived, the feeble spark of hope was extinguished, almost the moment it was ignited, by the recession.

The town is still a mass of narrow, treeless streets, lined with two-up, two-down terraced housing, only now they're one-way, a tangled maze of miniature roundabouts, iron fences and No Entry signs. The rows of old grey stone are interrupted by a rectangular red-brick health or community centre, looking as if it has landed from another planet. The High Street, protected from invading traffic, is largely unchanged and bustles as it ever did, though there are no pram or furniture shops, only charity and discount outlets, cheap food and fashion stores.

The north-eastern spirit may be bowed and bent a little, but it is still unbroken. It's Maundy Thursday and there's a holiday feel in the air. Despite a wintry Easter chill, people stand and chat in doorways and on street corners. I stop and ask the way. 'Why aye, pet, she lives just there, our MP,' and they point me towards an old, grey-stone, detached house, standing proudly alone on the edge of the shopping area.

'When you get here, go round the back. I'll never hear you otherwise,' said the indomitable Joan Carthy, Hilary's secretary, in her attractive, gravelly Geordie voice, when I rang to ask if I could trail Hilary around the constituency for the day. 'If she said you can, I suppose you can,' she growled, with the resignation of one long aware that no one's really taken in by the ferocious watchdog manner, and that any attempt to protect her territory is doomed to failure anyway by Hilary's openness to allcomers.

From the front the house is calm, serene, a quiet, private residence. At the back, where Joan has her office and sits with Hilary's large, permanently open diary on a desk piled high with mail, it is a hive of activity. The phone and doorbell ring incessantly. People come, people go. Some of us sit and wait. Hilary wanders in smiling, wearing trousers and blazer, casual, relaxed, looking ready for a round of golf, rather than a busy working day. A change of gear is obviously taking place. She is home, where she belongs.

For Joan it's busier than usual. 'The police want to talk to you about sheep rustling. There are problems with New Age travellers. What time are you going to fit the doctor in? Can you speak to a student about grants? There's a woman complaining about … oh, and a journalist wants to know your thoughts on …?'

Hilary nods accommodatingly, makes one or two suggested timings, then beckons me, coffee mug in hand, to follow her into an airy sitting room at the front of the house. In pride of place on the wall hangs a plate marking the 125th anniversary of the death of John Wesley. It says, 'I look upon all the world as my parish.' One armchair is occupied by a bulging plastic carrier bag, full of paperwork. She pokes it and sighs loudly. 'I was one and a half hours late leaving the office last night, and we didn't arrive back until the small hours. It's always like that in London – hectic.' She moves the bag to the floor, draws out a sheaf on the beef crisis – vital information, I gather, for a meeting later in the morning – and has just settled in the armchair when the doorbell goes.

'My first appointment.'

I follow her into what must have once been a back parlour, where the lady of the house would have sat with her embroidery or crochet, worrying about social engagements rather than social injustice. A woman, her husband, and her son, Keith, who is deaf, are waiting nervously for their MP.

'Tea? Coffee?'

She puts her head round the office door and relays the order to Joan's second-in-command.

'Do you lip-read, Keith?'

He nods.

She's thoughtful, considerate, moves slowly, hands in pockets, puts people at their ease almost at once.

Keith's mother explains that after seven years with the same company her son has been given the sack, unjustly and through personal prejudice, as far as she can see. She has all the details, including conversations with the management and tribunal dates, written in a notebook, and she recounts them to Hilary, looking from her husband to her son for confirmation. 'If I shed a few tears, it's not because of you,' she whispers to Keith, when Hilary goes to collect the tea tray, 'It's because I'm so angry.'

'Don't worry,' Hilary reassures her, overhearing it, as she comes back into the room. 'Everyone's worked up when they come to me. It's because I'm always the last in line.'

'I didn't know we could come to you. I didn't know Hilary Armstrong dealt with things like this.'

'Well, I don't know what I am here for if it's not for things like this.'

'They sacked him in December and sent him a birthday card in January. Do you see how cruel firms can be these days?'

Hilary nods. 'The problem is they're really up against it. The government have set them productivity targets which are very hard to meet.'

'It means they can sack anyone they like. The workforce is

terrified. There's hundreds waiting to take their place.'

'Well, I don't have much power. Being an MP doesn't mean they'll listen to me, but I'll do what I can.'

Hilary photocopies their correspondence with the union about an appeal, and I notice for the first time the poster on the wall above the photocopier. It's a quote from Archbishop Desmond Tutu, which says, 'I am puzzled about which Bible people are reading when they suggest religion and politics don't mix.'

'How do you cope with injustice when it's in your sitting room?' I ask her, as the mother herds her little brood out of the door, looking a little happier. 'It isn't just "out there" any more. For you, it has a very human face.'

'Serious injustice does make me feel helpless, especially if its due to bad policy and there's little I can do to change it. That's why the constituency is so important. I need to know what's happening to people, how national policies affect them personally. Local firms are being pushed to achieve impossible targets. That family is paying the price. It's important for me to see it from their perspective. It dominates their entire lives. I will fight for them. On the other hand, I can't let emotion rob me of my rational judgment. When someone feels picked on, who is the arbiter? I need to talk to everyone involved, to know all sides of the story. My social work training is useful. Although I'm affected by people's pain, I don't collapse under it.

'Did you notice it was the mother who took control of the situation?' she asks, as we head back to the sitting room and she dials the local police station. 'That's often the case in working-class communities. The women are strong, resourceful, the driving force. They've never had any real outlet for their capabilities, and that's a terrible waste. Yes, Inspector, what's happened this time?'

For ten minutes she 'hmms' and 'tuts', while law enforcement, balanced precariously between journalists and farmers, the local equivalent of the devil and deep blue sea, offloads its angst about the relationship between New Age travellers and increased sheep worrying. Occasionally she picks up the beef briefing and gives it a cursory glance.

'It's really about listening, isn't it?' I call after her, as we hurry out to her car, fractionally late for the next, crucial meeting of the day.

'We should be walking, not taking the car,' she says, apologetically. 'And I'm on the Shadow team for the environment! Local government's my actual brief – it's the only thing I really know about. I should know more about green issues.'

We drive at breakneck speed around the one-way system and appear to emerge almost where we started. 'I love being back in Crook. It's home. But when I'm in London, I love my Shadow responsibilities too. There's such variety in being an MP,' she says, as she negotiates a parking place right outside the Farmers' Union, then adds, as an afterthought, 'but you never quite feel on top of everything.'

How do you force 14 large male farmers and one MP into the tiny back room of a small terraced house? A beef crisis is probably the most effective way. This was the largest turnout there has ever been to any local NFU meeting. Scientists have suggested a link between BSE and Creutzfeldt-Jakob Disease (CJD). The European Community has banned all beef products. The price on the British market has dropped by 25p per kilo, wiping out the farmers' profits, and they are determined that their MP should be in no doubt about their mood.

Gathered are an assortment of Pickwickian characters, some with shiny bald heads, in smart overcoats; others in jeans, with drooping mustachios; a few in the statutory green wellies, flat caps and sleeveless, padded jackets. There's a hint of the smell of the soil. Or is my imagination working overtime, hallucinating from the effects of so much hot air? No one opens a window. The atmosphere, stuffier by the minute, is one of unremitting gloom and doom. They shake their heads and reflect on 'the longest fortnight in my life', and 'this once-in-a-lifetime tragedy', or they wag a warning finger and prophesy further national disaster: 'Eggs yesterday, beef today, what will it be tomorrow? The government needs to think about that.'

They want moves to restore public confidence in beef and the removal of the European ban. Hilary listens carefully for over an hour, maintaining eye contact throughout, thoughtful, affirming, only interrupting for clarification. She writes everything down and promises to relay their thoughts and feelings to the Minister, but admits there is little she can offer by way of reassurance. 'We expected some clarification in Thursday's debate, but were given few details.'

'They could have been far more belligerent,' she says as we climb back into the car, 'given that most of them vote Conservative.'

It occurs to me that in this instance it is probably a distinct advantage to be a socialist. I also wonder whether 14 men would have shown such restraint in the presence of another man. Old-fashioned courtesy is by no means dead in the Durham farming fraternity.

But carrying the party card is not a prerequisite for Hilary's concern. Perhaps they sense it, know it from previous experience. Perhaps this accounts for the lack of personal animosity.

'Some of my colleagues complain that farmers are always bleating on when they're rich. But that certainly isn't true round here. Some of them are on the breadline. This could really finish them.'

'They're not very keen on the media,' I comment.

'I don't think they ever realised before that people are interested in what they're eating. Public accountability comes as a bit of a shock.'

As we arrive back at the house, a delicious, mouth-watering smell meets us at the door. Paul, Hilary's husband, is cooking lunch – lamb. Joan has gone out for an hour and the phone is still ringing. I make myself a mental note never to complain about living in a vicarage again.

Hilary disappears into the office to answer calls and sort out her diary for the afternoon, while Paul, who looks the epitome of the new man, standing at the cooker in his pinny, continues to stir his concoction.

'There isn't much privacy, is there?' I comment, aware that I am probably the first in a long line of intrusions this Easter. 'It seems to me that when they're at home, MPs belong body, soul and mind to the constituency.'

'We have to leave the country to have a marriage,' he says affably, 'But I knew what I was taking on. And you get used to living in two places.'

They live, I gather, in Paul's flat in London mid-week. Hilary comes to Crook every weekend, and he joins her for one in every three. They met when Hilary taught social work at Sunderland Polytechnic, and Paul, a sociologist, was a member of staff. They married only four years ago, after a long friendship and a General Election.

'Our wedding was just down the road at Whitton Methodist Chapel. Half the Shadow Cabinet was there.'

'That must have been quite an event for the village?'

'In some ways. But they've become used to a police presence – because of Ernie.'

As Deputy Speaker, Ernie, I gathered, was eligible for a visit from the IRA.

Over lunch the conversation revolves around John Smith, and Hilary's role as his Parliamentary Private Secretary. I only have the vaguest notion of what's involved, based on the television serial, *To Play the King*, which is probably highly glamorised – and erroneous. 'A PPS is the political operator in the office, the link between the politician and the party. I had to sound out party opinion, try and assess which of his ideas they would wear, tell him about any rumblings.'

Looking back, she feels her greatest achievement was the one-member-one-vote decision, taken at the Labour Party Conference in 1992, which depended on persuading the Manufacturing Science and Finance Union, Hilary's own, to abstain.

'John was sitting on the platform looking thoroughly depressed, convinced the union wouldn't change its mind, that we would be defeated. I went up and whispered to him that they had promised to abstain. He could hardly believe it. It was a great triumph.'

She isn't sure why John chose her for the job. They had never been close friends and in fact, apart from their politics, had little in common other than their strong, nonconformist Christian beliefs. 'The party members used to complain, that's two of them with a moral conscience, we'll never get that past them!'

Socialism had for many years been dominated by intellectual rationalism. 'John's great bequest to the party,' says Hilary, 'was that he encouraged socialism to own and affirm its Christian roots.' He brought Christianity back from the fringes into the centre, not just of the Labour Party but of the entire political debate. And it was not entirely intentional. John Smith was not a man given to wearing his beliefs on his sleeve, might never have spoken out in public, but for a growing anger and sense of helplessness at what was happening to society with the disintegration of the local community. Hilary helped him prepare his seminal speech for the Christian Socialist Movement. She, with him, contributed to *Reclaiming the Ground*, a series of essays by Labour politicians, explaining how their Christian ideals influenced their political perspective. In many ways it constituted a radical re-evaluation of socialism. Looking back at the achievements of her paternal grandfather, many of them due to his Christian faith, Hilary attacked the notion that building strong communities must be at the cost of the individual. 'If we look not just at the lives of an earlier Labour Party, but also at ourselves, all of us developed our skills and ourselves as fully as we could in order to provide something real in public service … As a party we need to fight against the false idea that building a community means denying people the right to do well for themselves. Such an idea is one that cannot be found in Christianity, and it is one that should not be found in socialism. If we enter the next election with even a whiff of that antipathy in our policies, many people who would really rather like to vote for us will find that they cannot.' The boundaries between Carolyn Johnson's Christian toryism and Hilary's Christian socialism were becoming rather blurred.

John's sudden death was utterly devastating. Hilary was on her way to his home in Basildon to pick him up for a meeting when he had a heart attack in the shower. She arrived at the house to discover he had just died. 'I couldn't believe it. He was so full of life, always joking, full of fun, and unlike me, a real bon viveur. He was a bear with a sore head during Lent – because he gave up alcohol.'

This obviously rings a bell with Paul, who laughs loudly in agreement.

'But he was also a good man to work for, extremely loyal to his staff. He always listened to what I had to say, though he had a very good grasp on what the party was thinking anyway.'

He was, she explains, a typical 'House of Commons man'. Westminster is full of them, men away from home, with a semi-bachelor lifestyle. While the women dash off to sort out their domestic arrangements, they live and eat at the House, enjoy convivial company, and pick up, bye the bye, every nuance of what's going on.

'The loss to the party was enormous – but he wouldn't have wanted us to give up the fight, or try and do things the way he would have done them.'

The personal loss to Hilary was also immeasurable. John Smith's death robbed her of her political influence overnight.

'You had access to the top. Information is power. Do you miss having such a powerful job?'

She reflects for a moment.

'Yes – but I don't lie awake at night and worry about it.'

She gets up, clears the table, gathers her things, and we leave a smiling, genial Paul to make what he will of the debris we leave behind. A couple with a complaint about the social services are waiting for a visit from their MP.

~

'What about ambition?' I ask her, as we leap back into the car, and head for a council estate on the outskirts of the town.

'I'd like to be a minister one day, who wouldn't? But I'm not as ambitious as some of my colleagues.'

'Is ambition predominantly a male prerogative in Westminster?'

'I was naive at first. I thought so. But some women are just as ambitious as the men, just as susceptible to envy, and to the rat race. Once I'd worked that out it was okay. The problem is that it can be highly destructive of teamwork. And for me, teamwork is everything.'

'Isn't that more typically female?' I ask. It is in fact a recurrent theme as I speak to women about their approach to work.

'It may be,' she concedes, 'but then it was Tony Blair who said, "We're able to do more together than alone."'

We pull up outside a row of spruce, neat little houses, immaculate enough for a paint advertisement. Inside, everything is equally spick and span. A hint of bleach pervades the air. A pleasant, middle-aged couple explain at length their ongoing problems with the local social services. Hilary has to find her way through the complex tale of a son's second wife's child by a first marriage, who lives in London but ended up here with no one else to care for her. In her usual way she gives them space and time, though I am aware she has to be at a doctor's practice, on the other side of the constituency, 13 kilometres away, by three, and the minutes, measured by a large clock on the wall, are slowly ticking by.

But this is familiar ground for her. It also involves the well-being of a child. 'I think it's time I paid social services a visit,' she says, 'and see how things have changed since my day.' There are no specific promises, but we leave the couple looking reassured, no longer two lone individuals against the world – while we make a 70-mile-per-hour dash cross-country to Shotley Bridge, where the good doctor has already been waiting for more than 20 minutes.

He gets his own back. He is seeing a patient. Like anyone else Hilary has to wait her turn in the surgery waiting room, surrounded by screaming babies, anxious mums and old men with wracking coughs. 'I speed read,' she says, scanning yet another fat document, this time a policy for primary health care in the area. Acute medical care, including accident and emergency, has been moved out of Shotley Bridge to another hospital several miles away and there are real fears that the downgrading of the district general hospital is only the first step to its being closed altogether. The doctor has come up with a radical alternative, a medical centre responding to the needs of local GPs and their patients, providing all the basic and long-term care not available at the acute hospital. 'This is very exciting,' Hilary says, as she reaches the final paragraph, and the doctor ushers us into his room.

He explains in detail the potential power of local GPs, who know the particular needs of their patients, working together to commission health care for their area. He's young, enthusiastic. 'He's a marvel,' Hilary says to me later, with admiration. 'Imagine uniting a motley crowd of GPs, both fundholding and non-fundholding. That takes wisdom, and gut-hard work. I can foresee a bit of political flak, but I'll give him all the support I can.'

She has promised as much during the interview, listing the people she will lobby on his behalf, 'And if that doesn't work I'll go to government, see a minister, make it work.' I've lost count of all the people she has promised to see as a result of the people she has seen so far today. Her work seems to be governed by the law of exponential growth. The Easter break is in danger of becoming a distant dream.

We have an hour to spare before visiting the police station to pick up on the sheep rustling problem, and head for Phileas Fogg country to find a café. Consett, Britain's steel centre, used to have a highly skilled, highly paid workforce. Today the town centre has an air of general decline and despondency. We try several small cafés reeking of stale fried food, but it's 4.30 pm and long past Consett's time for a cuppa. The staff are clearing away, chairs turned upside-down on the tables. I wonder whether she'll be recognised, whether someone will say, 'It's our MP. For you, Hilary, we'll make a brew', but no joy. She is as incognito as I am – until we eventually find the only open café, and settle down for a deep and meaningful conversation.

'Look who it is! It's Hilary Armstrong, our MP. Do you remember when she helped your gran with that …'

She gets up, greets the people sitting at the table behind ours, asks after the rest of the family.

'How do you get on,' I ask her, when she finally returns, 'with all the officials you have to see to sort out the problems of the people we've met today?'

'It varies. Some are wary, which is a shame. I think they stereotype me as an aggressive woman, but I'm not that type at all.'

'Are there advantages in being a woman MP?'

Very definitely, she says, but not for the reasons I anticipate. No mention of the empathy or approachability I have witnessed, qualities I imagine she would say are shared out between the genders.

'The cultural expectations imposed upon women prepare them more than men for a life in Parliament. Women are much more used to taking responsibility for their own lives. No one sorts out the peripheries for us, so that we can devote ourselves to one main task. We have no one to organise us. We juggle all the plates ourselves. That's a useful lesson to learn, as Parliament is very unstructured. You have no targets, no goals, no guidelines except a bit of pink paper, which tells you when to vote. The men can find that very unnerving. Some of them bring their wives and secretaries with them to ensure that someone is in control of their lives. It was the opposite for me. I had to hand over bits of my life to a secretary and I hate it. I give her hell. If we manage to engineer our way through the selection process, I think women are far better equipped both to do the job and survive. It's no coincidence that all the scandals – both sexual and drink – involve male MPs. Left on their own, they're at a loose end, whereas a woman always finds something to do.'

I pick her up on her comment about the selection process. It is obviously a sore point. Does she agree with her party policy to legislate in favour of women candidates? As long as becoming an MP is seen as an unusual job for a woman, she does. 'The logjam is historical and cultural, and we have to take positive action to move it on. It isn't just about stereotyping. There are plenty of women in the public arena. The problem is that women don't instinctively see themselves as MPs. We have to push them into thinking about it. We have to get to the place where the public, and particularly selectors, see women as the obvious candidates.'

But then of course there is the cost, I remind her.

'Yes, it does take over your life. I always knew I'd never be a traditional wife and mother, but I don't think I ever consciously decided not to have children. Looking back, I think I would have been torn. It's one thing meeting the challenges of your job yourself, it's quite another to drag innocent kids into it.'

We talk a little of Harriet Harman at the centre of a political storm for sending her son to the private school of his choice.

'If I'd had children, would I have become an MP? It's hard to say. Some women manage it. You see them rushing away from the House to relieve the childminder. But Consett is the other side of the world, and child care isn't part of the culture here.'

Because she is a woman MP, everyone, including her colleagues, tends to assume she will be more interested in child care than in the economy. She finds it galling and is in fact very happy to be Opposition spokesperson for the Treasury and economic affairs. Her favourite role model and inspiration is Ellen Wilkinson, the great political campaigner who led the Jarrow marches. The North-east, we agree, breeds a tough, resilient kind of a woman. 'If you survive as a single woman in the North-east, it makes you strong. Westminster's a bit of a doddle after Durham County Hall.'

But there is no question about the real source of her strength. The pivot and motivating force, the energy for all she does, comes from her faith. 'Is God good for women? Yes, and He's good for men too, because He offers forgiveness and love, so that we can forgive and love ourselves, then go and take that forgiveness and love out into the community. The early Christian teacher Irenaeus said, "The glory of God is a person fully alive." It's that personal relationship with Christ which brings me constantly back to what my life is really about. It would be all too easy to get hooked into the seductive glamour of Westminster and the illusory sense of self-importance it can give you. When I come home and see my constituents, they bring me down to earth. So many of the women here haven't had the opportunities I have had. It's a privilege to serve them and I must do it as best I can.'

Hilary has no illusions about her ability to solve the world's problems. Sorting out Shotley Bridge Hospital would do, she says. 'All around me are people who have no one to listen to them, who feel they don't matter, who don't believe they have the capacity to achieve anything. But they do, so much more than they think. If the role of the Church is to bring God's kingdom on earth, my part of it is to give the people here the self-confidence to go out and fulfil their God-given potential as the human beings He loves.'

The Bible, she believes, makes it clear that working for others, contributing to the community and sharing the wealth of the earth all enable individuals to live stronger, healthier, happier lives. She doesn't see a great chasm between Conservative individualism and a socialist emphasis on community. They go hand in hand. One cannot thrive at the cost of the other. That to her seems the secret of the power of the early Church, a close-knit community of individuals who had the courage to face martyrdom for their beliefs.

How would she feel then, I ask her, if her party were never in government, or if she were condemned to a life on the back benches or, worse still, if she lost her seat?

'Status doesn't interest me. I'm called to better the life of my community, not necessarily to be an MP. I love it, you can see that. It isn't a burden at all. There are such rewards. But if I'm defeated by the electorate, either personally or as a party, I have no right to say to them, "You don't know what you're doing." This is a democracy. I must listen to what they're saying to me, especially the young, and constantly reassess and re-evaluate my views. The basic principle remains the same. We can't move with every shift of the wind – but listening involves changing, growing. We mustn't sacrifice people for our ideological dogma.'

'And what is the basic principle?' I ask her, as she hunts for her car keys and prepares to tango with the local police force. That will be followed by a surgery, anathema to every MP, a sports day for all the groaners and grousers. Hilary doesn't complain. It's all part of the job.

'Don't you stay,' she says, 'Go home to your family.'

'What is the basic principle?' I ask her again, as we walk back to the car.

'Love your neighbour as yourself.'

When the suffragettes won women the vote at the beginning of the twentieth century they assumed women would go on to play an equal part in the government of the country. They would introduce more sensitive, caring legislation. There would be less war. On the whole, they were wrong. The Hilary Armstrongs of this world, their faith in God and humanity intact in a hostile political environment, are a rare breed. Women, both in terms of numbers and influence, have not yet substantially affected the way we are governed, though the last election makes it more possible. The old-style feminists used to say that there is no such thing as specific 'feminine influence', and Margaret Thatcher with her Falklands War seems to bear that out. But it certainly isn't true for Jan Ransom or Ruth Clark in their respective male-oriented institutions. Perhaps it does boil down to numbers, to the fact that so few women are prepared for the life of an MP, make it into the Cabinet, and are able to remain true to themselves when they do. But even if, as Hilary suggests, a political career is incompatible with motherhood, where are the single women MPs, the older women MPs whose childrearing years are over? Where are the pioneering women who will change the culture of Westminster, as well as their world?

One of them is still out in the constituency, working a 15-hour day. As I set off I realise that I will have travelled 240 or so kilometres and be safely back home, long before Hilary returns to snatch what's left of the day with Paul. And that probably says it all.

Shortly after becoming Prime Minister, Tony Blair appointed Hilary Minister for Housing and Local Government. Following the election victory of 2001, Hilary was appointed to the position of Government Chief Whip.

CHAPTER 9

The Priest: Joy Carroll

Normality is obviously what it's all about. The BBC *Everyman* programme was at pains to prove how normal she is. As Susan Howatch says, the public suspects that the male clergy aren't. As far as their female equivalent is concerned, it is too early to say. The verdict is still out. So they showed her putting on her lipstick before a service, buying cans of beer, as well as the communion bread, at a local supermarket, hosting a 1970s 'bad taste' party at home. She is, after all, the model for the highly successful BBC sitcom series, *The Vicar of Dibley*, and you can't get more earthy, less pious, than its star, Dawn French.

Joy Carroll herself uses the word freely. Her childhood was, she says, normal, which, for a child of the vicarage, is not really normal at all. Vicarage life, particularly in an area of high social deprivation, can be rarefied, not altogether conducive to the development of a socially well-adjusted, well-integrated teenager. But Joy's parents were not what she calls 'the old-style, patronising, missionary types, who think they have something better than the local community, barricade themselves in the vicarage and never share the same social activities as the local people'. They were committed, 'lock, stock and barrel', to their parish. Joy and her brother went to the local grammar school and did without a 'pristine, private-school accent'. 'Who needs one, anyway?' she asks pertly.

Dark-haired and pretty like Dawn French, though somewhat slimmer, she looks in fact the epitome of the normal, fresh-faced south London girl. It was the fear she might no longer be able to enjoy the things normal girls enjoy, such as parties and pop concerts, that worried her about becoming a deaconess. In 1985 that was the only option open to a young woman wanting paid employment in the Church. As a child, she had never dreamed of becoming a priest like her father. It simply wasn't a possibility. Her brother, for whom it was, became a heating engineer.

Once, however, in a fit of pique, riled by restrictions on the time she should come in at night, she swore she would never marry a vicar – which was the next best thing to saying, 'I'll get as far away from this kind of life as I can.'

But it was a life she had imbibed from the cradle and, headstrong, determined as she was, she could not escape it – only reshape it in her own particular style and way. 'I'm a genuine product of the inner city. That's where I belong. There were 11 in the congregation in Stockwell when Dad arrived there as vicar. He played football with the local lads, started a boys' club, had the old Victorian church pulled down to make way for a community centre. I grew up with the regeneration of communal life revolving around the church.'

Yet it wasn't easy. If she won a prize at school, or received an award for good behaviour, it made her mad when the other children mocked, 'Just because you're the vicar's daughter.' When the kids off the street came to play in the vicarage garden – the only 'park' in the area – it made her feel uncomfortable. There was a growing awareness of the unfairness of privilege, especially in her teenage years in south Lambeth. 'I had a very close friend. We shared everything – the same taste in clothes and music. But she lived with her single mum in a council flat, and I lived in a palace. I knew that by a freak of birth our lives would go their separate ways. I went to college and she became a single parent. I married her and her partner last year. That was the first time she had ever moved house. There were no resources for the girls I grew up with, no encouragement. Your opportunities depend on your expectations.'

Joy is grateful she grew up to see that. When it comes to shouting about social injustice, there is no substitute, she believes, for first-hand experience. 'You can't really empathise from a distance.' Eight months as a volunteer in Haiti saved her from succumbing prematurely to compassion fatigue. Haiti made the poorest parts of London look positively affluent. She had never seen anything like the poverty she saw there, and returned to Britain, to teacher training college in Plymouth, with the determination to do something useful with her life.

'I was never an academic. I'm a doer, not a thinker. A qualification was simply a means to an end.' This was what her brother calls, her 'socialist phase'. She was 'a little wild', kicking the boundaries of her upbringing to see how far they would bend. 'My faith was never in question. But I didn't go to church. I wanted to explore life on my own terms – to have my cake and eat it. It was important for me to detach myself from the Church, so that when I came back it was with a clearer understanding that this was what I had chosen.'

Her childhood, faith, socialism, Haiti and even her father's example, though she was loath to admit it, were all combining to form a rich foundation for her future ministry. She was teaching five-year-olds, primarily Bangladeshi children, at Gonville Primary School in Thornton Heath, and involved in youth, children's and pastoral work at her local church in her spare time, when friends began to say, 'You're good at communicating religious ideas. Have you thought of becoming a deaconess?'

It conjured up images of spinsterly ladies in twinsets, tweed suits and pearls. Not, she says, that there is anything wrong with any of those. Some were wonderful women. 'They just weren't me.' The acid test was whether the Church of England would accept her exactly as she was, warts and all – or rather long, dangly earrings and all. She was not prepared to act her way through the selection process. To be turned down might even be a relief. 'I'm the sort of person who is often led by how passionate I feel, which isn't necessarily the best guide. Uncertainty, in this instance, was a good thing. You can't say, "I'm going to be a priest." A whole number of people, as well as the bishop, have to decide that with you.'

The testing of a possible calling is a gruelling business. It involves a three-day conference at which candidates are closely scrutinised to discover how well they listen, communicate, are open to new ideas and respond appropriately and pastorally. In 1984 most were men in their thirties and forties. A few were younger. Even fewer were women. A deaconess would always play second fiddle to a male priest. At a time when women were beginning to make serious inroads into the job market, when 'equal opportunities' was the rallying call, when Margaret Thatcher was the first woman prime minister, it was not the most attractive of propositions. But that was of little concern to Joy. Feminism had played no part in her socialist phase. When, to her surprise, she heard she had been accepted, there were other concerns on her mind. Shortly before she began training at Cranmer Hall Theological College, like a virgin about to take holy orders, at a Bruce Springsteen concert, she remembers saying to herself, 'This is my last summer of freedom.'

Cranmer Hall was far from monastic. Part of the rabbit warren of cobbled streets of St John's College at Durham University, it was a highly stimulating academic environment, which allowed her to think and question, and gave her the courage to be her own person. A term at the Roman Catholic seminary in Ushaw, work experience with hospital and prison chaplains, and a schizoid long summer placement in the USA, half with a black Lutheran church in Chicago, half with a white Episcopal church in racist, Ku-Klux Klan Virginia, broadened her theological and cultural perspectives.

Education and training for a woman, was, to all intents and purposes, the same as for a man, except that a man became a priest, but a woman remained a member of the laity. While many of her college friends, both male and female, found that untenable, women's ordination had never been a major issue for Joy. One day in 1985 that changed. 'We all sat round the radio waiting to hear whether Synod had voted to allow deaconesses to become deacons. The decision came as a huge surprise. It meant that priesthood for women was actually on the way. I never thought it would happen as quickly as that.' Now, Joy could go to her first parish as a member of the clergy – an eternal first-year curate, unable to administer communion, but clergy nonetheless, with the right to conduct weddings, wear a dog collar, and be addressed by the title 'Reverend.'

There were few surprises in her choice. What was unusual was the level of responsibility she was given for a first post – warden of the community centre and minister in charge of St Michael's, the daughter church of St James's Hatcham, at the centre of the predominantly Afro-Caribbean, disadvantaged Milton Court estate in Deptford. The 1950s community church centre had a gym, a coffee bar and a stage. There was no doubting its potential as a focal point for the entire estate. But it would take every ounce of energy Joy possessed. 'I was lucky. As a single woman without children I had only myself to consider.' In other words, there were no obstacles to her living in an urban priority area, or UPA, as they became known. She did not have to weigh up the cost of her commitment on a family – unlike her fellow ordinands, or her father when she was a child. For the possibility of being a minister in Britain's impoverished inner cities was no longer the exclusive domain of a conscious-stricken, lefty, clerical fringe. Urban poverty had become a central issue on the Church of England's agenda. While Joy was at Cranmer Hall a seed change had been sown which, for her, made the deaconing of women pale into insignificance: the publication of the *Faith in the City* report.

Gone, almost overnight, was the Church's image as 'the Tory Party at prayer', upholding the cherished religious traditions of hierarchical, rural England à la Dibley.

'What was that socialist tract you were spouting from the pulpit last Sunday?' asks the local Dibley landowner and councillor in the TV series.

'I've got a feeling it was the Sermon on the Mount,' replies the vicar, alias Dawn French.

'Jesus never said give away all your money to the poor.'

'I think you'll find that he did,' she says.

Hitherto one or two bishops, predominantly of Durham and Liverpool, had spoken out about the deepening divide between rich and poor, and had been rapped firmly over the knuckles by government ministers for confusing religion with politics. Now the Church put its weight behind them, saying publicly what Joy had known for some time, that it had a Christian duty to take a more active role in addressing the mounting social problems caused by the decline of the inner cities, whatever the political implications.

'The Church has a long history of social action. Take Wilberforce or Shaftesbury. But it lost its way when attendance became wrapped up in status – when it pandered to people's values, rather than challenging them.'

For Joy, *Faith in the City* signalled that the time had come for the Anglican Church to reclaim its heritage, 'To say, we're not here to offer tea and sympathy, but to be a radical life-changing force in society, with a powerful message of a God of justice Who values all human beings equally'. It led to the setting up of the Church Urban Fund, spawning hundreds of exciting projects all over the country. 'It challenged the very basis of Conservative policies. That's why so many Tory MPs dismissed the report as wacky and Marxist. They knew that once the Church had made up its mind to be an agent for change it could be an invincible opponent – and they were afraid.'

As a lone clergywoman on the Milton Court Estate, this for Joy was sink-or-swim time. She had been thrown in at the deepest possible end of church ministry. There were few clerical models for women, even fewer for a woman committed to the kind of environment where for years the Church had largely been an irrelevancy. Her ideals would be put to the test. On the positive side, she says, there was nothing to compare herself with. Whatever she did would be pioneering, unique.

Her father always got stuck in. So did she. But that was as far as the similarity went. Joy was determined to carve out her own style of ministry. 'Dad and I love each other dearly, but we're so alike that we can't spend too much time together without arguing. There is a part of me which is Daddy's little girl, wanting his approval. And that's always going to be a struggle. But growing up is about becoming your own person, adopting your own set of beliefs, your own way of doing things.'

Life in that little community was a hotch-potch of contrasting experiences and conflicting emotions – aggressive and demanding, but drawing on reserves of protectiveness and tenderness she barely knew she possessed. There was no greenery anywhere. In every direction every view was hard and angular. At times she felt hemmed in by concrete, a prisoner within brick walls. Survival seemed to sap her strength. Some nights the constant whine of car alarms, the blare of radios, the sounds of argument, violence and distress kept her awake and frayed her nerves.

On the other hand, the depressing side of life in the inner city was only half the story. 'It can be energising too, particularly when its characters are allowed to flourish, to use their gifts and talents. They can be such fun. The Afro-Caribbean culture is colourful and rich. We started a dance workshop and discovered some brilliant dancers. They ended up performing all over the area.'

With financial support from City Challenge and the Church Urban Fund she initiated all kinds of projects: an after-school club for children, a parent and toddler club and a toy library. Church members built a community garden on a piece of wasteland behind the centre. They planted shrubs and trees, created a play area and built a patio for barbecues, all surrounded with a high iron fence, painted buttercup yellow, to keep marauders and stray dogs out. Building yet another fence seemed counter-productive at first, but it worked, kept the garden safe, and gave access to those who would love and cherish it. 'It's still there today,' she says with excitement and pride, 'yellow, green and lush, a riot of colour in the middle of all that concrete'. Local people book it free of charge. It becomes their garden for the day if they are planning to hold a special event.

For her, as well as for the residents, the garden became a sign of hope. If God's intention is to make every human being whole, she maintains the Church should have a humanitarian as well as a spiritual role. 'We all have an inbuilt desire to know who we are, where we've come from, whether there is a God. We were simply saying, here is Christ, right in the centre of your community. That's only fulfilling the original intention of the Church of England to be "a presence" by dividing every part of England into a parish.'

Community life was easier to nurture than church attendance. If the measuring rod of a minister's achievement was the quantity rather than the quality of a congregation, Joy admits that she would not be regarded as a great success. 'You learn about failure in the inner city. The church grows slowly. Middle-class Christians with middle-class gifts which stimulate growth, like being able to play the piano or having organisational ability, always manage to be "called" to nice parishes. It makes me very suspicious about the whole idea of calling! On an estate like that everyone used up their energy simply surviving. There was little left over for innovation. If anyone had a creative idea, they were the only one who could make it happen. No one else would run with it. I was drained to the point of utter exhaustion.'

A tutor at Cranmer Hall had written in one of her reports, 'Joy will never be prone to becoming a workaholic', a rather more astute and useful observation than 'Joy's theology has improved substantially.' In Deptford, where life and work were inextricably entwined, where parishioners needed a great deal more than the usual level of clerical support, workaholism was an almost unavoidable professional hazard. The concerts, films and parties, the London social life outside the parish which Joy feared she might lose before she went to Cranmer Hall, now became a lifeline. 'I'd seen enough of vicarage life to know I didn't want to be destroyed by it. Too many clergy mess up their marriages, neglect their kids or drink themselves to death because they lose their sense of perspective. They're swallowed up by the role. I learned to preserve my real self, to switch off. I made sure I had a network of friends outside the church. I took in lodgers. Even now, I go down to the gym, where I don't have to talk to anyone.'

For the people of Milton Cross, having a young woman as their minister was never an issue. It riled her from time to time that she should have to call in her vicar to give the congregation communion, since she had so deeply identified with the life of the people and was looking after them in every other way. Nor did it make much sense to them. If she could take their weddings, christenings and funerals, why should a man suddenly appear at certain services to say the magic words? Despite her frustration, she never became a campaigning member of the Movement for the Ordination of Women. 'I didn't stand on the cathedral steps waving banners or placards. That's not my style. I pursued my goal in a different way. I felt I could best bring about change by working within the structures, using the gentle art of persuasion. I felt instinctively that some who had been put off by the more militant feminist approach would warm to someone simply sharing their experiences over a cup of tea.'

The opportunity came in 1990, two years after she went to live in Deptford, when she was elected to General Synod. At 29 she was the youngest clergy member. Initially, it was a very daunting experience. Several hundred members of the Church of England's equivalent of Parliament meet in a magnificent, domed circular chamber in Westminster. The rows graduate slightly upwards, less than in an amphitheatre, and all around, above, in the gallery, members of the press and public watch the sport below. It is what Joy calls 'a male arena', dominated by grey and black suits with the occasional flash of an episcopal purple shirt. The coughing and clearing of the throat, the assenting grunts or dissenting guffaws echoing around the vaulted ceiling are essentially male. So is the characteristic synodical slouch, legs stretched out in front, head well back and hands resting on well-fed stomach. Speakers are numbered and named with their diocese, and are predominantly, though not exclusively, men. 'I used to wonder what contribution I had to this very male, very clever theological environment. I remember walking into the tea room thinking, "What on earth am I going to talk about?" But actually, if you're brave enough to breach this initial barrier you discover these people are really quite nice and normal. I know that because my dad is one of them. I suppose that helped me not to feel too intimidated – even with bishops – so that I could hold an intelligent conversation and express my opinion on a debate without feeling they were looking down on me, or thinking, "What is that silly woman talking about?" But it does take some getting used to.'

One day will remain etched on her memory, the day in 1992 that the Synod agreed to the ordination of women to the priesthood. There was no doubt that the majority of the British public saw no reason why the vicar should not be female. From early morning the crowds had begun to gather outside Westminster with sandwiches and flasks, listening to the debate on their radios. As dusk began to fall on a dank, grey November afternoon the tension mounted. Thousands now waited in semi-silence for the results of the historic vote.

Inside Synod it had been a long, hard day with intense, passionate debate for and against the motion. It was impossible to tell which way the vote would go. The majority of the house of clergy seemed in favour. The house of laity was another matter altogether. The non-clerical members of Synod were often the most committed to maintaining the status quo. Joy wouldn't leave the chamber, not even for a cup of tea, for fear of missing a single moment. When, eventually, the members were asked to record their votes she was convinced the motion would be defeated.

The counters seemed to take an eternity. Conversation was unusually muted. 'The Archbishop of Canterbury got up to read the results with a deadpan face. We knew we had to have a two-thirds majority in both the houses. But there was such a complex numerical system that we couldn't work out what he was saying. Had we won or hadn't we? It was only when he said, "The motion is carried", that we knew for sure.'

Knowing what pain the result would inevitably mean for some, George Carey had asked that it be received with a dignified silence. 'It was hard. We so desperately wanted to cheer, to acknowledge such a significant moment in the life of the Church, but we had to sit there hanging on to our emotions.

Around me one or two women began to cry – with sheer relief. The first thought that went through my mind was, "Thank God we don't have spend the next ten years pouring our energy into this, when there are so many more important things for us to be doing in the parish."'

Outside Westminster there was no such restraint. At the announcement of the result the crowds broke into wild cheering. Later, when Joy walked out into the quadrangle the partying was well under way. People were laughing and dancing, champagne bottles were popping. 'That was the place to be. It was absolutely lovely.'

Eighty women were ordained in the Southwark diocese. They all went on retreat together. Some had only been waiting for a few months or years. Others had been waiting for almost the whole of their lives. 'We were like brides preparing for their big day. There was a tremendous sense of excitement, of solidarity, of celebration, as if we had been on a long journey together and had finally reached our destination. It was a real privilege to share the occasion with women who were older, wiser and more experienced than I was, women like my RE teacher at school, a deaconess who had had a profound influence on me when I was a teenager and had begun to wonder whether this moment would ever come.'

There were three ordination services, morning, afternoon and evening. Joy was priested in the afternoon in a cathedral packed with her friends and family. Her father was one of the three sponsoring clergy she invited to lay hands on her head. It was, she says, like a dream come true.

But the next day, Sunday, was better still as she celebrated Holy Communion for the first time – in her new parish in Streatham. Congregation and parishioners turned out in force to show their minister their love and support. 'We had to push back the doors to make room for everyone. It was a wonderful occasion.'

Being a priest, she admits, made little practical difference to the way she did her job on Monday morning. The liturgical duties could now be shared out equally with her male colleague. She could say the special words at communion, pronounce the absolution after the confession of sins, say a blessing, three ostensibly minor additions. 'But in fact it's bigger than that. People perceive you differently when you are a priest. It made sense of everything else I had been doing the rest of the week.'

And so she quietly continued with her work – until the introduction of a motion in Synod so challenged her integrity that she felt she could no longer keep silent. In many ways the ordination of women was the beginning, not the end, of a tidal wave of change. In its wake it left many disgruntled members, clergy and lay, who felt betrayed. The goalposts had shifted, they said, it was no longer the Church they knew. Some felt that in order to represent Christ, the priest must be male. Others said that since He appointed no female disciples, He can't have intended women to lead. Others still resorted to the apostle Paul, who forbade a woman to speak in church or have authority over a man. They all felt that a bishop who had ordained a woman would be tainted by it, and that the churches would be left without pastoral support. What they requested were several 'flying bishops', or 'provincial episcopal visitors', as they became known, who would keep themselves free from contamination and provide the necessary care.

The general feeling among those who had fought for women's ordination was, 'We've got what we want. Let's be gracious. Let's give them their special bishops.' To Joy, that smacked of collusion. 'The pastoral side of me, which likes unity, harmony and peace, which dislikes confrontation, felt we should give in to the request. The other side of me said, "This is an unacceptable compromise. It says women are somehow unclean. How can we have two kinds of bishops, one sort which has touched a woman and can no longer look after his clergy, and the other sort which hasn't?"'

So she rose to her feet and, in a prepared speech, said, 'Last year those of you who voted against the ordination of women said, "It's not you as women we're against. It's not a gender issue. It's theologically impossible for us to vote for you." Don't you think that felt like, "We don't want you"? And I just wonder if this was all about provision for people opposed to the ordination of black people, would the Synod be as gracious about it? What I'm voting against is inconsistency and bad theology – for fear that the Church may find herself bent so far backwards that she might fall over.'

She sat down to resounding applause. Some told her they were delighted she had had the courage to put what they felt into words. In the end it didn't sway the result. She knew it wouldn't. But it was an objection that had to be made as part of the debate. And now, with hindsight, she feels there is no doubt the decision proved retrograde and counter-productive.

In the gallery that day, watching her performance, was the writer of *Blackadder* and *Four Weddings and a Funeral*, Richard Curtis. He had written one episode of *The Vicar of Dibley* and was looking for further inspiration.

⌒

Streatham is a far cry from the lush green pastures of Dibley. Immanuel and St Andrew's, where she came as assistant priest in 1993, is a Victorian monstrosity parked on the frenetically busy main road, blackened by years of soot, grime and fumes. Whatever serenity it once knew vanished long ago when its surroundings sank from chic suburbia into inner-London sprawl. This is bedsit land, where the elderly eke out their days and people with mental health problems come to terms with the lonely and often frightening implications of 'care in the community'.

The church's shopfront is the Beehive Community Café. Here blond and beautiful Jessica, the Amazon of a manageress, cooks up casseroles, snacks and big fried breakfasts for £1.50. The delicious smell wafting incongruously down the road from the local church draws in passers-by, second-hand traders, the residents of hostels with nowhere to go after 10 am, the elderly and ill, too tired and frail to prepare a meal at home, the unemployed, left to their own devices day after day. They sit round the tables, which are cheerfully decked in gingham cloths, with china salt and pepper pots. They unburden themselves to

Jessica, whose heart is big enough to absorb the whole of London, let alone this small corner of it. They chat, stay warm, while away the endless, lonely hours.

It was here, after morning prayers, that I met Joy. She was wearing blue denim jeans and a white angora sweater. Her hair was tied back in a ponytail, which swung, with her earrings, when she spoke. She looked incredibly young and anything but vicar-like. Our conversation was interrupted dozens of times by people who just wanted 'a quick word', about a problem with benefits, or a friend who needed a visit, or an upset with the landlady. She is gentle, very soft-spoken, and gives her complete attention to whoever needs it.

That, she claims, though I would never have guessed it, is an acquired art. She worries she may not be a very good listener, especially on Sundays, when so much is going on around her that she goes into major organisational mode. 'When I get stressed I get bossy. I hear myself beginning to sound like a schoolmistress. I rush round sorting everything and everyone out. I have to make a conscious effort to stop and be aware of what's going on. I don't find it easy to pray either. That's why morning prayers are an important discipline for me.'

She takes me on a tour of the building. It is standard church-hall interior, stark, unappealing and badly in need of restoration. 'Regeneration' is the word Joy uses. Her face lights up as she looks around. She can see what I can't – potential. With the neighbouring United Reformed Church they have just com-pleted a parish audit to assess the needs of the community, and whether they, the Church, can help. 'There were no surprises. The elderly, the unemployed, and particularly people with mental health problems all need facilities. Care in the community is a good idea in principle, but it doesn't really work. Many are not cared for, they don't feel secure, they're not taking their medication and they are surrounded by people who cannot handle their strange behaviour. If we can find the financial backing, either from local businesses, the Church Urban Fund or from the lottery – though that is controversial since it bleeds money from vulnerable members of communities like this –

then in two years' time we could come up with a first-rate community centre.'

A quick estimation tells me it will take at least £1 million to transform this archaic site into anything vaguely useful. I don't want to dampen her enthusiasm but I wonder whether she isn't simply shielding the government from facing up to its responsibilities. 'The government should fill the gaps in the community,' she agrees, 'and the Church should pressurise it to do so, but if we wait until it does, we may wait forever. Besides, we are responsible for our neighbours. I can't understand people who say religion and politics don't mix. Politics is just the organised life of the city. If Christians were not commanded to improve the lives of ordinary people, then I don't know what they think they're doing.'

She came to Streatham having heard of the vacancy and feeling desperate for a change. The bishop had been surprised by her request. 'But Joy,' he said, 'isn't this a sideways move? Why do you want to be an assistant minister? Shouldn't you be looking for your own parish?' She told him she thought being a minister meant being a servant. 'I was tired of working on my own. I desperately wanted to be part of a team, to have others who would affirm me and build up my gifts again.'

Two years later, in fact, her colleague moved on to a new job, and she was left in charge as acting vicar. 'I prefer working with others. I think that's a very female thing. We're instinctively more collaborative than men – though not automatically so. Taking on a traditionally male role, it's important women don't also take on a male way of doing things. I think that's what I was trying to say to the bishop, that seeing a career in the Church in terms of promotion is male, rather than Christian.'

On the other hand, the bishop must be receiving some very mixed messages. It isn't easy finding suitable jobs for women priests. Many churches looking for a new vicar state a preference for a male, married at that. Joy is part of a group of women priests in her diocese who meet to share that and other problems. On one occasion they invited the bishop, and asked him to ensure women were represented in roles of high responsibility. He agreed. He is very supportive. 'One day soon,' says Joy, 'we may no longer need to meet, but meanwhile we have to go on pushing the boundaries, make sure we remain high-profile or we will simply be passed over.'

Some of her senior female colleagues aim to get to the top, and have the ability to get there, but she herself has no such ambition. She has, she admits, a problem with the whole concept of power. It came to a head when she was invited, with three other women priests, to represent the Church of England at a consultation on 'Women's Leadership in the Anglican Communion' in Washington, DC, chaired by the Rt Revd Penny Jamieson, Bishop of Auckland in New Zealand. The prospect filled her with a certain amount of trepidation. In her mind she had an image of dauntingly powerful American women fearlessly making their way in the Church, pioneers in inclusive language and feminist theology, the first to become priests, then bishops. 'The caution I felt probably had something to do with the fact that we had spent a long time in England trying to calm the fears of our male colleagues, reassuring them that we, the women of the Church of England, were not like the more extreme American feminists, and they needn't worry.'

Her stereotype proved false. Far from extreme, the women she feared were understanding and supportive. Some were persecuted and in great pain. One, who had been appointed to a high position in the Episcopalian Church, had been the victim of an organised campaign to discredit her. Letters, with a forged signature, were sent round the diocese saying she was resigning because of a drug habit. She had survived – but just.

As they shared their experiences a deep bond developed between women from America, Canada, New Zealand, England and South Africa. Hesitantly, Joy described her own ambivalence about being in a position of authority and responsibility for the first time and, to her relief, others understood exactly what she was trying to say. She began to think she might actually be comfortable being called a feminist, particularly when feminism was defined as 'the firm conviction that we male and female were made equal before God'.

It was an exploration of the meaning of power that she found most helpful of all. 'At first it felt very strange to be speaking about exercising power. The word had such negative associations for me – male, exclusive and hierarchical. I was much more comfortable with the good old Church of England model of "the servant leader". But I began to see that power could be an enabling force, something which can be given away. It's a myth that there is only a limited amount to go round. The proper exercise of power creates more power and more creative ways of using it. It's at its most life-transforming when it grows out of prayer and is a reflection of Christ working through us.'

A South African priest gave a moving example of how a group of apparently powerless women in her neighbourhood used power positively. A child of a poor family was being sexually abused by her father. The mother knew what was happening and was afraid, angry and in despair. To go to the police and have her husband arrested would leave her without a source of income and, ultimately, with no home. One day the women of the village got together, walked to the man's house, and simply stood, face to face with him, in angry silence. It was a very powerful gesture. Since no words were spoken he had nothing to fight. In their silent solidarity the women had become a protective force. They had told him in no uncertain terms that his behaviour was not going to be tolerated.

Joy came home with an increased realisation of the contribution she, as a woman, could make to the Church. 'Women priests are pioneering. We're the first. We're trailblazers. Everything is up for grabs. We can introduce all kinds of new ideas.' At a time when many parishioners cohabit rather than marry she would like to encourage them towards a public commitment by putting an affordable marriage package together – service, dress, buffet, cake, photos, all for £500, with a small profit margin. The resources, she says, are in the Church. It's just a matter of getting round to doing it.

'God has to be good for women. He offers us the opportunity to fulfil our potential. Women are so often held back by the social structures, stereotyping, discrimination, abusive relationships or the sins of others. God makes us whole. We are great reconcilers, often bringing harmony in the midst of chaos and conflict. We should be liberating one another. At its best, that is what the Church is all about. At its worst it colludes in holding women back.'

Some churches are good for women, some are not, she says. Like all women priests, she has suffered her fair share of the latter. 'My own colleagues have all been very supportive and enabling – often pushing me further than I wanted to go. But there are local clergy who refuse to take part in ecumenical events if I'm invited to preach. It's hardly a good example to the next generation.'

I wonder how that kind of rejection feels, and whether she is used to it and now takes it in her stride.

'It still makes me very bolshy,' she says.

'Is it a genuine matter of conscience, or bigotry?'

'I think for many Catholics it's a matter of tradition. But I have a hunch that if a man, particularly a young man, is really antagonistic to women priests, it can reflect some problem with his sexuality – from childhood, in his marriage, or in his orientation.'

Every institution, we agree, has its awkward, prickly people. Is she ever tempted to leave it to its rather fatuous internal squabbles?

'For me there's a difference between the institution, which I find quite difficult, and God. I stay in the institution because I believe in a God Who isn't bound by it.'

We are interrupted again, and she decides to take me back to her house, so that we can finish our conversation in peace. It's a small semi in a quiet suburban street about a kilometre from the church. The interior is anything but suburban. Her choice of decor reflects individuality and character, polished floorboards, interesting hangings, comfortable sofas, bold primary colours. In the sitting room one wall is pink, the other green, and it works. The house is peaceful, quiet after the buzz of the Beehive. A French window leads into a secluded, leafy garden. She has created a haven.

On a wall in the hallway hangs a large, arty photograph of the faces of Joy and Dawn French, side by side, in soft focus, both in black shirt and dog collar. Joy describes how for some days she kept getting messages on her answering machine from someone called Richard Curtis, who said he was a writer and wanted to speak to her. 'He was terribly modest, never mentioned *Blackadder*' and, since she gets a great number of calls from journalists, she never bothered to get back to him.

When he eventually managed to catch her, he explained that he had written the first episode of a comedy series for the BBC about a woman vicar, and needed a little bit of extra help. He was entirely convinced that women were needed in the Church. It seemed perverse to him to put middle-aged men in charge. Mothers were so much more interested than fathers in their children's romances, joys and heartaches. To do women priests justice he wanted to create a real human being, not a fictional cardboard cut-out. Joy was the right kind of age and the exact image he had in mind. Could he come and see her?

He came, and brought Dawn French with him. Dawn visited Streatham several times to watch Joy take christenings and funerals and preach, but she appeared to want to know more than the practical basics of the job. 'She wanted to know what made me tick, why was I a Christian, what made me want to be a priest? She was very bouncy, very quippy in the car when we travelled from one place to another. But she's also highly professional. And a serious thinker.'

Did Joy feel the series reflected the real issues?

'I think it was a very positive introduction to women's ministry. The vicar of Dibley is funnier than I am, and yet, in an uncanny way, she was very like me – in the way I relate to people, the way I cut my hair, and even in the clothes I wear.'

I remember the day I saw Joy Carroll for the first time, at a meeting for women priests in Synod. It struck me then that she was wearing the same kind of long pinafore dress I had seen on Dawn French and thought it must be coincidence. Nothing as uncalculated, of course, with the BBC.

Much is made of the fact that Dibley's vicar, while having the normal sexual appetites of any healthy young woman, hasn't a man in tow. It cannot be easy to meet Mr Right once there is a dog collar around the clerical neck. 'If I'm out socially, I hate it if people introduce me as "Joy, the vicar". It's a real conversation killer. People are not interested in getting to know you after that because they attach an image to you of what they think you should be like.' Although she is unmarried at the moment, she is at pains to stress that it's not because she is a priest. There have been men, she says with a twinkle in her eye, many of them, and there may well be "an interest" on the horizon at just this moment. 'Like many career women, I'm independent, opinionated and single-minded. I think men find that difficult.'

Does that cause problems for her when working with a male colleague?

'When a man and a woman work together, as they often do in the Church, they have to be fairly secure about their own identity, so that they can play different roles when it's necessary, take it in turns to be the decision-maker or dependent. It's only difficult when one of them feels threatened. But I suppose that's just as true when a man and a woman are in a partnership.'

If she ever finds the right partner she insists it will be for her, not for the Church. 'I feel strongly about that. I don't have a job description at the back of my mind which says, "has to be in church every Sunday, arranges flowers, and bakes cakes". There have been some horrendous expectations of vicars' wives.'

But what about their expectations of the clergy, I ask her, to be saintly, gracious, available, smiling? But I know the answer in advance. It is there in the disarming way she looks straight at you, plays with her ponytail or holds out the palms of her hands. She will only be who she is, an approachable, vulnerable young woman. 'I do feel overwhelmed sometimes at people's expectations of me and I do feel humble when they come to me to talk about their spiritual problems.'

Come they do, many who feel much more comfortable baring their soul to a woman than to a man. But then Joy is an easy, outgoing, eminently 'normal' human being. A few days after Synod's decision to ordain women, the *Daily Mail* ran a feature on the Revd Carroll, complete with photograph of her in mini skirt, and the inevitable earrings. Several letters of complaint turned up in her post – from both men and women. Their problem? They couldn't cope with the mix of body and spirit. 'Men cover their sexuality with black or grey suits, by being bland. A woman can't – not, for example, if she's pregnant.'

Confronting this deep, unnatural ambivalence is, she feels, at the heart of what women have to offer the Church. 'I think women priests are going to have a profound affect on the Church in the long run, on this tendency to separate body and soul, what is spiritual from what is not, and one of the things women will bring is more of an integration and wholeness. I think it's going to make the whole of the priesthood much more accessible to modern women and therefore the human race in general.'

———————————

Joy Carroll is now married to Jim Wallis, the well-known American Christian political activist. She and Jim and their son, Luke, live in Columbia Heights, Washington, an area known for its social problems, and they continue to fight for a better deal for the world's poor.

CHAPTER 10

The Chief Executive: Angela Sarkis

A stone's throw from number 7 Millbank, separated by an exclusive restaurant and health club, is number 1, home of the Church Commissioners, they who in the late 1980s managed to divest the Church of England, on paper at any rate, of £800 million in one or two unfortunate property deals, thereby putting my husband's precious pension at risk. But I haven't come on any personal pecuniary pilgrimage. I have come to meet the newly appointed Chief Executive of that other, rather different organisation also housed here, the one committed to bringing hope to the poor and voiceless, and a strange, somewhat uncomfortable bedfellow for this world of capitalist, high-finance dabbling, the Church Urban Fund.

From the outside, both buildings are serene, elegant, standing proudly on the banks of the Thames, but there any similarity ends. Inside, number 1 is as different from number 7 as Wormwood Scrubs from Buckingham Palace. No purposeful, pushing parliamentarians, bureaucrats or civil servants in pin-stripe suits, no smoky glass screen separating the officials from the plebs, little sense of the great matters of state being decided in this location.

There is security, but it is relaxed, genial, and 'Just sign the visitors' book'. I am consigned to a heavy, weary-looking armchair, marooned in the middle of a high-ceilinged, stone-floored entrance hall. Pinned to a board nearby a notice reads, 'Stuff for CUF. Do you want to do something meaningful with your lunch break? We need volunteers to fill 1,000 envelopes with our quarterly newsletter. Make new friends. You'll be surprised to discover the fun that can be had from stuffing and sticking.'

It's a terribly jolly Anglican notice, incongruous in the austere surroundings. An unworthy thought passes through my mind, an ever-present hazard for a clergy wife, 'How typical of the C of E to do things on the cheap.' I dismiss it. Think positive. They obviously do. The Church Urban Fund has far better things to do with its money than spend it on administration.

While I wait, two excited children on half-term, harassed mother in tow, rush past looking for Dad. A man in overalls appears, pats them proudly on the head and dismisses them with a meaningful nod at the woman. An echoey silence is restored, interrupted only by the heavy footfall of one or two occasional grave, grey-haired gentlemen in glasses and pin-striped trousers. A purple shirt or two with tousled head shambles past, newspaper tucked under the arm, cross swinging across the chest. The episcopal hierarchy peer at me with curiosity, searching some internal database for a possible identity. The Church of England is after all just one big, happy family.

Into the heart of that family, just a few months ago, like a long-lost child given up for adoption, bounced Angela Sarkis. Her appointment as Chief Executive of the Church Urban Fund worried some, shocked a few and filled the visionary with a sense of excitement. She was, after all, a rank outsider in every sense of the word: a woman in secular employment, a Pentecostal and black. The Church Urban Fund, like almost all of the Church of England, had always been managed by white, middle- or vaguely upper-class males. Her selection, said one Trustee, was a vote for fresh inspiration, radical new ideas, against the status quo. It was bound to unsettle one or two of the more traditional old uncles.

As for Angela, she sees herself a personal embodiment of the restoration of a much-needed rich cultural diversity, forfeited in the 1950s, when an established, rather bourgeois British church rejected the Caribbean children who came expecting acceptance and instead found marginalisation, leaving them with little alternative but to set up their own churches. As a Jew in the Church, conscious of a longer, centuries-old rejection, I have a deep sense of identification with Angela's feelings. She is someone I very much want to meet.

Ignoring the large, old-fashioned iron cage of a lift in its centre, Michelle, Angela's PA, escorts me up an imposing circular staircase and along kilometres of mosaic-floored, oak-panelled corridor to a suite of offices at one extreme end of the premises, separated from the rest like an afterthought by heavy glass fire doors. Beyond the doors the atmosphere changes. It is light, bright, whitewashed. The corridor is heavily carpeted. In rooms on either side, groups of people are bent, heads down, in easy discussion. Angela's room is at the end of the corridor. Her door, like every other, is unnamed. No sign says 'Chief Executive'. The room has been transformed, I have been warned in advance, much less civil service, no more in-trays piled high with paper, no more dark and heavy desk and leatherette furniture.

As she walks across to me greeting me like a long-lost friend though we are meeting for the first time, I take in the bright, modern pine desk unit, newly painted walls, family photographs – and a strikingly attractive lady with a broad smile, smartly yet comfortably dressed, with the inevitable pearl earrings, as necessary for the executive woman, said my *Good Housekeeping* magazine, as a decent tie is for the man. She beckons me to join her at a simple, round pine table in one corner of the room beneath a large window looking out over London. 'Lots of coffee, Michelle, thanks, now and in an hour. I think we're going to need it.'

'She is wonderful,' she says with admiration, as Michelle discreetly leaves the room. 'A first-rate PA is a must. That's why I brought her with me from my last job. Now you know how brazen I am.'

I also know she doesn't take herself too seriously, a professional hazard for anyone in management, let alone someone peddling such sobering issues. I warm to her at once. She is open, natural and vivacious, makes no attempt to patronise, or pull rank, appears completely relaxed about who she is and what she has to do. Her enthusiasm for the new job is infectious. She is very aware of the privilege of heading an organisation that, since its launch in 1987 in response to the *Faith in the City* report, has given £23 million in grants to over 14,000 projects all over the country. She's proud of all CUF (she pronounces it affectionately 'cuff') has achieved, proprietorial – surprisingly so for someone coming in from outside – except that, however it may seem, she doesn't see herself as an outsider. She is a Christian first, a Pentecostal second. 'I worship in a Pentecostal church because it suits me. It's a way of life. But CUF had to come from the Church of England, the established Church. It would never have had the same impact, never have been as effective, if it had come from the Pentecostals. The Anglican Church can draw in and work with other churches in attacking poverty together.'

As a social worker, most of her professional life was spent under the political leadership of Margaret Thatcher, whose basic philosophy was anathema to her. 'Thatcherism said, "It's out there if you want it, so go and get it." But we all know it was a lie.' While an ever-deepening chasm opened between the haves and have-nots, the Church remained deafeningly silent. Until 1985. The *Faith in the City* report finally put the Church on the offensive and saved it, in Angela's eyes, from becoming a sad irrelevancy. At last it not only recognised the problem, but also wanted to be part of the solution. 'It was ready at last to take the gospel to the driest parts of the land, to go beyond all the normal boundaries and reach people where they were.'

CUF's strength, she says, has been its versatility. No two projects are ever identical. Each reflects a particular local need, and that means weighing up the dozens of requests for funding that land on her desk almost daily. 'We don't just throw money at any old problem. Before we give a grant we make sure a project is relevant, supported by local people and has a real chance of success. The aim to involve churches and local communities in working together, learning from and enriching the other. It's about giving local people, who often feel voiceless, a new confidence and power. It's a bottom-up approach.'

From her personal perspective her job is a tremendous

opportunity to enable a motley band of civil servants with administrative responsibility to be men and women with vision for all CUF can achieve. 'None of us can get away from loving our neighbour as ourselves. Christians have a duty to work with the disadvantaged as Christ did – but that doesn't mean going out converting everyone. It will mean different things to different people. For some it will mean financial giving, for others voluntary work or a certain career path, and for yet others becoming a campaigner.'

I don't ask which she is. I don't have to. It is written all over her face, a face that would be hard-pressed to hide any emotion. For her the real challenge is not overseeing countless different community projects, vital though they may be – but a chance, now that CUF has earned its credibility, to enable the Church to speak on poverty issues at national and government level. The poor and vulnerable, she maintains, have been sanitised by politicians. They have had the lid put on them to make them invisible. Her aim, quite simply, is to take the lid off.

Her strong sense of calling is unmistakable. I am here in her office, propelled by her reputation for straight talking and the interesting, mixed reaction to her appointment. 'I was headhunted,' she says coyly. 'I never sought or asked for this post, but I've found one which demands and uses all my skills. Looking back, I've been so lucky. I've identified with all the jobs I have done. But this one has a Christian dimension which the others hadn't. It's as if I was prepared and waiting just for this.'

Her parents were from Jamaica. Her father, a saddler by name and profession, was a skilled leatherworker and good businessman, her mother an efficient, clever seamstress, but they were lured away from the island of palm and mango trees in the 1950s British government recruitment drive with promises of a better life. The thousands of immigrants from the West Indies who poured into Britain to take their chances soon witnessed the destruction of all their dreams. The promises were vain and empty, the standard of living little, if at all, better than at home. All that was available to them were low-paid, low-status jobs and inadequate, poor-quality housing. White communities were suspicious and unwelcoming. There was open discrimination, often in the streets.

The sense of shock, of cultural disorientation and bitter disappointment were more than many could bear. Some had come for the adventure, intending to make a bit of money, then return and die in peace in their beloved homeland. The reality was very different. Once here, it was hard enough to find the wherewithal to survive, let alone the fare to go home.

Adversity forces people together and black communities supported one another. Angela's father decided on Nottingham, where a sizeable black population had already settled and where he had one or two useful contacts. British Rail offered him a job almost at once, and there he stayed for the rest of his working life, being promoted slowly and painfully through the system. It was not what he had planned or anticipated. The pay and status were hardly a fair reflection of his skills, but providing a family with security, paying the rent and basic survival were higher on the agenda than personal satisfaction.

By the time Angela was six months old he had secured enough money to send for his wife. Angela, the daughter he had never seen, was left in Jamaica with her grandmother. The overcrowded house in Nottingham her father shared with many others was hardly suitable for a child. While she enjoyed what she remembers as an idyllic childhood, cosseted and spoiled by her adoring grandparents and large band of aunts and uncles, her parents struggled to come to terms with the dank climate, depressing surroundings and open hostility that constituted their strange new life.

Her mother found a job in a sewing factory, but it was not dressmaking as she knew it, creating a high-quality garment from beginning to end. As one member of a production line she was condemned to a stultifying week of side seams or hems or knicker elastic, without the satisfaction of ever seeing the finished product. But she was fast, which was a huge advantage in piece-work and would have been quite lucrative if she hadn't given away so much to friends she felt were in greater need. 'Goodness, they worked hard,' Angela sighs, reflecting on her parents' stamina in those early years in Britain, 'But they would never have coped with unemployment. They instilled in us the value of work. I think I get my work ethic from them. It's a bit of a problem at times, this inner drive, and not the best of the qualities I inherited.'

Two years later another daughter was born and Angela's mother was faced with major child-care problems. 'Black women took it for granted that they would work. That's what they came to Britain to do. But it caused a great deal of animosity.' Respectable middle-class white women did not go out to work. The working class women who did, resented the arrival of an industrious, cheaper workforce. They were hardly going to look after their babies. Furthermore, there were no laws on child care. Black women, who often gave birth in appallingly inadequate living conditions, were forced in desperation to make whatever child-minding arrangements they could, and some of their experiences were nothing less than hair-raising.

The Church was no more accommodating. At home in the West Indies Angela's parents, like many Jamaicans, had been very active members of the well-established Pentecostal New Testament Church. No such denomination existed in Nottingham, so they tried hard to integrate into local white churches, with little success. The message was as clear as if it had been spoken. 'Come and look, but don't expect to play a major part.' There was no place for their culture or their gifts in this stalwart, reactionary arm of the British Establishment, and they left to become founder members of the Nottingham New Testament Church.

'At immense cost to a white, British church,' I prompt. 'The music, the colour, the dynamism of that rich culture was lost to us forever.'

Angela agrees and disagrees. 'It was lost – but not forever. In the 1950s the Church was in great danger of becoming a dying institution. So many different groups felt excluded. Because of my background I understand the resentment that breeds. Progress involved opening wide its arms, being prepared to have meaning for all kinds of people's lives. That's what CUF is doing, bridging the old boundaries, taking the Church into every community, bringing back diversity.'

I see now why, as the daughter of those passed over by the Church, she is so excited about being CUF's Chief Executive. It is an extraordinary about-turn, a full circle, almost an admission and repentance of past wrongs, a restoration of what was lost. It is certainly no coincidence.

In August 1962, when she was seven years old, leaving her much-loved grandparents behind, she flew alone on a plane to England, feeling very vulnerable, and desperately wishing she didn't have to go. 'I had never met my father or sister before. The first thing I realised was that I had a broad West Indian accent. My sister sounded terribly English. There we were, two girls used to exclusive attention, now sharing our busy parents. Inevitably it meant a certain amount of sibling rivalry.'

England was a profound shock. In her childish fantasies Angela had imagined something far grander than life in Jamaica, and found it hard to reconcile the reality of the semi-detached in a rather grey, built-up, working-class area. At home in the Caribbean they had had family land, wide open spaces, lush scenery. Here everything seemed restricted, poky, confined. She made up her mind she would go back to Jamaica one day. It was the goal that sustained her through the difficult early years. 'The dream didn't finally disappear until very late. I counted every year from seven until I was 14. That was when I realised I had lived longer here than there. I was staying, so I'd better get on with life.'

Above all, she remembers being made to feel different. Other children pointed at her hair, mocked her accent, called her names. That first frozen winter she was initiated to her new school by being dragged face-down along an ice slide in the school playground. Her face was scarred for some time. 'I saw in that moment what discrimination looked like for me, and made up my mind never to give in to it.'

Children grow up much quicker in the West Indies. From an

early age they are encouraged to share in the running of the family home, use their initiative and make decisions. Angela was in fact very independent and mature for her years compared to her classmates, which enabled her to stand on her own two feet. Being part of a loving, close-knit West Indian church family also boosted her instinctive self-confidence. 'It wasn't just a place to go to on Sundays. It was my life. Black-led churches really empower members of the congregation. Most people can have a go at most things. By the time I was nine I was singing in front of large audiences and never felt intimidated by it. My children haven't had that kind of opportunity, and it makes me quite sad.'

'Children are marginalised in our society?' I query.

'A bit of an embarrassment, really,' she says conspiratorially.

Angela's extrovert personality was a useful weapon against the harsher realities of racism. 'The more I felt under attack, the more I projected myself. I was mad. I used to stand on the top of the school steps in the lunch break and shout, "Roll up, roll up, opportunity knocks", and put on my own singing and dancing show. I probably missed my real vocation in life.'

Few, if any children from Angela's estate went to the local grammar school. By the time her opportunity came, the system had been changed. The eleven-plus was abolished and the grammar and secondary modern schools amalgamated into what was called a 'bilateral school', an excuse for two distinctive streams, two schools within the same building. Angela automatically found herself in the lower stream, but she didn't stay there for long. 'I felt I had a responsibility to achieve. I wanted to make my parents and my community proud of me and I applied myself. But all the time there was a kind of undercurrent from the staff which went, "Black girls don't get into the grammar stream. If you don't work you know where you'll end up." Expectations of us were so low. Girls like me never went to university.'

When she was 15, as an attempt to help her find her future life's work, the school arranged for a trip around a sewing factory, specialising in inserting elastic. 'I was good at sewing, like my mother. So I suppose I can hardly blame them for jumping to conclusions. But I took one look and said, "No thanks", and went to Baseford College.' She left three years later with ten O levels, three A levels, a place at Leeds University and the intention of teaching theology. 'My faith was my life, a powerful motivating force throughout my teenage years.'

At ten she had responded to an altar call in her church to become a Christian in her own right. 'Altar calls were a regular feature of our church life but, nonetheless, that was my very own dramatic moment. Something undeniably real happened as I walked forward. It was world-changing. I was a different person. I no longer felt alone. And I suppose that sense of no longer being alone is still the fuelling passion for all I do today.'

Living in Leeds opened up a new world. She went to the cinema for the first time. Her parents had been strict and Angela had never been exposed before to life outside the Christian community. Many of her old school friends had been expelled, or were pregnant, caught up in the vortex of a social system that would drag them down every time they aspired to something more. But she had not socialised with them, or met them out of school, had not understood the forces that denied them the chance of anything better.

In Leeds, confronted on all sides by urban deprivation, she began to wonder at what age a person's future was signed and sealed. Where was Christ in the horrendous social problems she now saw? It was not in her nature to be a passive observer. Theology was of no use unless it was practical. While other first-year theology students walked by, Angela became a volunteer in the probation services, helping to run Saturday clubs for young people who didn't do well at school. 'It wasn't that they were not academic. They were just demoralised. All self-worth had been removed. If a child feels excluded, it will be excluded. It seemed to me that the gospel was about teaching people to value themselves, and that may mean cutting through bureaucratic red tape to help them do so.'

At the end of her first year the theology degree meta-morphosed into a joint degree with sociology. 'It was probably the thought of all that Hebrew which put me off,' she says, raising her eyes to heaven. 'I'm a woman of action, not an academic.'

A two-year postgraduate course in probation work at Leicester University, significant predominantly for the first tentative signs of a deepening friendship with fellow student, Ted Sarkis, launched Angela into ten years of social work in London. 'Working with those who had offended against themselves and society truly was my abiding passion. I knew, because of my own working-class background, how easily people go off the rails and then can't get back on. I felt Christians had a responsibility to go to the least cosy, least fashionable places, offering love and hope.'

Neither marriage nor motherhood deflected her from her calling, though they did cramp her style somewhat in their own inimitable way. She married Ted Sarkis in 1980, after a three-year courtship. 'Ted is Armenian, and came from a more middle-class family, which meant we had all kinds of racial and cultural issues to work through together. I wasn't bothered about how other people would view our relationship. I can deal with others if I feel secure. That's why we had to be clear.' In the end they decided that Angela had outgrown aspects of her background, while Ted had rejected chunks of his. On the one hand they represented a whole spectrum of race and culture, on the other they met in the middle. 'It was a very happy meeting,' she says on reflection.

Matthew was born in 1983, and Laura in 1985. At this point Angela leaps up and presents me with the family photograph. Looking straight back at me are two beautiful, round-eyed children, the very picture of wholeness and happiness. 'I'm a proud, possessive mother, you see. My children are immensely precious to me.'

From now on her loyalties would be divided as never before.

The history of black women is a long stony path, trodden barefoot. If white women have bloodied their fists beating on the glass ceiling, black women have bruised and broken toes from the countless sharp obstacles waiting to impede their progress. Within their own community they are the lynchpin, strong and powerful, bearing burdens of responsibility that would break the back of lesser mortals – for their spouses, their siblings, their children, grandchildren, parents and elderly neighbours. They are ministers in the church, sustaining it in every area of its life, from preaching and teaching to cleaning and cooking. They provide for their families financially. It is marginally easier for black women to get jobs than their men. They present less of a threat. For outside of their own community, few expectations are made of them and they have little status. To succeed with such a backpack, to climb painfully to the professional top, usually requires exceptional determination.

Angela doesn't see herself as being particularly determined or ambitious. 'I have achieved because I work hard and believe in what I do – that's a winning combination.' Many doors have opened for her. Some she walked through, some she walked past, especially when the children were young. 'I didn't seek promotion then. I hadn't the confidence. I felt I would be achieving at their or Ted's expense. It's the old guilt thing all mothers face.'

Nonetheless she continued to work herself almost into the ground, admitting it's only what all mothers do, since they want to give their children as much time as they can. She went back to work when Matthew was eight months old, having gone to great lengths to arrange the best possible child care, her mother's bad experience all those years ago never far from her hypersensitive imagination. 'I was terribly torn. I wanted to be a good mother. As a social worker I had seen what a lack of proper parenting could do. If I hadn't felt passionately about what I did, hadn't felt I was helping to change people's lives, I'd have been sorely tempted to give up. Money was not the issue. I was passionate about mothering and passionate about the work I was doing.'

Laura's arrival compounded her ambivalence. She took a year off and then returned to work only part-time. Even then she felt anxious about it, relaxing a little when her mother offered to travel down from Nottingham on the coach every Sunday night, staying with the children until Thursday evening. 'It was a huge sacrifice, not only for my mother, but for my father too, who had to do without her during the week. On the other hand, it was very consistent with the West Indian way of life. My mum had missed out on those very significant years of my life. Now she had the chance to enjoy them in my children instead.' She dismisses the highly mobile nuclear family, self-sufficient, exclusive, as a particularly sad reflection of contemporary British life. 'There are, however, ways round it.'

The arrangement lasted for about a year. When Laura was two Angela took a week off work to settle her into a nursery. On the first day, she went to collect her after an hour or so, having decided to introduce her to the idea gently, but Laura protested and demanded to stay. 'I saw then who had the problem. Laura was secure and independent, while I was thinking, "Charming, my child doesn't need me." So I had a week's holiday instead.'

By now the couple were both beginning to experience a certain dissatisfaction with their work in the probation services. Ted felt he needed a new challenge, which rising through the hierarchy wouldn't give him, and Angela became convinced that she was doing little more than sticking a plaster on an open sore. Her youngest clients were 17, and that was already too late to enable them to change their lives. While Ted opted for a career in law, later becoming involved in a large amount of legal aid work, Angela got a job as a manager with the Family Service Unit, a voluntary charity used by the social and probation services, providing therapy for families in crisis. She was now in charge of a team of social workers, counsellors and therapists, who together had the skills that could enable families to handle major behavioural problems. 'It was tremendously exciting. Here at last was a chance to go to the root of the problem, not merely deal with the symptom. It seemed a much more holistic approach. An individual young man, for example, was not just an offender. He was a son, a brother or a father as well. He had as many roles as I have, as we all have, and deserved to be seen in that wider context. You have to get deeply involved in people's lives if you want to help them to change, and my faith told me that it was possible for people who felt valued at last to recognise their responsibility and realise they were accountable to those around them.'

At the FSU she discovered her natural flair for management, despite the fact that each subsequent rise meant further distance from the actual practice of her chosen career. 'I value practitioners because I love the actual hands-on. But management gives the opportunity to be involved in policy-making, which is crucial. We need both. A manager who loses her grip on practice is no longer a good manager. There are few practice-focussed managers around today. Because I am black, a woman and working-class, my roots are buried deep in the earth of injustice and disadvantage. It's unlikely that practice will ever become irrelevant to me. It's part of my life.'

Less than three years later a new challenge came her way in the shape of the Intermediate Treatment Fund, a government quango, which gave grants to fund a host of schemes for young offenders or those in danger of offending. The government was winding down its support. As assistant director, Angela had 18 months in which to turn the organisation into an independent charity, hanging on to as many grants as she could. She succeeded. The new charity was renamed Divert and Angela became its director.

'I slogged my guts out for Divert,' she says with feeling. It was a job that gave greater scope for her communication and public-speaking skills. The little girl who had stood at the top of the school steps, entertaining the playground, now enthused government ministers, diplomats, lords and bureaucrats for a project, which, under normal circumstances, was hardly likely to touch their hearts, let alone their pockets. 'My mother always said I should be on the stage.'

Her undoubted ability to inspire and to communicate unpalatable, unpopular truths in a compelling way, began to bring her a certain amount of attention and respect. In 1996 the Church Urban Fund was in its tenth year. Its success was unquestioned, but some within its ranks felt this was no time for resting on past laurels. The most successful ventures run out of steam without fresh drive and impetus. It needed new, visionary leadership.

After five years with Divert, Angela was approached and asked if she would consider applying for the post of Chief Executive. 'It was unexpected, daunting in many ways – yet, in another, obvious. I'd been aware for some time that working for a secular charity would never fully satisfy me. It took no account of a spiritual dimension. CUF, on the other hand, was openly committed to tackling the moral and spiritual malaise in urban priority areas, as well as the chronic economic, physical hardships facing individuals. It seemed to me an irresistible opportunity to have a prophetic voice.'

On an average day she's in the office at about 8.15 in the morning, sorting out paperwork, seeing key staff members, responding to messages, before she is sucked into the relentless, inevitable merry-go-round of meetings that seem an essential part of any higher managerial job. 'I prioritise,' she says unashamedly, when I ask her about the dangers of falling victim to meeting-itis. 'It's important to go to the right meetings.' Being a prophetic voice means taking the Church into the most influential places, where national policies are conceived, although often aborted at embryo stage. But whether it's the Association of Charitable Foundations, a political or church gathering, a staff meeting or a strategic review with the Trustees, 'I always know what I want from a meeting in advance, and get a tremendous buzz when I can involve other people in facilitating CUF's long-term plans.'

In the afternoon she'll try to fit in a trip to one of the dioceses to see some of CUF's projects in action. It may not be what was expected of a chief bureaucrat, but these chances to escape the ivory tower, she tells me with almost schoolgirl delight, are inspirational to her and keep her focussed. She loves meeting people and learning. Her first visit was to the Wakefield diocese, where she went to see a church that had been completely restructured inside so that it could provide facilities for the local Asian and Afro-Caribbean communities, becoming a focal point for the neighbourhood. The vicar told her how the project had earned the church respect, giving it a voice in local decision-making, as well as access to local authority funding.

The Wakefield diocese had received £750,000 of grants for 28 projects since 1978, matched the amount from their own resources and used the combined total to attract a further £7 million from other sources. A wonderful example, Angela says, of how the Church can be a living demonstration of the gospel, making a significant impact on local communities while shaping urban policy at the same time. Which is why, when she visits a diocese, she also makes it her business to call on local MPs, councillors and officials, as well as project workers, youth and social workers, not to mention, of course, the bishop.

While many might find it a little daunting to be face to face with a bishop in his living room, not Angela. As a Pentecostal she isn't, she says, seduced by status and power, the hierarchical structures within the Church of England. 'Of course I'm a challenge to male seniority. It must be difficult to relate to a younger, black woman on equal terms, given the Church's history, but it doesn't faze me. I bounce in. That's my personality. I've learned to be confident. If you doubt yourself, you don't get anywhere.' She has been known to halt a bishop holding forth about his expectations of CUF, mid-flow, with, 'Excuse me, bishop, can I now share my vision with you?'

Besides, she says, in the voluntary, grant-aided world in which she has moved for most of her professional life, she has rubbed shoulders with many well-known dignitaries, viscounts, barons and one or two film stars. Receptions at the House of Lords became a regular part of her life. Her previous chairman was a lord. They are not intimidating. They are simply men. And every white man will find a black woman in authority threatening.

It is a reality never far from personal experience. At a recent formal reception, a young man taking photographs as the guests walked in, put down his camera as she entered the room with a junior, white, male colleague. They were manifestly not interesting enough to snap. Later, when the photographer was alerted to the fact that the Chief Executive of CUF had arrived, he came back, photographed the junior colleague and asked him about the organisation. 'I was obviously the secretary,' she says with a wry smile. 'That was his stereotypical perception. Power, race, gender, all the issues were there.' The colleague was acutely embarrassed and apologised profusely, but Angela dismisses it, laughing. 'It happens all the time. And sometimes the worst offenders are our beneficiaries. You'd think if a project is receiving money from us, it would make more sense for them to talk to me.'

It is, she thinks, a cruel world for women – especially black women. 'Once we get to the top we're watched for every mistake and that can be off-putting, a blow to our confidence. It can make us decide not to take things on in the first place.'

Given the hard and chequered history of black women, the struggle for recognition and acceptance, I wonder whether they feel they are putting their faith in a good God. Is He good for black women?

'No more so than for anyone else,' she says. 'God is good for all people, but the Christian message is often exploited. People manipulate it for their own ends. So while many churches are kept going by the good offices of women, who, let's face it, do most of the unsung hard work, men take most of the credit.'

Despite her interest in issues affecting women, Angela has no time for feminism, at least, her perception of it. 'It's a luxury for the idle middle classes who have the time to argue about it, while the rest of us use up all our energy getting on with our lives.' Strong stuff from one whose deep commitment to equality on every level could justifiably earn her a feminist label, but Angela feels feminist attitudes have been hijacked by what she calls a 'godless view of things': that to achieve, a woman can't be a real woman, she must become a kind of a man. 'I'm very conscious that God is good for me. It's my faith which has enabled me to juggle a thousand commitments, achieve what I have and still hang on to my femininity. I love being a woman. I celebrate the differences between men and women. I like being pampered by my husband and praised by my dad. I don't expect Ted to be as soppy about the kids as I am. I bet he doesn't show their photograph to all his colleagues and clients. But I hotly dispute the kind of unspoken attitude which makes female managers uncomfortable talking about their children at work. I'm a mother as well as a chief executive. Both tasks are equally important.'

Being a woman for her involves that special feeling she gets in the morning when she puts on nice clothes, 'fully colour co-ordinated, of course', sees to her hair and her face. If she's late for work because of an appointment at the hairdressers', so be it. There are priorities in a woman's life and feeling good is one of them. 'I like getting dolled up – that's female for you. But self-esteem is important and I'm very aware of the need to be a positive role model for Laura. I bring her in to work. She sees the articles I write. Then I change into jeans and we go to the cinema together. I want my daughter to understand that she can have an education, career, family, beauty and faith.'

'Can a woman have it all?' I ask her.

'Well, there's no harm in trying,' she chuckles. 'If you don't aim, you never get.' But she feels very sad for the women, often black women, whose career ambitions and achievements have necessitated their staying single. It's too great a sacrifice. 'While it takes men all their time to cope with their work, providing what support at home they can manage, women have the capacity to take on so much more: marriage, a career, motherhood, being a positive role model for your children, voluntary work and caring for parents. Men are more impatient. They want everything at once, while we have more endurance. We reach our pinnacle later. We postpone promotion until our children are older. Maybe women can have it all – but not all at once.'

What about managing men? Do men find it difficult being managed by a woman?

'Of course they do. But it is a terrible weakness in a man if he really cannot tolerate it. Some women bosses make men suffer for it. I try not to.'

She works on the principle that exploiting another person's weakness is never acceptable. In time respect must earn respect.

There was at the beginning a bit of what she calls the inevitable 'jostling', as there always is when a woman is appointed chief for the first time, accompanied by a verbal and non-verbal undercurrent. What is she like? Can I get my own way? Is she a real woman or a woman posing as a man? Will she respond to flirting?

'I'm very careful about my body language with men. It can so easily be misread. Women are much looser about how we communicate. Men are more dogmatic, less flexible, economic with words. They tend to hold us to what we say, and come back and challenge us if we don't do what they think they have heard. They're more functional, they do the business and off they go, while a woman is often prepared to have a longer, more open-ended conversation.'

The merest suggestion of flirting is out altogether. It is a game she finds demeaning and she simply will not play it. It constitutes a concession to unacceptable stereotyping. She deplores the widespread tendency to judge women by the way they look, rather than the quality of their gifts and character. It has made women hypersensitive about being the right age, size and colour and, because of her own background, she feels duty-bound not to collude in such destructive behaviour patterns. 'On certain occasions that may mean I come across as a bit of a cold fish', but if that is the price for defending a woman's right to be respected for who, not what she is, she is more than willing to pay it. 'I remember interviewing a woman who was extremely unattractive facially. I made myself engage with her, looked her straight in the eye. It's so important for us all to remember that it's our perception of beauty which is defective.'

When she introduces herself she says she is Angela Sarkis of the Church Urban Fund. 'That's gender for you. Men usually like people to know how important they are. I try and play it down.' Once her full title is known she then has to cope with the response, be it disappointment, disbelief, shock or false admiration. 'And that's race for you,' she says, with a grin which spreads quickly from one ear to the other.

And her own weaknesses?

Many, she says, too many, but off the top of her head, and in the context of her job, number one would have to be administration. The very word fills her with an obvious distaste, which she tells me she struggles by the moment to overcome. 'I'm people-oriented. I want to be out there doing. But the truth is that what you get down on paper matters. That's why men make it a priority – even if it's only to cover their backs. I think women tend to go into high-powered jobs highly motivated, deeply committed, but unable to face the consequences.' And one inevitable consequence of her position, however hassled it makes her, however much of a daily penance it seems, is paperwork. It is the price to be paid for power.

Not that she rates power for itself. Raised with powerlessness, working with those who experience the lack of it in every part of their lives, she has no illusions about its seductive influence, political and personal, its dangerous tendency to build barriers and harden the heart. In fact, like Joy Carroll, she struggles with the concept, and has redefined it in her own inimitable way. The first law is recognising it for what it is, a useful opportunity to make the best possible decisions, both for the 23 staff members and those the organisation serves. The second is to remember how arbitrary it is, here today and gone tomorrow, but for the good will of her colleagues. That is why she doesn't have a sign saying 'Chief Executive' on her door. It worried everyone at first. 'The title doesn't confer the authority. I'm only Chief Executive as long as the staff allow it, as long as they think I'm worth working for. I'm an ordinary person, like any other. Hence the round table where all are equal. I'm only as good as my team.'

She herself is directly accountable to the Trustees, chaired by the Archbishop of Canterbury, who is too busy to get involved in the day-to-day running of CUF, but maintains a lively interest from a distance. He has expressed the view that it needs to reflect on its past ten years, learn from the people involved in local projects and bridge the gulf between the Church and the community even more. This is music to Angela's ears. 'CUF is the jewel in the Anglican crown, a pearl of redemption at a time when it was in huge danger of losing its way. At last the Church of England had a huge success on its hands, and I'm not sure it knew what to do with it. You have to polish a jewel to make it shine. It needs regular attention. My aim is to build and capitalise on the successes of the past ten years. Having got stuck in to so many communities, we've earned the right to demand hope for the hopeless, to speak up for communities where aspirations lie in the dust, to influence national policies on urban poverty.' If that means dragging the Church kicking and screaming into a new arena, to shout instead of maintaining a comfortable silence, to force policy-makers to confront the issues head on, then Angela is prepared to do it. 'Christ was involved politically. He had no pretensions about it. He cared about the poor, cut through red tape, challenged bureaucracy, healed and nurtured individuals, not just the masses. We need practical, as well as heartfelt compassion.' In Angela Sarkis's hands, as well as a celebration of the past, CUF's tenth anniversary year could be a dynamic new beginning.

This summer she went back to Jamaica for the first time since she left it in the year of its independence, 34 years ago. It was a very emotional journey. The country had changed almost beyond recognition. There were signs of deterioration, pockets of immense wealth, largely for the tourists, 'which I enjoyed to the full', and pockets of great poverty. 'It brought my job into sharp focus.' She made a point of visiting local churches and discovered that in the poorest, sustained by their faith and the hope of something better, were the most dedicated, faithful Christians. 'A candle shines more brightly in the dark. So it is with the Church Urban Fund. We have created society, we must deal with the consequences. The Church of England is facing a financial crisis such as it has never known before. The temptation is to retract, clamp down and give in to all the problems. This is just the time when we can refuse to be overcome by the darkness that surrounds us and shine out brighter than ever before.'

She returned to England with a sense of immense gratitude for a childhood richer than many. 'I like to think I'm still the same happy, secure little girl who flew here when she was seven and worked so hard to make my parents proud of me – and they are, almost to nauseating lengths. I may not have the West Indian or Nottingham accent. I may not be quite as working-class as I used to be. That's the price I've paid for an education. But I believe we have a duty as Christians, and that goes especially for women, so quick to give up and lose our confidence under the pressures we face, to seek out all the gifts God has given us and use them for His glory.'

_____

While working at CUF Angela was seconded, part-time, as a member of the government's Social Exclusion Unit, advising the Prime Minister on poverty issues. She moved on from CUF in January 2002 to establish her independent consultancy providing support to charities and the public sector. In 2002 she was appointed a governor of the BBC, a non-executive director on the Correctional Service Board at the Home Office and an adviser to the DFES on teacher workload management. She has an ongoing commitment to help churches and faith communities to engage with their local communities and use their experience to influence government policy.

CHAPTER 11

The Survivor: Mandy Moore

I grew up in Smackhead City. We moved there when I was nine – from a high-rise block into the house of our dreams: semi-detached, nice furnishings, a bit of a garden. Some clever dick in high places had this idea of planting scallies with the decent stuff. The scallies took over, like weeds in the garden, and what they got was Croxteth, Liverpool's answer to hell.

My mam was a screamer, my dad was a drunk. She earned the money, he spent it – every spare penny – on booze. She suffered from exhaustion. He wore her out. So did the neighbourhood. It was built on a bog. The drainage wasn't fit for anything. We lived in rows, all on top of each other, front to back and back to front, rabbits and guinea pigs separated by high walls and narrow alleys called 'jiggers'. Facing us, across the jigger, was someone's outhouse and bin shed. On either side of us were high walls. You felt as if they were coming down on you. Either you barricaded yourself in or you came out fighting. 'Do unto others before they do it unto you.' That was the local motto. Every time I set foot out of the front door I was hammered. So I learned to hammer back. Girl or boy, it didn't matter. I had a reputation for being vicious – a punk rocker with an attitude. I never started a fight, but I finished plenty.

My dad only tried to get me to do something once – to stay in at night, like Mam said – but I knocked him down the stairs.

'Don't ever tell me what to do again.' The fool, how could he stop me? He'd be drunk in an hour. I never saw much of him. He went out at 5.30 in the morning to the paint factory, and came back slaughtered late every night.

Sometimes, for a laugh, me and Jimmy from our close would go down the bars looking for each other's dads. One night, when Mam went off the rails, like she did, Jimmy couldn't find them. So the social worker took me to my cousin Betty's. Our Betty goes to church, fancies herself as the respectable one in the family. If my mother's a screaming banshee, she's the wailing wall. My godmother, I was 12, and she wouldn't take me in. Her Stan said, 'Her da drinks, her ma drinks, smokes and swears. She'll never amount to much. Put her back in the gutter where she belongs.' That really hurt.

My mam and I were hard on each other. I threw all my aggro at her. She used to batter me. The only place I knew I was safe was at my grandparents'. She never got on to me there. I know why battered wives say nothing. It's easier. Sometimes she'd give me a hug, then dig a bony finger into my ribs until it hurt, and say, 'See, that's what your friends will do to you one day.' She was right. She toughened me up. It was the only way to survive. Most of the friends I grew up with are heroin addicts now and well on their way to dying. It's one way out of Crocky.

I'd cry for them if I could – but I can't. I still can't. You weren't allowed to cry. Tears were a sign of weakness. They killed your street cred. Mine were dammed up at source. The feelings were there – but they'd no way out, not even when my best friend committed suicide. Inside I was a mess. Outside, no give-away signs, the same old Mandy, hard as granite, brazening out the world.

I hated authority and that meant teachers. I wasn't going to let them gossip about me in the staffroom. There was a gang of us stood up for each other. Jimmy was good with his mouth. I was good with my fists. I had plenty of practice – in the Bow and Arrow. We drank snakebites. Half a pint of the strongest lager mixed with half a pint of the strongest cider. The blue balls floating on top sent it slime green. One of those took your inhibitions away. Two and you couldn't stand up. Three drove you mad. If a fight started you went over to the jukebox until someone was thrown in your direction – then they were all yours. Grief, it was rough. Hatchets, Stanley knives, lump hammers – they all did the rounds. It's guns now. I couldn't stand it.

One night a girl pulled a Stanley knife on me and slashed my new keks from the knee to my shoes. I've still got the scar down my leg to show for it. I picked up a brick and battered her – for ruining my jeans. It was horrendous. There were seven panda cars. If you were quick you got away. Nine out ten times no one pressed charges anyway.

Yes, I ended up in Risley Remand Centre. This is where it gets really difficult. I don't like talking about it. The only way I cope with it now is by blotting it out. It was my last year at school. I had this friend called Paula whose dad wanted her to be a lady – not like the rest of us – and used to give her the belt and buckle. She was a nervous wreck, chain-smoked like she couldn't live without it. This particular day Sharon nicked her ciggies. She thought it was funny, but Paula was in a real state. At break I said, 'Sharon, give Paula her fags.' She slapped me across the face. 'Sharon, give Paula her fags back.' In the redness of my mind all I could see were the buckle marks on Paula's skin. Sharon slapped me again. She must have slapped me across the face about five times when I started to bang her head off the brick wall. I went completely mad. The PE staff came out and I started on them. They told me after it took eight people to get me into the police van. I don't remember much about it.

Sharon was on a life-support machine for a while. But she recovered. I took some flowers to the hospital to say I was sorry. She panicked and wouldn't see me. I can't think why. In the end, I was charged with 'defacing the Queen's uniform'. I'd managed to rip the sleeve off a policeman's uniform. 'How did you manage to rip the sleeve off a policeman's uniform?' the judge asked in Crown Court. I said it must have been shoddy workmanship, made in Taiwan. I wasn't being funny. I was too nervous for that. It was a genuine answer to the question, but the judge thought I was being cocky and bawled me out. I got six weeks in the young offenders' block, and a 10-year police record for violent behaviour.

If Crocky's hell I don't know what that place is. They put me in a cell on my own because I was labelled violent. The screws are awful. They didn't care about anyone. Not even a girl who was pregnant. Hygiene and cleanliness isn't exactly at the top of their list either. It made me more paranoid than ever, wary of everyone.

The only person in authority who ever got through to me was my art teacher, Mr Spicer. He wanted me to go to art college and was gutted when I said I wouldn't. He took all the rubbish I threw at him and came back for more. He was the only one who ever believed in me and stuck up for me. I'd like to see him now, but I'm too much of a coward to tell anyone they were right. 'What do you want out of life, Mandy?' he used to say to me. I was clever, you see, in the top set. I said, 'To get out of this hell-hole.' Half the girls in my class were pregnant and set to move in three doors down from their mams. I didn't want any kid of mine to grow up in a scally area and be branded a troublemaker from birth.

I left school at 16 with nine O levels and moved in with Mike. Mam had kicked me out. 'I won't set foot in this house again,' I screamed at her, not that I'm stubborn, or anything.

Mike lived in Tuebrook. It was only a few miles down the road, but after Crocky, it was like being in heaven. I felt I was leaving Jimmy and the rest on the dung heap. I got a job at my dad's paint factory – with no help from him – and ended up as packing and distribution supervisor when I left to have our Kelly two years later.

I was five-and-a-half-months pregnant when she was born, weighing 1lb 12oz. I was desperately ill – and she wasn't too good either. They told Mike they didn't hold out much hope for us. He came in just as they were rushing me down for emergency surgery, blubbering. I yelled, 'Get out of here, you nancy boy. Don't cry all over me.' I was always kicking him out, and he always came back. I booted hell out of him when Kelly had a stroke when she was 18 months old, and I found him in the hospital chapel. It didn't bother me where we were. I thought he should have been on the ward with his daughter, not wasting his time on his knees in some church.

Kelly was one of the best things that ever happened to me. That's her as a baby, that photo on the wall, and that's her at five. Wasn't she lovely? She didn't crawl like other babies. She didn't walk until she was two. There was always something wrong with her right side. It wasn't diagnosed as cerebral palsy until later. It was difficult to get her to do ordinary things. These days, the more the doctors tell her what she can't do, the more determined she is to do them. Stubborn old thing. Takes after her father! She taught me patience. I thought, 'No one was ever patient with me. No one ever gave me the time of day. But I'm going to give her forever.'

But I had to go back to work when she was two. There was no choice. Mike was a builder, times were hard. I managed to stay out of trouble for four years – until Mike was ill. When he was a kid a beer barrel had fallen off the back of a lorry on to his head. No, that's the truth. The chain had come loose. This is even funnier. It was Good Friday, and his mam, a good Catholic woman, was at mass. Anyway, he'd been having these terrible headaches for a while. He used to punch in the back door and break a window or two with the pain. But he never touched me. He's not like that, Mike. I found him blacked out on the back steps. The blow years ago had splintered his skull, and bits had been moving around in his brain, building up pressure. He needed urgent surgery.

I couldn't earn enough to keep us all. There were so many things I needed to make our Kelly's life more comfortable. So I started taking commissions – £50 a time – to dig someone. You don't understand what I'm talking about, do you? I mean, to put their lights out. Give them a good hiding. Beat them up. Because they'd given somebody a hard time, got on someone's nerves. There was plenty of work like that to be found at the Bow and Arrow, or at the Eagle and Child. All I wanted was the best for our Kelly. I never thought about whether there was a best for me. Or anyone else for that matter. And then, circumstances beyond my control, as they say, changed the course of my life.

We were getting off the bus one day, as Mike's cousin Alan was getting on. He used to go into the Bow and Arrow with his mates, and had a bit of a reputation as a hard case, but I hadn't seen him for years. Somehow we managed to scribble down addresses while the bus was at the stop. After that Alan started to come down regularly on a Thursday night, to take Mike off to mass at the Catholic church, then out for a drink. I wasn't going. I thought the pair of them had lost their bottle. Anyway, I was a Protty.

One Thursday night sticks in my memory, like it stuck in my throat then. I couldn't really forget it, given what happened. That particular night Alan seemed really agitated. He paced the floor, backwards and forwards, for ages, then turned to me all of a sudden and said, 'Jesus is what you need, Mandy, you know.' It wasn't new. He was always saying it, and I argued that night like I always did, saying all the things I always said – the things you say when you know you're right and the other person's a total idiot.

'Okay, okay,' he said, 'I'll make a deal with you. When I die, come and see me when they lay me out. If I've a smile on my face, you'll know what I'm saying is true, because it means our Billy' – his dead brother – 'will be holding one of my hands, and Jesus the other.' Honest, he brought me out in goose-bumps.

I said, 'Alan, don't be so stupid, you're only 32. At your age you're not about to die.'

He was like a dog with a bone. He wouldn't leave it alone. 'No, promise me,' he kept saying, 'And I'll never mention it again after tonight. If I die smiling, you'll go to church and check out what I've been telling you.'

What could I do? I remember thinking, well at least I won't have to do anything about it for a long time yet.

We didn't discuss it after that, but as he was leaving he turned back in our hallway, looked straight at me and said, 'Remember your promise, Mandy.'

Three days later he was dead. It was Sunday afternoon, the day of his little girl's sixth birthday party. There was a knock at our door. Alan's ten-year-old was standing there.

'Me dad's dead,' he said.

I told him to stop messing. It was a terrible thing to say.

'But it's true. Me mam found him dead in bed this morning. A thrombo – summat.'

We went up to the house just as we'd planned – though it wasn't for any birthday party. I don't remember what I was thinking as I went up to the bedroom. I wasn't afraid. I'd worked in a mortuary and seen dead bodies before. I'd washed them ready for the coffin. The faces were usually distorted with the pain. But even before I got close to the bed I knew what I was going to see. Yet when I saw it – the enormous smile from ear to ear, the kind of smile he had on his face when he and Mike arrived back from a good night at the pub – it shocked me rigid. I stood there looking at him, and it felt like he was grinning straight at me.

'You little …,' I screamed at him. 'You've done this to me on purpose.'

'Promise me, Mandy.' I couldn't get it out of my head. A promise is a promise. If Crocky had taught me anything decent it was that. To this day I don't make promises lightly. I say, 'I'll do my best', or 'I'll try'. Promises have to be kept. And anyway, Kelly wanted to go to Sunday school. It was as good an excuse as any for getting me to church – St Cyprian's, the local C of E on the corner. I waited for her outside.

'Did you go to church?' Mike asked when I got back.

I said I had.

'Into the bit where there's an altar and pews, Mandy?'

He's far too cunning, Mike.

The following week I went in, but sat outside the main bit in a lounge, so that I could just about see the altar and pews. A lovely old boy called Reg asked me if I wanted to go inside. He'd sit with me if I was on my own and needed a bit of company. I thought, 'Mandy, this is stupid. You promised Alan – so do it.'

They were asking for people to go to a meeting to plan the Christmas fair. So I went. I'm always full of ideas – but they didn't half give me a grilling. They seemed a bit … wary. I wonder why. I was only the next best thing to a hedgehog. Too close and you could be impaled on one of the spines. And I couldn't be doing with praying and all that stuff.

Joke a minute, wind them up, give them aggro, keep them

away at any cost. No, there was no overnight change, no sudden transformation. But something was definitely going on, because after a few weeks I remember saying to myself, 'Mandy, what do you put up all these barriers for? You don't have to take the world on to prove you're as good as the next person', and then the next minute I'd think, 'God, what's happening to me? I'm going a bit soft in the head.'

And then the major miracles began – minor to anyone else. First, I got married. I'd never wanted the formal ceremony before – not because I was afraid of commitment, but because I wanted to be sure there was a God, so I wasn't just using the church. I'm many things but a hypocrite isn't one of them. My dress was ivory – not white. After all Mike and I had been together for 12 years.

It was funny how it happened. This particular Saturday afternoon we went up to Grandma's, as we always did on Saturdays. She rules the roost, my grandma. She knew I'd started going to church. 'I've bought your wedding dress, Mandy,' she said. Like it was the next thing to do. So I went with the flow and we were married two months later.

We had nine bridesmaids – in sky blue, I think, I can't remember, I didn't pick them. Our Michelle did. Kelly was one. David, the vicar, prayed for the three of us. After the service the family wouldn't let me change back into my jeans in the vestry. And they wouldn't let me travel to the do in the coach with everyone else and join in the sing-song. Me and Mike had to drive round alone in the special car. I was really mad. It was dead boring.

I've been with Mike longer now than I've been without him. You're right, that's quite an achievement considering how long relationships usually last round here. I said to him the other day, 'Do you realise we've been together 16 years? I've served longer than a life sentence. Isn't that a depressing thought?' No, not really. Why have we lasted? Well you met him. You tell me. Stubbornness, I suppose. He told you he didn't go to church? He would. Did he tell you about his faith? Don't let him fool you. He keeps mine going.

The other miracles? I suppose the most telling was that I gave up my 'job on the side'. Fifty pounds was a lot of money. But I knew I didn't want to fight any more. I certainly didn't want paying to do someone else's dirty work. Big JC and his 'turn the other cheek' stuff was getting under my skin. Mandy Moore of Croxteth began to ask herself whether revenge was really worth it. The hard centre had started to melt.

I only noticed the change a few months later when Jimmy, my old Crocky friend, became caretaker at the local school. I could see the chip on his shoulder, heavier than a 20-foot post, at 100 yards, and felt sorry for him. Mine was shrivelling fast. And I knew it.

'You've changed,' he said. 'I take it you cut people down with words these days?'

'No,' I said to him, 'you've got it wrong. There's been no exchange of weapons. I'm a different person.'

That was what I'd always wanted. To be different. To be a person I could respect. But I never knew how to go about it. I couldn't change myself, couldn't let go of the aggression. It was the only thing that protected me from rejection.

I had almighty fights with the Big JC – still do. No one had ever just accepted me as I was before. I'd always had to fight for everything that was worth anything. 'You can have your clever ideas,' I used to rant at Him, 'I've done what you said, turned the other cheek, now just leave the major decisions to me. I've always been in charge of my own life. I know how to handle myself.' Crazy, eh, to think you can even take God on?

When I get to heaven I'm going to get that Alan. 'Lord, let me dig him – just once. I'll never settle till I do.' He'll probably be waiting for me anyway – with the policeman whose uniform I defaced.

⤳

Is God good for women? He's been good for me. I never had the opportunities other women have. There's no future, no hope, no life for a Crocky kid. I could never say, 'I'm going to be a doctor or a solicitor or a teacher.' Everyone thinks you're brainless if you've been to Crocky Comp. I knew I wasn't, but what did it matter? They put you down faster than you can pick yourself up. But here I am doing a university degree in psychology and sociology.

I gave up work a few years ago because Kelly needed a bit of extra support at school (she should have had a carer – some hope!), and started doing courses in computer studies and drama at the Parents' Centre. Five of us saw an advert for a part-time degree course linked to Liverpool University, and decided to apply. We thought it was a bit of a laugh. We never expected we'd be accepted, especially me, but we said to each other, 'It doesn't matter if don't get in, we'll do the access course and try again later.' Who do you think was the only one with the right qualifications? I love it. I've a student pass card. I feel like a voice is saying, 'Here's your big chance, Crocky kid.'

If God's good for women, I'm not so sure the Church is. Funny that, isn't it? God gives you a chance, but the Church doesn't. It's the only place where I ever feel discrimination – not at our local – I mean at a higher level. I've been the treasurer at St Cyp's for six years now and once a year I'm summoned to a formal diocesan finance meeting. A fuddy old official usually holds forth at length in a monotonous voice about some new measure to rescue the church's budget by lifting more money out of the pockets of the poor suckers in the pew – those of us who can barely afford to survive as it is. What do they know about what it's like to live on benefit or income support? What do they know about real poverty? But I notice that whenever I get up and ask a perfectly sensible question, they look up at me over the tops of their spectacles, and weigh me up and down as if I've just crawled out of an apple. You can see 'woman' register on their faces, closely followed by 'thick'. Well, you must be, mustn't you? Since when does a woman understand anything about finance, budgets and deficits? They answer in that tone of voice which says, 'Well, my dear, this is all a bit hard for you. You'll just have to take our word for it' – when I know they're talking a load of rubbish. All I want is a straight answer to a straight question, without having to apologise for my sex.

The way I was raised there was nothing a girl couldn't do:

wallpaper, plaster, change a plug, deck a lad if he asked for it. The boys learned to iron and to cook. In fact the poorer people are, the more they share the chores. My grandma's word is law in our family. My grandy makes the tea for 23 of us every Saturday afternoon. First the kids eat together in the kitchen. Then the men eat, while the women look after the kids in the other room. Then the women eat together while the men look after the kids. We eat last because we do most gabbing. We usually manage about 20 cups of tea each. If a child dares to stray into the room, my grandma shouts, 'You've had your pleasure, there is no leisure. Get the kids out!'

She's the putty that cements the family together: a Catholic who married a Prot. 'The priest can come to my house whenever he likes, as long as he knows who's boss in it,' she says. On New Year's Day she makes us all sit down together round the table. You're told where to sit, and it's always next to the person you've had a row with, or you don't get on with, so that you have to talk to them. 'Don't carry any excess baggage with you into the new year,' my grandma says. 'Leave it behind.'

It was Grandy taught me to read and write before I went to school. He showed me a man can be tender. But my grandma showed me a woman's a force to be reckoned with, whatever she does. In Liverpool the woman is the boss. The men think they are – but they're just figureheads.

There are lots of things a man can't do. If I'd been a man I wouldn't have been able to give up work, go to school with Kelly to take care of her or teach the kids with learning difficulties to read. I wouldn't have had the chance of doing a degree. I'd have been a bricky or a roofie, a plumber or a plasterer. I'd have worked myself into the ground. And I'd have hated it.

Mike never wanted to be a builder. He stood at that fireplace one day and told me how he'd always dreamed of being a nurse. But there's so little money in nursing, especially at first.

'Go for it,' I said to him, 'Don't ever tell me I've got in the way of your doing what you really want.'

He made it in the end, but he didn't half take some stick from his family.

'Is Nurse Nancy there?' they'd say on the phone.

One of his brothers bought him a pair of tights for Christmas. 'He prefers stockings – black fishnet with suspenders,' I said.

They made me so mad. Maybe there are definite advantages in being a woman. No one has ever tried to stop me from doing what I felt I had to do.

And there's so much more I want to do. I've only just begun. The community hasn't had enough of me yet. All the important things I ever wanted for myself I've got, thank God. No, the house isn't really immaculate. You're not looking hard enough. Anyway, material things don't matter. They mean almost nothing to me. It's self-respect that counts, the courage to walk away from trouble. But that's something those kids out there – those ones throwing bricks at the cars – is that one your car? – may never know. Some of them can't read, write, do basic maths. That's why I got involved at the school. I couldn't just help our Kelly and do nothing for the rest of them. Eleven years old with an average reading age of eight – that's the good ones. So I teach them to read. All I want is for them to have the chances I never had till now. I was never allowed to be a child. Everything was thrown at me – bricks, stones, buckets of water. Treat a child little better than an animal and that's how it'll behave, because that's how it will feel.

They come to the door selling things and I know they've been stealing. 'We don't sell you robbed stuff, Mandy,' they say, 'We know you don't agree with it. We'll show you the receipts.'

Once they stole from the local grocer's on principle, because he'd accused them of robbing him when they hadn't. I ask you, people invite trouble. These kids have a highly developed sense of justice. They need somewhere to go. No Crocky kid was ever allowed in the local youth club. We were too rough. That's why we ended up drinking snake bites in the Bow and Arrow. Mike's set up a local football team for them. He's having his chest waxed to raise funds. Well, where can they play round here?

In my spare time I'm doing a course for children with special needs. That grew out of the church parent and toddler club I run with Nancy. We had three special needs kids. I don't think there's another club in this area that could take them. What's so difficult about accommodating a Down's Syndrome child or one in a wheelchair? They're disadvantaged, not disabled. How would I have felt if Kelly had been rejected? It's just a case of knowing what these kids need. That's why I'm doing the course.

I had to wait years to do it. That 10-year record still hanging over me, still dominating my life. It seemed to last forever. They wouldn't let me near kids with my 'violent' tag. I know what I did was wrong. But if I'd been done for manslaughter I wouldn't have been held over a barrel for ten years. It's unfair. There should be a way of checking up how you're doing every so often to see if you've changed.

I love kids – always have – especially special needs kids. At Crocky Comp, if you were bad they sent you to work at the place for handicapped kids as a punishment. I used to be bad deliberately so they'd send me there. I looked after the deaf kids. Now I look back I see how important that was. Nothing's wasted. It's just funny it had to be a punishment.

Now I want to help the club parents too. They all come round with their troubles – when the kids are ill or having problems or giving them heartache. When they're worried or upset. Officials don't explain what's going on. There's no one to speak up for them or support them. I write letters to councillors, contact the social workers, bully the doctors and the hospitals and the teachers. That degree's proving useful.

We've taken in quite a few homeless people. What's a home unless you share it? Stephen was 13 when he came to live with us. He didn't know right from wrong. He stole the neighbour's milk one day because we'd run out. I made him go and put it back. No one had ever made him do something like that before. He just couldn't understand. We were beginning to make progress when the social worker took him back to his mother, and all because of some technicality or other. The day he left was the nearest I'd ever been to crying. I dread that lump in my throat. I still say, 'God, don't do this to me. You can change me in any way you want – but not that.'

Stephen got into trouble with police. We knew he would, but

one day there was a knock at our door, and there he was. 'I'm sorry, Mandy,' he said. At least he now seemed to know what honesty was.

And then there was Sandra who'd had a breakdown when her husband left her. She used to ask us if we thought she was mental. Mike said, 'Yes, at the moment, but you're going to get better.' She did, and remarried. Her little girl is our goddaughter. I love being a godmother. I've bought her her first Bible. Look at the pictures. Can't you get lovely books for kids now?

Would I be doing this if it weren't for JC? You're joking. I'd probably be serving time for assault. There's a woman three doors down who smashed into my car a few months ago. She wasn't insured. Now she won't pay up. She'd have been dead if I'd have been the Mandy I used to be. He turned a bundle of aggravation, who was a cowering heap inside, into a woman who's glad to be who she is.

Most of the time. I still have loads of loose ends I try and keep tied up. But sometimes the ribbon frays. A tiny comment can send me wild. It puts me right back in Crocky. Like when we were discussing the church refurbishment I heard someone say, 'Don't get one of those Italian lifts. They're rubbish.' That hit on a nerve. My family are of Italian extraction. I was flaming angry. But where do you get off? I know the answer. JC wants 100 per cent. I'm just not ready for such a risk. I'll do the Pepsi Max challenge. I'll give it my heart and soul. But when it comes to JC, I'm still facing the final frontier. I still can't make the ultimate commitment, trust myself to someone else completely. I keep thinking one of these days He'll get hold of me by the scruff of the neck and give me a size-seven kick up the backside, and say, 'I've taken enough nonsense from you.' That's why I keep running away. But He never does. The truth is, and I don't know why, but He just never lets go.

Like Kelly. She drives me ballistic. She keeps saying, 'You've no faith, Mum, that's your problem.' She's all I ever dreamed a daughter would be, all I imagined a fulfilled young woman could be. I wanted to give her the security I never had. I didn't want to pass on my hang-ups. She'd have enough of her own. She's turned out to be independent, strong-willed and stubborn. Well, who does she take after? Her dad, of course! She did a 24-hour famine for Oxfam. The doctors said she shouldn't. Twelve hours was enough. But would she listen? Would she heck! She won't let any of her physical problems beat her. She said, 'Mum, you have to fight for what you believe in.' She cares passionately about justice, can't stand discrimination and stands up for the underdog. It's only what I expected of her. It was just I thought it would start when she was 25, not 15.

She's almost grown-up. Soon, she won't need me as much, so what shall I do with my life? The street gets worse. Sometimes you can't sleep for the sound of the sirens. Mike wants to move. I take his point. He's got a good job as a psychiatric nurse. We could get a bank loan, have a house with three bedrooms and a bit of a garden. He says I could still go to St Cyp's. But what would I tell the mums of the toddler club? They need someone to be there for them, to listen to them, to identify with them. How could I say, 'I'm committed to the community', then go and live in the next parish?

You could say I was a woman with a mission. I suppose I have this vision of being a bit like Grandma one day, taking not just my own family but the whole community into my heart. I don't want status or power. They don't interest me. Just wisdom. Out there there are so many people like I used to be, alone and frightened. I want them to see that I don't have the monopoly on opportunity. There's plenty to go round. I have this notion that there's a better world for all of us round here – one where there's justice and love – and it may only take one woman to lay the foundations.

Kelly now has a degree in graphic design. After she got her degree Mandy began to work with disadvantaged young people in Croxteth, part-time. She now heads a full-time team of four detached youth workers in the area.

CHAPTER 12

The Consultant Gynaecologist:
Anne Garden

I couldn't complete any quest for women of achievement without making a special effort to explore one of the great mysteries of our times – why, despite the increasing influence of women in the world of medicine, are there so few female obstetrician-gynaecologists? Only 4 per cent of consultant surgeons are female, and an astounding 94 per cent of consultants with special responsibility for the working of women's nether portions are men. This is a puzzle to which I have always wanted to find a solution, ever since I had my two children, one in Manchester, under the care of a male consultant whom I never saw and whose staff showed scant regard for the wishes of the mother; and the other in Nottingham, a dramatic Caesarean delivery, almost less traumatic than the normal birth, thanks to a wonderful female consultant and her team, who never left my side. Was my experience a reflection of professionalism or gender? Did one have any bearing on the other?

With these questions in mind I set off for the brand new Women's Hospital in Liverpool. There, I felt sure, I would find answers which could affect the well-being of millions of women. If God is good for us, then He must take some interest in, even responsibility for, the correct functioning of those uniquely female parts He made, those bits and pieces that rule our lives, have a habit of letting us down at the least convenient moment, and are a complete mystery to most men. In fact, when I asked Directory Enquiries for the number of the Royal College of Obstetricians, so that I could check out my statistics, a male operator, in a state of some confusion, gave me the number of the Royal College of Osteopaths. He was after all in the right sort of area, if on the wrong side of the body.

My first impression of the largest women's hospital in the UK, probably in Europe, took me by surprise. A monster reception desk, efficiently and busily manned, sits as if lowered from outer space, in a pool of light, a dazzling focal point in a large and bustling thoroughfare. I didn't expect pink frills, but nor did I anticipate an American TV soap hospital, spacious, gleaming and sophisticated. 'Take a seat, please.' I am pointed towards a cluster of comfortable chairs in a lounge area, where two women in dressing gowns are making a listless attempt at conversation. Gradually, as my eyes get accustomed to the glare, the soothing furnishings and scouse voices work their magic. Were it not for the worried-looking men scurrying past with bouquets and the wan-looking young women in denim jeans, hanging weakly on the arm of a boyfriend, this might almost be the lobby of a suite of expensive executive offices.

Behind me, a magnificent piece of appliqué in satin and silk conveying scenes of Liverpool life fills one wall, so tactile I can't resist reaching out a finger – and set off an alarm, which makes everyone jump, even the two washed-out women in dressing gowns. The receptionists, barely visible behind their desk, laugh and give me the thumbs up. This, evidently, has happened before, probably several times a day since they opened a few months earlier.

The noise subsides, but not my fascination.

'Don't you love it? Look, there are the Walton sextuplets. You can just make out the little pink bows.'

Senior lecturer and consultant in obstetrics and gynaecology, Anne Garden, has appeared at my side.

I have come to see her because of her reputation.

'Go and see Anne Garden,' several people said to me when my

uterus not only outgrew its usefulness, but began to protest the fact rather too loudly. 'Don't go to a man. She's the only one to see.' I never did go to her as a patient, a fact I view with some regret, but I am here now.

'I thought you would send one of your minions down for me.'

She laughs out loud.

'Och, no, where are you living?'

She's wearing a floaty, floral skirt, pastel-coloured sweater and rows of beads, and with her soft golden bob and hint of make-up looks younger and much prettier than I had imagined. I'm living 15 years in the past, I decide, when I had my babies and consultants looked like consultants, and put 1,000 miles, let alone a reasonable distance, between themselves and their patients.

'Ah yes,' she recalls, in a lilting Scottish accent, 'it was about 15 years ago that things really began to change. Up till then most obstetricians regarded the National Childbirth Trust as a load of wacky women.'

We agree, as we walk to her room in the university part of the hospital, that that was because most consultant obstetricians were men.

'Why?' I ask her. That after all, is what I'm here to find out.

She's not sure why, but thinks it may have something to do with the nature of the job. 'Obstetrics is seen as being an incredibly demanding aspect of medicine. Physically demanding. An on-call in any other discipline may mean being up all night. In obstetrics you can guarantee you'll be up all night. I don't know that I could have got this far if I had married and had children. The cost to any family would have been enormous. My work takes over my life.'

From the names on the doors we pass I notice the number of professors on her corridor and wonder whether she aspires to the title. There have been female professors of obs and gynae, she says, but not many. No, senior lecturer and consultant is good enough for her, thank you. She's satisfied with her lot. Administration isn't her strong point. I see what she means when we go inside her room. The piles of correspondence, the demands of our increasingly litigious society, leave her near to despair.

That lack of determination to get to the top seems to be a recurrent theme in women's lives, I say to her, while she moves the paperwork to make room for us.

She nods in agreement.

'I think you have hit on a basic difference between men and women. I don't know whether ambition is the issue, or whether women are simply more aware of their limitations. Or are we just more cautious? Unlike my male colleagues, no matter how prestigious the job, I'm not tempted if I don't think I can handle all of it.'

She thumbs through a pile of files, sighs and deposits them on her desk, and I remember that I have heard somewhere that when a job is advertised, men will see the 75 per cent they can do, while women will see the 25 per cent they cannot do. Anne Garden seems to prove the point.

If women are that hesitant, if there are such hurdles for women in this particular field of medicine, how did she get into it in the first place?

'My students always ask me that,' she says, laughing, 'and the answer is I fell into it.'

Raised in Macduff, a small fishing village on the Moray Firth in the north-east of Scotland, where her father was the much-loved local solicitor, she knew she wanted to do a caring job and decided to become a nurse. 'I said to myself, "Annie, it takes six years to qualify as a doctor. By that time you'll be on the shelf." This was the 1960s, remember, in a very quiet backwater. I thought there was no life if I didn't marry. My mother had given up work when she married my father. Theirs was a very happy relationship – but rather traditional.'

She had been accepted at the Edinburgh Royal Infirmary as a nurse when her deputy head at the local school she attended tried to persuade her to opt for medicine instead. Her mother was concerned. Anne's father, though content to be a solicitor, had always dreamed of being a farmer, and would have been, but for his mother. Anne's mother was determined her children wouldn't be faced with that kind of pressure. She only wanted them to be happy, and said so to the school. In the end Anne decided to wait and see what came her way. Her natural diffidence convinced her she'd fail her exams and end up on the nursing course anyway. But that was not to be. She won a place at Aberdeen University to study medicine.

Only a third of her fellow students were women, but she remembers no discrimination. Later on there was some pressure to become a GP, the more acceptable, more accommodating job for a woman, but serving her elective in India in 1972 had fired her with the ambition to be a missionary doctor, and that required a specialist knowledge of either obstetrics or anaesthesia. 'Officially, I went to India to study family planning in the context of a rural health project, but it was really just an excuse for travel. I had no idea when I went out to Jamkhed Maharashtra that I was going to a mission hospital, but it radically affected my perspective on life.'

In India, for the first time, she became aware of her privileged existence as a Western woman. 'What had I done to deserve being born in a country where I lived in relative riches, could study and become a doctor, when, equally, I could have been an Indian village woman condemned to a life of poverty and hardship?'

It pained her that the Hindu culture appeared to collude in keeping the women in their place. It was their lot, their karma. They were no one's responsibility. On public transport to the clinic one day, an Indian man turned to her and said, 'Only the Christians come here to work.' She saw then that Christianity, if it really meant loving your neighbour, could and should make a difference.

The dawning of her own faith had been something of a non-event. 'We Scots have a very highly developed sense of duty. I'd always gone to church. I was a bit of a brat, but I'd never been a really bad girl. So when in my fifth year as a medical student the penny finally dropped that I didn't have to earn God's acceptance, outwardly little changed. Yet inside it certainly had. I began to see people, not patients, individuals uniquely made, rather than a man or a woman presenting this or that condition.'

The appalling deprivation she saw in India was a shock for the sheltered young woman from a nice home. Women bore the brunt of its poverty-related problems. Whereas pregnancy and childbirth had usually been a cause for some joy in her familiar surroundings in Scotland, 'I saw for the first time the despair a woman's reproductive system could cause her.' Little did she guess that Liverpool, not Lahore, would one day be her major mission field.

She returned perplexed, unsure which specialty to pursue. Anaesthesia, with its more reasonable working hours, had a higher proportion of female specialists than any other area of medicine. It was the obvious choice. In addition, she knew that her new faith would make obstetrics and gynaecology a much more difficult option, because of the ethical problems she would face. But in the end, the decision was taken out of her hands. Back in Aberdeen and 'doing a spell on maternity', she found herself working for a consultant with a reputation for seeing how many female medical students he could reduce to tears on a ward round. 'I came on duty late one evening and asked the Sister if there were any patients who needed special attention. She sent me to have a look at one particular woman. I was barely back in the Duty Room when the consultant rang and asked how the woman was. I told him – in detail. To be honest, having just come from her bed, I could have told him how many get-well cards she had and the colour of her bedsocks. He told me a few days later that he was very impressed with the way I seemed to know my patients, and offered me a research post.'

Intimidated as she was by the consultant's reputation, Anne had to recognise that this was too good a job to refuse. 'We actually got on like a house on fire. I don't know why, because I'm really very timid inside. Standing up to people doesn't come to me naturally. But once I started the job, I never looked back. I knew then that it was obstetrics I really wanted to do, not anaesthesia. I'd found a job that used all my gifts.'

What particular gifts, I wonder, does a consultant obstetrician and gynaecologist need? Are there advantages in being a woman?

'Muchty, yes,' she exclaims with surprise, as if it's self-evident.

'You need to understand what it is a woman's complaining of, and why she's frightened. We doctors have tended to assume a woman understands how her body works much more than she actually does.'

In a place like Liverpool, she explains, with huge variations in social backgrounds, there are vast differences, not only in how much a woman comprehends her basic biological functions, but in how much she wants to understand. What all patients do want is kindness and compassion. 'Women don't have a monopoly on these qualities. My male colleagues are wonderful, extremely caring, but because an initial barrier needs breaking down between a woman and a male gynaecologist, it takes longer for the patient to discover the compassion that is there. Given the restrictions of time imposed by the demands of the NHS on a consultation these days, it may never be long enough to form a relationship and have meaningful communication.

'When a woman walks into my consulting room she knows she doesn't have to explain about periods. I understand how awful it is to have to carry sanitary protection in your handbag, to worry about whether you'll be able to go to the works dance, or take the kids swimming. She'll probably assume I know all about having children. More meaningful communication would pass between us in ten minutes, than would have ever occurred with a male equivalent. The initial barrier isn't there.'

I'm impressed to hear her admit the barrier exists. I thought doctors dismissed the idea as nonsense, an affront to their professionalism. With some amusement she relates how she discovered, to her immense surprise, that it existed even for her. 'I'd always told myself I was a doctor, I couldn't care less who looked at my nether regions – until I had to have a smear test. When I rang up to change the appointment because I had a busy antenatal clinic, I discovered for the first time that it would be performed by a doctor, not a nurse. The thought that the doctor might be a man was a shock to my system. I didn't want it.'

She smiles, and pushes her hair behind her ears.

'It made me realise how patients feel, how vulnerable and threatened by such a loss of privacy and dignity. On the other hand,

I have a brilliant male colleague who is a breast cancer specialist. If I had a lump I'd feel very comfortable about letting him treat me.'

Does the old-style obstetrician-gynaecologist exist, I want to know, the consultant schooled in paternalism, who wears a spotted bow tie, kisses the hand of his private patients and thinks women ought to be grateful for his knight-errant intervention in her life? She thinks there is still a vestige around, but not at her hospital. I tell her about the one who told me with obvious pride, 'We have ways and means of stopping women's periods.' He manifestly thought I would be impressed, that periods were the worst thing with which we poor woman had to contend.

'There are huge dangers in sweeping generalisations of that kind,' she says firmly, pushing up her sleeves. 'No two women with gynaecological problems will react the same way. It's a nonsense, and a denial of our uniqueness to think they will. One woman will stop at nothing to keep her uterus, another will be equally determined to get rid of hers. We don't know why.'

She shows me a recent report in the *British Medical Journal* suggesting that socio-economic grouping does seem to make a difference. The more limited a woman's education, the more likely she is to have a hysterectomy at an early age.

'We need to take the implications on board, to have a careful, honest look at our attitude to the patient and how we interact. Are we performing hysterectomies unnecessarily?'

This is, she admits, an emotive subject. It worries her that there are still 85,000 hysterectomies a year, and so few alternatives, though it's hard for a consultant to get the chance to learn new tricks anyway. 'I slipped my disc when I was supposed to be learning how to do an endometrial resection, the removal of the womb lining, a less invasive procedure, and once I was back at work, found it impossible to get time off. I'm still not sure about it anyway. The verdict is still out. Sometimes we don't know whether a procedure is really effective until it's five or even ten years old. But I would like to be able to offer women a variety of choices.'

Whatever the patient's opinion, Anne is delighted when she

hears it. Decision-making, however difficult, is a joint responsibility for a woman and her doctor. 'I believe people should get involved in their own health care, particularly in pregnancy and childbirth, and I'm really pleased when they say they want this or that in labour, for example, that they don't want to be cut if it's possible, or that they want their partner there all the way through, whatever the difficulty. We must work with the mother. After all, it is her body.'

We sit for a while, reflecting on how radical a concept that once was – especially for the doctor. 'It's taken years for us to concede that childbirth is not an illness. A few vociferous, educated women have had to shout very loudly – and it's led to a positive partnership with their doctors. I hope they'll go on shouting – about breast cancer, osteoporosis, rheumatoid arthritis, and all the other conditions where women should have a great deal more input into the kind of treatment they receive. I also hope that women who are not as well-heeled and educated will learn not to defer to us to such an extent. It's not, "What do you think, doctor?" but what do they think? It's so hard to get some women to say what they want. Women always want to please.'

I ask her why she thinks that is.

'I don't know. I've puzzled and puzzled over it. Even with another woman, they find it hard to mention that worrying little subject greatly implicated in the whole reproductive process – sex.'

I can't imagine anyone being intimidated by Anne Garden. As she sits playing with her beads, she looks more like a benevolent primary-school teacher than a consultant. There is a warmth and naturalness about her that would relax the most nervous of patients, an openness which should put anyone at ease. But women, as I have been hearing repeatedly, are not confident, especially with the medical profession. There's a long history of badgering, bullying, suspicion and hostility to overcome.

I remember a Relate counsellor once telling me how hard women find it to say what they really want. That was why their men found it so difficult to please them. They didn't know what it was they were or weren't doing that caused the relationship to break down. Women tend to put their own needs at the end of their list of priorities. To express them is to appear unwomanly, aggressive or demanding.

'Have you noticed,' Anne asks me, 'how, if a woman gets a little shirty about something, she's dismissed as being premenstrual, whereas a man is simply making a point?'

Little has changed, it seems, since New Testament times, when a woman who had been haemorrhaging for 12 years, who was regarded as unclean by the entire community and had been messed about by countless doctors, reached out in utter desperation, to touch the bottom of Jesus' robe. She didn't dare tell him what she wanted. But Jesus affirmed her for her faith and confidence, and made her well. Not surprisingly, it's one of Anne's favourite Gospel stories.

'When any of my male colleagues are being a little stroppy, I say to them, "Touch of PMT, is it?"'

Most consultants are men, and men are not on the whole clairvoyant. They're not even experts at reading hidden female vibes, the multiplicity of unspoken fears and hopes that accompany a malfunction of those essential female organs. So it seems that in all our relationships women will have to develop the confidence to say what it is we really want.

I vividly remember the extraordinary moment when I held my first baby in my arms and it seemed as if we were a tiny part of some great cosmic miracle. Is Anne Garden, from her very different perspective, aware of that personally? Is delivering babies just a job for her, or is there more to it than that?

'You mean does childbirth ever lose it sense of wonder?'

That is what I mean, and the answer is plain, before she opens her mouth.

'No, never,' she says, her face alive with excitement just at the thought of it, 'and I hope it never will. I do so few deliveries these days, usually when there's been or likely to be a problem, which makes it all the more poignant. At that moment when a couple hold their brand new baby in their arms I feel like an intruder. I have a little snuffle at one end of the bed, while they have theirs at the other.'

She pauses for a moment, and grins.

'If my male colleagues heard me saying that they would definitely think I was loopy.' But then, on reflection, she says firmly, 'I think we're meant to walk through the world with a childlike sense of awe. When we lose it our lives are so much the poorer. I'm fortunate because I work in an environment where it suddenly takes you by surprise at all kinds of unguarded moments – when you see a fetus on the scanner and it's wriggling or sucking its thumb. The whole of the birth process is truly amazing – a great privilege – and it was given to women. That must mean God is good for us. With all the hassles it involves, it has to be the greatest gift in the world.'

If it is the greatest gift, then, I wonder, does it ever hurt that it's one God has denied her?

'Yes, of course. I'd have made a good mum.'

A picture forms in my mind – a band of golden-haired children, hanging on to the apron strings of this gentle, vivacious Scottish woman.

'You would,' I say to her.

'It wasn't to be,' she says, smiling.

'Was it a conscious decision to stay single?' I feel I'm barging into very private territory.

She blushes a little, then laughing, dismisses my apology with a wave of her hand. 'No, no, I don't mind talking about it. I don't think any woman makes a conscious decision about something like that. There was someone once, a very long time ago, but it didn't work out. Then I used to wonder in the early days what I would do about my job if someone came along. I decided I'd deal with it if and when it happened. There was a time when I was in my thirties and attending a house church when it really got to me. The only women with any clout were leaders' wives. You were made to feel half a woman if you didn't have a man. Silly ideas began to pass through my mind like, "If you're not good enough for a man, are you good enough for God?" And yet I know that marriage isn't the fulfilment of every dream. I've seen too many unhappy relationships to believe that.'

What fazes her, she admits, is walking alone into a party or a crowded room, when all her colleagues have partners. 'That's hugely daunting. But on the whole I'm much more positive about being single these days. I have opportunities denied most women. The idea of using a dating agency makes me want to spit. If you believe your life has a special calling and purpose, you must accept and embrace it. Whether you marry or not may be crucial consideration in what you achieve.'

She tells me then about the celebrated Dr Ida Scudder of Vellore, and how powerfully the missionary doctor's story has influenced her life. Ida, the daughter of missionaries in India at the turn of the twentieth century, was a fun-loving, young American woman, educated in the States, where she planned to stay, wanting only marriage and a comfortable life – until one fateful night. In India, caring for her mother who was ill, she was woken on three separate occasions by young Indian men, each begging her to attend to his wife who was having difficulty in childbirth. Each time Ida tried to explain that her father was the doctor. She wouldn't be of any help. She didn't know what to do. Each of the men turned angrily away, refusing to let a male doctor attend their wife. In a Muslim or Brahmin culture, it was unthinkable for a man to go anywhere near a woman.

The following day Ida tried to find out what had happened to the women. To her horror, she discovered that all three and their babies had died during the night. After long hours of agony and tears, she made up her mind, despite every obstacle to women – and there were many – to train as a doctor, and improve the quality of life for the women of India.

She began with a tiny clinic in Vellore, working all day and most of the night, battling against misinformation, superstition, and suspicion. Over the years that clinic became a huge hospital campus and medical school, offering most of the major medical specialties. Ida Scudder was the first to train women doctors in India, and the fact that in the late 1940s, in the new government of an independent India, the first Minister of Health was a woman, was in no small measure thanks to her efforts. Today the staff continue the obstetric and gynaecological side of the work she started in Vellore. Anne Garden goes out there whenever she can and loves the chance she usually gets of training the student doctors.

'When you ask whether God is good for women, do you mean here – or in India? Looking at the miracle of childbirth, looking at the opportunities and privileges I have in this country, I'd have to say a resounding, "Yes, He is." Looking at the lives of women in developing countries, I'd be much more guarded. I'd have to say God is good for women, but men are not. In India, Africa and Asia, every country where men own women's bodies, they commit them to a life of misery and pain. It is a terrible denial of the equality men and women were given at creation to reduce woman to a mere possession.'

In India, she tells me, many men refuse to use contraception and the women are worn out with childbearing. In parts of Africa female circumcision is still a way of life. When she was a locum in Abu Dhabi and needed a husband's permission to perform a Caesarean section, he always managed to be missing at the crucial moment. It made her feel positively murderous. In many parts of the world women have to travel so far for help once they are in labour, often in bullock carts, that the baby bores a fistula or hole through the vagina into the bladder or bowel, leaving them incontinent and social outcasts, as their husbands no longer want them. Australian missionaries have at last set up a special 'fistula repair' hospital in Addis Ababa, as it is a relatively easy piece of surgery but, says Anne, it's like closing the stable door once the horse has bolted. Prevention is better than cure, but the resources for antenatal care and the early referral of potential problem cases are simply not there.

A million women die every year, not of any major disease, but in childbirth, usually because their men won't let them have access to medical care. And the number is rising. So much, she says, for international conferences and slogans such as, 'Health for all in the year 2000'!

Her passion for women in the developing countries presented the greatest challenge to her code of medical ethics. Throughout the world, one of the main causes of death for women is unsafe abortion. 'As a newly qualified doctor I wouldn't perform abortions. Life was too precious. Then I spent a year in South Africa saving the lives of women dying of septicaemia after back-street terminations. In India too, for very poor families, it's often the only way out. Another child is too awful to contemplate. I came to the conclusion that we live in a fallen, not an ideal, world where there will always be unwanted pregnancy. If the choice is between a safe or unsafe abortion, there is no choice at all. My job was to perform the operation as efficiently as I could, with maximum respect for the mother's life.'

This is Liverpool, David Alton territory. Alton is the Liberal Democrat MP who has consistently argued for a lowering of the maximum duration of pregnancy up to which an abortion is permitted. Anne Garden admires him enormously for standing up for what he believes. For someone in her position, there is a very difficult path to tread. She does not perform abortions on demand but weighs up each situation according to its own merits. She has, however, huge reservations about telling the parents of an abnormal fetus what they should or shouldn't do. 'Unless we are going to be involved in the raising of that child we have no right to pontificate. For example, I find it difficult when Catholic priests who are celibate, with no commitment to the care of the child, dictate God's will to my patients. If we take the place of God and say, "You must not terminate this pregnancy", the next logical step is to do what He would have done, and help them cope by sharing in the care, taking the child at weekends to give them a break. It also means fighting for the rights of disabled people to ensure they have access to maximum resources and all public facilities. There's no cost attached to pontificating. There is in commitment.'

When she speaks of inequality, injustice, the oppression of the weak and vulnerable – whether in this country or abroad – the legendary fire and passion of the Scots flashes in her eyes. Here is a woman who will never be content to stand on the sidelines while others fight her battles for her. She claims she isn't a feminist – not in this country at least. She finds feminists a little daunting, a little too intense, but agrees that the predicament of women in the two poorest thirds of the world could turn the mildest human being into a raging protestor. She also acknowledges that Western men don't always make the perfect partners. There are times when she finds their behaviour utterly incomprehensible, more like men in India or South Africa and bitterly disappointing. 'I had one patient who was allergic to her husband's semen. It caused her immense discomfort and pain. Thankfully, that's a very rare condition, easily dealt with by using a condom. The husband refused categorically. Can you believe it?'

She has noticed too – how could she not? – that men tend to pass off all responsibility for the reproductive process to their women. When there are fertility difficulties, the men still send their women to 'get sorted out', though the problem may in fact be theirs.

Despite the challenges of an obstetrics career in Liverpool, India draws her back year after year. She'll probably take early retirement, she says, and go for a much longer stint. But that's a way off yet. Meanwhile, she's enjoying all the resources and refinements of the new hospital, built with women in mind.

'It's great, isn't it?' she says, as she escorts me slowly back towards the main entrance. 'The architect was a woman, the chairman is a woman, all the midwives and nurses are women, the only male patients are babies.'

'A pity that only two of the consultants are women,' I remind her.

She agrees, but says the environment still feels female, and that matters. 'Look, only a woman could have made that.' She points to a wall hanging made of hoops and squares, lilac and pink, gingham and spots, buttons and beads.

'I love being a woman. It saddens me when patients say that next time they're coming back as a man, whether they mean it as a joke or not. I always say to them, "Who'd want to be a man? Just wait until you're 70, and he's trotting back and forwards to the loo ten times a night with his prostate, while you're tucked up all cosy in your bed."'

Is she ever tempted, as a consultant, to take on a certain image and play at being a man?

'No,' she says firmly, 'I'm happy to break the mould. I'm not the authoritarian type. I'm so afraid of behaving like a man that I probably don't push my authority enough. I've seen female obstetricians in India shouting at their patients. They haven't yet learned that power doesn't mean behaving in a stereotypical male way. It's power to improve the quality of people's lives.'

That being the case, how does she handle confrontation?

'I hate confrontation. Fortunately, the only time I have to resort to it is when a junior member of staff is sloppy and hasn't shown the necessary level of care, or when a patient, or even a GP, is unnecessarily rude or aggressive with a member of staff. That makes my blood boil, and I launch in instinctively out of a sense of justice, rather than any sense of authority.'

And does she ever challenge her male colleagues? I couldn't help but notice one or two decidedly pointed cartoons pinned to the board in her room. One is of two toddlers side by side, looking down at what's inside their knickers. 'Ooh,' says the one with the bow, 'that explains our difference in pay.' Another, less apt for a gynaecologist, but pertinent all the same, is of a board meeting. 'Very good suggestion, Miss Trigg,' says the chairman, 'would one of the men like to make it?'

'I tease my colleagues mercilessly,' she grins '"Typical male response!" I say to them, when they get on their high horse. When all your patients are women it's easy to fall into the trap of thinking that only women have problems.'

A young man walks past us at speed in the opposite direction.

'Hi,' she calls after him, 'she's fine, still speaking to me – but only just.'

It might be a colleague. It is in fact the husband of a patient who has had six failed pregnancies, and is now waiting, in desperation, for a safe seventh attempt.

'How do people cope?' she says, shaking her head in wonder.

'Because you're a woman do you get more emotionally involved with your patients?' I ask her, remembering a quotation from the missionary doctor Denis Burkitt, pinned among the cartoons to the notice board in her room:

Attitudes are more important than abilities.
Motives are more important than methods.
Character is more important than cleverness
And the heart takes precedence over the head.

'Yes, I think women do find it easier to get alongside those who suffer. We tend to be more sensitive – and probably more neurotic! Male colleagues say to me, "Don't let it get to you, Annie", so I suppose that means the emotional trauma of my patients must affect me quite deeply. But how can it not when you're with women at the best and worst moments of their lives? No pain compares with the loss of a child. When there's a stillbirth here a pall hangs over us all. You can feel it in the air.'

She stops suddenly. 'I'd better not let my male colleagues hear me saying that either. They'll say Annie has really gone off her trolley this time. I'm not saying they don't have feelings – they just build higher defences. Some are atheists because of the suffering they've seen, the congenital malformations, the inexplicable tragedies. I never know what to say to them. Ethical dilemmas, human misery and suffering, we face such enormous theological issues in this field of medicine. I knew that when I took it on and it doesn't get any easier. I struggle my way through and sometimes have to admit I don't know the answers. All I have is a deep-seated certainty that one day, in the light of eternity, all the great mysteries of life will be made clear.'

We have arrived at the front door. She is off to have supper with a friend. 'Patients can become friends too,' she tells me as an afterthought, 'particularly if there's a long history of problems in pregnancy, and I spend a great deal of time with them'.

There is one couple of whom she is particularly fond. They had years of problems. The mother eventually managed to give birth to twins but, tragically, one died of renal failure. Anne is godmother to the surviving twin, and it means a great deal to her. Several of the babies she has delivered are her godchildren, and she tries to keep in touch with them all.

'I don't think we should be afraid of emotional engagement – as long as we do keep a certain distance too – for survival's sake,' she says. Survival for her is leaving the consultant behind at the hospital and having somewhere she can simply be herself.

The last thing she tells me is that when the hospital had its official opening by Diana, Princess of Wales, she wasn't there. She had a prior engagement – in India, training obstetricians. The irony seems to please her. 'You can read into that whatever you like,' she says with a huge grin, as the automatic door slides shut behind her.

I watch her slowly disappear into the night, the woman who thought she would never make a doctor and yet became one of a rare breed of consultants. With the calling came the cost. In a more perfect world, she might have managed to combine marriage, motherhood and a career in obstetrics and gynae-cology. It is essential in the future that women do. This is why Carolyn Johnson at the Preston Hospitals is so attached to flexible working hours and job sharing, for women and men, so that women can become consultants, and men more committed husbands and fathers.

But for the moment such words as 'choice' and 'sacrifice' are very real in women's vocabulary. Ruth Clark, Jan Ransom and Anne Garden have all adopted an almost nineteenth-century approach to pioneering in embracing singleness as a necessary prerequisite for career success. Victorian pioneers such as Florence Nightingale had little choice. She knew marriage would have robbed her of any chance of real achievement, let alone a career. She despised women who could not resist the temptations of the flesh the way she did. Today there is more, if not unlimited, choice, and perhaps that is why Anne Garden's seems so poignant.

But she neither laments what might have been, nor blames God. He has enabled her to fulfil her potential in ways she never expected. Self-pity is not in her nature. She is more than satisfied with her lot.

Some are born pioneers. Some have it thrust upon them. Anne belongs to the latter category. She is a pioneer not by nature, but by dint of the job she decided to do. Her achievement rests not so much in introducing radical new surgical techniques but in her more holistic approach to being a consultant, in her openness with her patients, in her unashamed emotional involvement with them, in encouraging women to make choices about their own care, all of which will, nonetheless, in time, play its part in the developing relationship between women and their doctors in this uniquely female part of their lives.

I left the hospital with most of the answers to my questions. Women are not necessarily better obstetricians or gynaecologists than men, but they may empathise more and be better able to fight our cause. What I never expected, in my blinkered, self-centred state of mind, was to be alerted to the suffering of sisters in the other two-thirds of the world. It would be far too easy, having met women in this country with access to power and influence, to sit complacently down and imagine a God who smiles benignly down on women, pats us on the head, opens the doors and shoves us through. It's harder to remember that for many women in the world there are no doors, only brick walls. While so many do not have access to basic rights, let alone opportunities, we may not be as morally free as we would like to enjoy ours. Anne Garden is a timely reminder that if God is good for women, we who believe it must be prepared to take on the cultures, societies and institutions that behave as if He isn't.

Anne is now Professor of Medical Education at the University of Liverpool – which she claims shows that God has a sense of humour! She is still involved in a small amount of clinical work – concentrating on what has become her specialist area – paediatric and adolescent gynaecology. Although the decision to reduce her involvement in clinical work was hard, Anne felt a real sense that this was God's leading for her life.

Conclusion

All the women in this book think God is good for women. They are not so sure about religious institutions. But then, whatever is man-made can be changed. If God is good for women, women will be good for religion.

They have their own unique contribution to make. Men tend to be linear thinkers. The line may be circular, but the task is all-absorbing. Women appear to have a built-in radar system. They think and work in wide sweeps, encompassing many activities at once – childrearing, homemaking, leisure and professional commitments, family relationships, friendships. They switch easily from one to another, carrying with them a consciousness of all the rest. A friend's birthday, Mother's gammy leg, the neighbour's shopping and a child's clean underwear are as important as a board meeting. That's what makes them instinctive carers, their attention to practical details, an awareness of body as well as mind and spirit.

All the women here enjoy being women. Society, it seems, has become too pushy, driving and insensitive, too hooked on a limited concept of achievement, too 'masculine'. Their God-ordained task is to bring back the feminine, to create a healthy, whole, more balanced approach to life and work for both men and women. Feminists from the 1960s, the 1970s and even some from the 1980s said, 'I am as good as a man because I am a man.' The new-millennium woman says, 'I am as good as a man because I am a woman.' These women say, 'God is good for all of us' – but they are glad to be female nonetheless.

Not only do they refuse to be restricted by their gender, they have learned to use it to great effect. Only Helen Taylor-Thompson believed there might be advantages in being a man. But would a man have got away with building a hospice for gay men with AIDS? Would a man have dared confront the Church with its ostrich-like attitude to the doubtful morality of some of its clergymen, or be conscious enough of the importance of body image to pioneer specialist fashion designing for people who are disabled? In fact most of the 'coping' agencies, support groups and respite care facilities for the elderly, the terminally ill and their carers have been set up by women. That, says Julia Neuberger in *Whatever's Happening to Women?*, is no coincidence. As little girls, women learn to cope, to put up with things, to make the best of a bad job, which is very different from boys, who are taught to change things. 'Women look for new and imaginative ways of living with the unliveable, of coping with the most difficult of situations.' This is what turns an ordinary woman into a miniature superwoman, a virago in the face of human misery, a pioneer at the very least.

Few of these women deliberately aimed for the top. Why not? Instinctive female self-deprecation, as for Anne Garden, who felt she couldn't become a professor of obstetrics because administration was not her forte? A good senior manager might have said, 'Go for it, Annie, and I'll provide you with extra secretarial back-up.' She would then have to decide whether she wanted promotion, not whether she was competent enough. Or do women pursue a different set of goals anyway, such as personal fulfilment and contentment?

The nesting instinct is undeniable. On the whole, most women, married or single, view the home, not the office, as their base. If recent statistics are right and 90 per cent still do the majority of the housework and take responsibility for the domestic arrangements, there may not be much energy, creative, emotional or physical, left over for the workplace.

Most of these women know that. They are not convinced they can have it all: a high-powered career, a perfect 'new man', secure, well-behaved children, creative space, spiritual insight and a modicum of sanity. Both Carolyn Johnson and Angela Sarkis waited until their children were at school before they took their own career prospects seriously. Anne Garden, Ruth Clark and Jan Ransom would probably have waved goodbye to their respective institutions and sailed into the sunset had they met the man of their dreams. Both Susan Howatch and Jan Ransom believe their singleness enables them to sublimate vital energy into their work. Hilary Armstrong, MP, made a conscious decision not to inflict her lifestyle on a child. How many men would take such considerations into account?

But then, every calling has a cost – for both the sexes. Women, if they can afford it, reserve the right to make choices, which a man, because of cultural expectations, neither would nor could. They choose whether to marry or not, to have children or not, whether to work in or out of the home, and for how many hours a week. But then, since there is so little support for carers, either from the government or from what is left of local communities, how real are the choices?

The great American suffragette Elizabeth Cady Stanton once said, 'The woman is greater than the wife or mother; and in consenting to take upon herself these relations, she should never sacrifice one iota of her individuality.' The theory is all very well. Reality is another matter. At a recent church event I was introduced by a clergyman as 'journalist, writer, PR consultant but, most important of all, wife and mother'. Unlike men, and despite their achievements, women, it seems, are still defined and constrained by the roles they play. But with my children in their late teens and about to fly the nest, the best and major part of my mothering is almost over. It was a wonderful, unbelievably short hiatus, and I miss it terribly. If it had been my all, what would I now have left? Small wonder that many middle-aged women succumb to depression and a sense of uselessness at this stage. But perhaps, like Nellie Thornton of Ilkley, or Helen Taylor-Thompson of Mildmay, I shall now discover my great life's work. Since women tend to live longer than men, there's more chance of doing so.

It's all a case of overcoming that basic lack of self-confidence that robs so many women of their potential. Even Helen Taylor-Thompson, if she couldn't see it in herself, could see it in others, the women in her church wives' group who spent time discussing submission to their husbands when they could have been changing the world.

It is their faith, these women say, that is the source of their confidence, the impetus to go out, rise to a challenge and make a difference. Like Abraham, the patriarch and Deborah, the judge, they set off as commanded, their hand in God's, make the most of the opportunities along the way and, on the whole, are surprised to see where they have ended up. Susan Howatch is convinced God inspired the Starbridge novels. Helen Taylor-Thompson saved a hospital without knowing what for. Nellie Thornton never imagined having the money to make her dream come true. Several of the others talk about finding a job that used all their gifts, as if it plopped, neatly packaged and beribboned, from the heavens into their hands. That suggests a denial of the years of sacrifice, gut-hard work, not to mention their ability and their talent. What they mean is that they haven't had to be grasping or underhand to get it. For years Hilary Armstrong resisted taking the jobs her father's reputation could get her. When God is on their side, there is no need for wily manipulation. No one is deliberately trodden over on the way up. As senior managers, Angela Sarkis, Carolyn Johnson, Julia Neuberger and Jan Ransom know their own mind but they also know there is a way of sharing, rather than imposing it, without destroying the self-esteem of those in their path. Helen Taylor-Thompson may be a bit of a steamroller when it comes to human red tape – but an entrepreneur needs obstinacy, and flattened bureaucrats have a way of popping back up.

This kind of confidence does rather depend on a woman's concept of God. All the women here have had a fairly positive experience of human parenting. A bad or inadequate father might have led them to see God as patriarchal, restrictive and oppressive. In fact, such is their faith that discrimination, difficulties and opposition, far from crushing their spirit or pushing them into passive submission, only fuel their fire to fight the injustices they see.

God is as good for women, says Jan Ransom, as they let Him be. If a woman is hide-bound by convention or social mores, if she has imbibed the doormat mentality or martyr spirit that condemns her to a life of meek passivity, ugly clothes and non-existent sexuality, she is limiting His goodness and her opportunities. A woman should be gutsy. If religion doesn't have this effect on her, there is something wrong with the brand of religion, not with a God who has made human beings what they are and has their best interests at heart.

It takes guts to survive in institutions like the army, the police force, the NHS and the government, let alone change them. Julia Neuberger believes that the more women have access to power the more positive an influence they will be, and that seems to be true, if Jan Ransom's and Ruth Clark's experiences are anything to go by. In remaining fully female, fully in touch with their true selves, they produced a subtle change of culture in their corner of the army and the police force, two institutions notoriously resistant to a woman's touch.

Even the Church is finally beginning to yield to the inevitable influence of women priests. It is beginning to appear that churches led by women priests grow. Women lead differently. They are more interested in nurturing the inner life of the Church, of developing relationships, than in making a success of their ministry. They don't fall into the trap of measuring their effectiveness by the number of bottoms on pews, so don't become as stressed as their male counterparts.

They also appear to prefer working as part of a team. Power without accountability is dangerous. When, like Margaret Thatcher, women behave like men, and wield it alone, they may be tempted to abuse the privilege, use it as an oppressive tool, a means of control. Ruth Clark saw it as responsibility, Anne Garden as opportunity, Angela Sarkis and Joy Carroll as a creative, enabling force.

In many ways my journey was circular. Helen Taylor-Thompson, at the beginning of the book, and Anne Garden at the end, worried about the ongoing damage inflicted on countless women in two-thirds of the world by the refusal of many men to wear condoms. Most of the women in this book judge God by the freedoms they have experienced in the West. But God doesn't appear to be so good for Jan Ransom's Filipino friends, who work as servants, separated from husbands and children, to try to earn the money to keep them alive. Or for Anne Garden's Indian patients, condemned to endless, unwanted pregnancies, appalled by the birth of a female baby. Or for the many women victims of AIDS Helen Taylor-Thompson saw in Africa.

Yet these women have much to teach their Western sisters. The black South African priest Joy Carroll met in the USA did not believe the pain or the limitations facing women in her society were a reflection of God's basic intention. Their faith made the women of her village an invincible force. He was good for them, even if their world wasn't. So they found a way of quietly and forcefully out-manoeuvring the restrictions imposed upon them, of rising up together and curbing the activities of a child abuser. They redefined power. And they became unbeatable.

There is an ancient Indian fable about a mouse who is afraid of cats, so he asks the magician to turn him into a cat. But the cat is afraid of dogs, and asks the magician if he can become a dog. The story continues until the mouse finally becomes a lion. But the lion is afraid of the hunter. The magician finally gives up and says, 'I might as well turn you back into a mouse, because although you are a lion, you have the heart of a mouse.'

Many women feel like a mouse inside. They take a peek at their possibilities, see only pitfalls and problems, and cower in a corner. But throughout history there have been women willing to respond to the call to go beyond their usual limitations, to rub against hard and difficult man-made structures in an attempt to make their world a better, fairer, godlier place. The friction reveals the true metal. 'Iron sharpens iron, so one person sharpens another,' says the old proverb. Esther in the Bible conquered her fear of the tyrant to whom she was married, risked her life and rescued her people. Nellie Thornton, Jan Ransom, Ruth Clark, Angela Sarkis and all the other brave women here, not to mention their courageous sisters in the developing world, rise above their fears to challenge basic assumptions, institutions, governments and even the Church, when integrity, authenticity and justice demand it. This is what they mean by women having a prophetic voice. They prove that a God who is good for women intends them to have the heart, the mind and the roar of a lioness.

Note
1. Julia Neuberger, *Whatever's Happening to Women?* (Kyle Cathie, 1991), p. 63.

National Distributors

Trusted
All Over the World

Daily Devotionals

Books and Videos

Day and Residential Courses

Counselling Training

Biblical Study Courses

Regional Seminars

Ministry to Women

CWR have been providing training and resources for Christians since the 1960s. From our headquarters at Waverley Abbey House we have been serving God's people with a vision to help apply God's Word to everyday life and relationships. The daily devotional *Every Day with Jesus* is read by over three-quarters of a million people in more than 150 countries, and our unique courses in biblical studies and pastoral care are respected all over the world.

For a free brochure about our seminars and courses or a catalogue of CWR resources please contact us at the following address:

**CWR,
Waverley Abbey House,
Waverley Lane,
Farnham,
Surrey GU9 8EP**

**Telephone: 01252 784700
Email: mail@cwr.org.uk
Website: www.cwr.org.uk**

WR CRUSADE FOR WORLD REVIVAL *Applying God's Word to everyday life and relationship*

Inspiring Women Every Day

The NEW daily devotional by women, for women, from the publishers of *Every Day with Jesus*.

Inspiring Women Every Day is a life-enriching daily devotional designed to be a source of inspiration and encouragement for women of all ages. Readers will gain a deeper insight into Scripture and know a more intimate relationship with God.

- 2 key women authors each issue
- Readings for each weekday and weekend
- Prayers, commentary, thoughts and reflections
- Bimonthly

£1.95 per issue
£11 one-year subscription